THE COMPLETE ACTOR

STANLEY L. GLENN

Department of Dramatic Art
University of California, Santa Barbara

ALLYN AND BACON, INC.

Boston • London • Sydney • Toronto

*This book is dedicated
to my acting students,
from whom
I learned so much
and without whom
this book
would not have been possible.*

Library of Congress Cataloging in Publication Data

Glenn, Stanley L
   The complete actor.

   Bibliography: p.
   Includes index.
   1. Acting. I. Title.
PN2061.G63   792'.028   76-41227
ISBN 0-205-05580-X

CONTENTS

PHOTOGRAPHS

PREFACE

The original title of this book was to have been *The Actor: Interpreter and Creator.* Its emphasis was to have been on the fundamentals of acting with a more comprehensive development of interpretation than normally might be found in most beginning acting texts. As the writing of the book progressed, however, it became clear to me that in terms of the fundamental needs of what most of us conceive to be the complete actor, the scope of my intentions was too narrow. After all, creation and interpretation for the actor surely must include the influence of style and genre, which are aspects of interpretation and whose expression in action is an aspect of the actor's creativity. Few acting texts, I find, recognize this, and those that do include discussions of style and genre that lack the comprehensiveness with which other basic materials are treated.

My decision to explore these important areas more deeply should be regarded as an expansion rather than a reduction of what normally might be expected in a beginning acting text. Rather than treat the various stages of the actor's development as necessary but unrelated concerns, this book attempts to demonstrate their organic relationship. The challenges of tragic styles and of the various forms of comedy cannot be met successfully without honesty, belief, awareness, and an appropriate use of the imagination, as well as the development of the actor's physical instruments. In turn, exercises in style and genre should expand and make more meaningful the earlier psychic and physical training of the actor. For example, although an actor may never be cast in a Greek tragedy, the exercises that explore its unique conventions should make more stringent demands upon the actors' body, voice, and imagination, and result in their greater range and flexibility.

There is a chronological order for the actor's development, which is proposed in this book's organization. It suggests that the actor's work on himself with an emphasis on improvisation should precede the interpretation of character and the performance of scenes from actual plays. The rationale for this sequence is that textual work becomes more meaningful and more manipulable after the actor has learned to be comfortable on the stage and has attempted to explore his own creative and imaginative powers. It is necessary, however, to maintain the organic concept of actor training by demonstrating the relevance of the earlier work to specific characters in plays, and the later work with textual drama to the fundamental principles and approaches of the earlier. One device that makes this possible is the use of five specific plays for illustrative purposes.

Essentially, each of these plays has been selected to demonstrate a particular aspect of actor training. It requires that every student in the class be familiar with these plays so that demonstrations and exercises will be more meaningful. Scene work with plays familiar to everyone in a class may then be viewed and discussed with appropriate judgment. Strindberg's *Miss Julie* and Molière's *The Would-Be Invalid* provide interesting contrasts in terms of interpretation and characterization, and both plays serve to illustrate how the actor's work on himself is relevant to the demands of the stage. Euripides' *Medea* is used for the Greek tragic style but is also used in an earlier chapter to demonstrate an aspect of relating. Shakespeare's *Richard II* demonstrates Elizabethan tragic style as well as poetic drama. *The Would-Be Invalid* crops up again for farce demonstration, and Congreve's *The Way of the World* serves the exploration of high comedy. Specific translations of *Miss Julie, The Would-Be Invalid,* and *Medea* are used and recommended, but it is possible to substitute other translations if they are more convenient.

The approaches to acting in this book are as eclectic and varied as today's theatrical fare. The first part of the book is Stanislavski-oriented, because after having experimented with most of the "post-method" methods I have concluded that Stanislavski's principles continue to be the most effective, pragmatic, and universal approach to acting. They not only have proven to be the most effective way to introduce the student to acting, but are invaluable in their application to all forms of theatre. Finding the appropriate action, being as honest and having as great a sense of belief when dealing with poetic drama as with prose, and always basing characterization upon those questions that stimulate dramatic action are a few of the principles that serve as guidelines in this book. While methods and techniques other than those of Stanislavski are integrated into various parts of the book, they still serve the principles just enumerated. What I hope will be consistent despite my eclecticism, is the stance that no "method" of acting should be viewed as an end in itself. This is as true of misconceived Stanislavski trends such as the "as long as I feel it that's all that matters" school of American method acting as those which suggest that the purpose of acting is for "fun and games," or the exhibition of the actor's therapeutic explorations, or other self-indulgences. The purpose of this book is to assist the actor in finding a personal style without resorting to exhibitionism; to encourage him to serve the character, the play, and the audience rather than his own ego, and to extend his capacity to face the challenges of the varieties of drama, both old and new.

Stanley L. Glenn

ACKNOWLEDGMENTS

I would like to express my deepest appreciation to the following who contributed in some way to this book: Alan Armstrong, Theodore Hatlen, and Kathy White of the University of California at Santa Barbara; Michel Langinieux, colleague, friend, and collaborator; Robert Morgan, costume designer at ACT, San Francisco; the Academy of Motion Picture Arts and Sciences; Le Strasburg, scene designer at the University of California at Santa Barbara, for the line drawings upon which the materials in this book are based, and various actor-friends of the Royal Shakespeare Company for their inspirational examples of acting excellence.

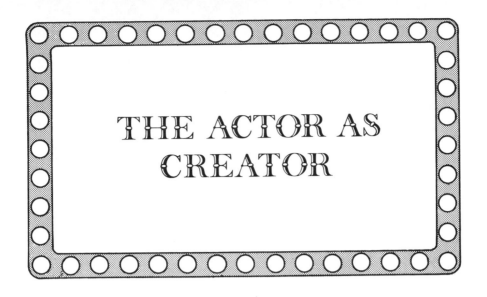

THE ACTOR AS CREATOR

PART I

INTRODUCTION

The actor's art is the art of action. To be able, thoroughly and brilliantly, to analyze a character may be the achievement of persons who have neither the inclination nor the ability to perform. The actor's responsibility is to enact—to bring to vibrant and believable life the character whose only existence heretofore has been on the printed page. His understanding must transcend the intellectual yet control the intuitive and subjective forces that are as necessary to him as is inspiration to the artist.

The character on the printed page is incomplete—deliberately so. The playwright is aware that the art of theatre is the art of collaboration—that his characters await embodiment and ultimately their full fruition in the living actor. One of the differences between narrative literature and drama is that, in the former, character is the result of collaboration between writer and reader. The writer uses words to describe the thoughts, actions, and appearance of his characters, and the reader supplies his imagination to complete *his* visualization of them. The dramatist, like the composer, must rely upon another agent between his creation and its impact upon an audience.

1

The actor supplies his imagination to complete *his* visualization of the character, and what the audience experiences is the living enactment of what previously had been words on paper.

The usual play manuscript describes vocal and physical action only minimally—if at all. Pre-nineteenth century dramatists, including the Greeks, Shakespeare, and Molière, provide practically no stage directions concerning facial, physical, or vocal expression. It is up to the actor to determine what Oedipus does when he appears before the chorus with blood streaming from his self-inflicted wounds. The actor playing Lear must decide what force, inflections, and timing to use for "Never, never, never, never, never," as he holds his dead Cordelia in his arms. Argan's rages, Toinette's sauciness, Béline's hypocrisy, and Angélique's frustration in *The Would-Be Invalid* depend upon the actions of actors and actresses for their fullest expression.

Writers such as Strindberg, Shaw, and O'Neill, knowing that they write for a reading public as well as for the theatre, include more detailed descriptions of the physical appearance and occasional actions of their characters, but never enough to commit the actor to a fully preconceived performance. In *Miss Julie,* Strindberg frequently uses adverbs and descriptive phrases to help us imagine how his characters respond overtly. Here are a few of those descriptions selected at random from the play: *shyly, very becomingly, agonized, innocently, stunned, tense and nervous.* On the printed page, however, these are still mere words. As readers, we must try to imagine expressions of shyness or nervousness. As actors, we must not only imagine expression, but find the best and most appropriate means at our command of enacting it.

Just as there will be inevitable differences between the way in which a playwright originally imagined his action, and the way in which it may be interpreted by either reader or performer, there will be major differences between various actors' performances of the same role. Tennessee Williams may have had his own sister in mind when he created the role of Laura in *The Glass Menagerie,* but she did not and probably could not play it on the stage. Julie Hayden performed it in its Broadway introduction, and another actress, Jane Wyman, played Laura in the motion picture version. The mother, Amanda, was played by Laurette Taylor, who was acclaimed for her interpretation of the role on the New York stage, but when Gertrude Lawrence played it in the motion picture, and Katharine Hepburn on television, no one expected imitations of Miss Taylor. Miss Lawrence and Miss Hepburn, stars in their own right, were expected to bring their personal insights to the role. In the theatre, each actor must find his correct way of expressing his interpretation of character. In literature, and especially in drama, a certain degree of latitude in interpretation is inevitable. Each of us allows experience to filter through in terms of our own capacities and limitations. See what *Hamlet* means to so many different capable critics and actors! The actress who plays Miss Julie allows a certain concept to be formed as a result of *her* adaptation of the manuscript character to *her own imagination*. She will then utilize *her* own experience in finding what *she* believes to be the correct actions for the enactment of *her* interpretation.

Variations in interpretation are inevitable in acting because of the individuality of the actor. Differences in the means of expression are determined by major factors that we shall term the *physical* and the *experiential*. Included in the physical are differences in external appearance and voice. Basically, humans vary in height, weight, coloring, hair texture, and facial features. They differ, too, in their manner of behavior—in their physical tone, tempo, rhythm, and personal idiosyncrasies. Voices vary in their combinations of quality, pitch, volume, tempo, and rhythm. The external individuality of a human being is determined by endlessly possible combinations of vocal and physical characteristics, so that even if two actors visualize a character in exactly the same way, their performances must vary. Two different musical instruments may play the same melody, but the sound may vary because of the inherent differences of the instruments.

The second category, the experiential, is concerned with the realm of the subjective. Just as individuals vary in external appearance, they vary in their ways of seeing and reacting. These variations are a result of the unique life experiences of separate individuals. None of us "sees" in exactly the same way, because the process of seeing involves more than just viewing, it involves a *way* of viewing. Two persons in the same room will differ not only in their way of perceiving, but in what they choose to perceive. The housewife may notice the dust on the piano, the cabinet maker will notice its wood and craftsmanship, the artist its spatial values and color, and the musician its potential for music making. Two writers asked to describe a room after seeing it at exactly the same time will vary in their views of what is important in the room, and in their response to the room: one may find it amusing, the other nostalgic. One may describe its details objectively, the other emotionally.

The play is a writer's view of some aspect of life that he has selected, and toward which he has developed and expressed an attitude. The characters he creates from his own vision and experience are to be interpreted by, and embodied in, actors whose eventual characterizations will be affected by their own physical and experiential capacities. The initiator of the character must depend for its completion upon the actor, and therefore must expect the final result to be another individual's interpretation of life. This imposes an enormous responsibility upon the actor. There is always the danger, in interpretative art, that the interpreter will exploit the writer's dependence upon him, and using the justification of individual differences, may ignore the fact that he is *completing* a character rather than *creating* one. The writer is at the mercy of actors who fail to study the character sufficiently well, actors who distort character for the sake of indulging themselves by imposing irrelevant concerns upon the text, or actors who use the role for the sake of demonstrating their own virtuosities.

The ethical actor recognizes his dependence upon the writer, as well as the fact that his function and duty are to fulfil and enrich the potentialities created by the script. This is why, before he enacts, the actor must try to understand; then, in the process of enacting, he must continue to explore the writer's intentions, both as a stimulus and as a justification for action. He constantly must be preparing himself for the most effective adaptation of his physical and experiential being to the character he is to portray. Since the success of his performance will depend upon the use of the self to bring a character to life, the actor must realize that for the variety of characters he may be called upon to portray, he must develop—in the broadest and most flexible way—his physical and experiential being.

CHAPTER 1

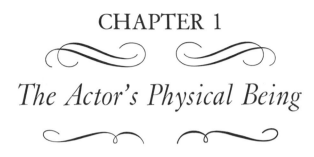

The Actor's Physical Being

When the issue of the physical being of the actor was first mentioned, it was in connection with the necessity of recognizing that the writer's conception of a character must necessarily be incomplete. On the other hand, the actor must understand that while there are certain aspects of his physical self that cannot be altered, there are others that, when required by the role, can be changed radically, depending upon the tone and flexibility of the actor's muscles.

Because of the tendency in our time to stress the psychological forces at work in the actor's art and skill, the media through which those forces must be expressed have been sadly neglected. There is validity surely in the theory (later to be explored) that the actor, by finding the appropriate internal stimuli, is more likely to produce the appropriate external expression; but without responsive or well-trained instruments, the expression of the actor's beliefs may be thwarted and unrealized. A pianist may know a sonata thoroughly, his body and soul may be infused with it, but if his wrists and fingers are sluggish and stiff, if his piano is out of tune or inadequate, he will have no means by which he may fully express his strongly felt conception of the sonata. In the same way, the actor who aspires to play Argan may understand Argan's objectives; he may have found for himself the appropriate internal stimuli for Argan's actions and emotions, but without physical and vocal vitality, without muscles that will respond to the necessary physical alterations and demands of the hypochondriac, without the ability to enlarge and project his truthful discoveries about the character, he is bound to fail. The actress playing Miss Julie must be able to control and

FIGURE 1-1. *Scene from Molière's* The Would-Be Invalid.
Comédie Française.

define the projection of neuroses that cause the character to fluctuate between arrogance and fear, hysteria and frozen immobility. Feeling and understanding will not be enough. She will be lost without the physical and vocal mechanism that is capable of responding, projecting, and controlling the character's sharp fluctuations in emotion and attitude.

THE BODY

The versatile actor must be as physically well-conditioned as the athlete. His body must respond quickly and with agility to external and internal stimuli. Later, we shall be concerned with learning how to develop such stimuli, but for the present, our chief concern is with the potential ability of the actor to allow them to function. Because many of the external stimuli that take place on the stage are make-believe, the actor is responsible, through his response to the imagined causes, to make the audience believe that such causes exist. For example, the actor may have to convince his audience that the environment is excessively hot or cold, dry or moist, dark or bright. His success in physically creating appropriate responses to such stimuli depends to a large extent upon his ability to express those responses through his entire body. Much will depend upon the actor's imagination and sensory awareness, but these are of little value when the body fails to respond with conviction. The actor who suggests that he is bitterly cold by merely blowing on his hands and stamping his feet may not merely be relying upon clichés, but may lack the tone and agility to activate the muscular response of the head, neck, torso, arms, legs, and digits that are affected by extreme cold. The emotions, too, demand outward responses (even the restraint of emotions must be expressed). A lazy, unconditioned body cannot be expected to respond adequately to the anger, violence, and fury of Othello in his most barbaric moments, or even a Iago in his most subtle ones.

Tonality and flexibility also are required for control of the external character traits that have been selected by the actor through various processes of observation and imagination. He will find that facial and physical distortion, both subtle and obvious, are demanded for the adequate playing of many roles. Parts that require him to assume postures excessively straight or bent in a variety of degrees, facial habits and idiosyncrasies such as a jutting jaw, constantly raised eyebrows, pulling all the facial muscles up or down, excessive loosening or tightening of the facial muscles, tics, and the strength to sustain such attitudes for several hours—all these can be fully realized only by the well-conditioned actor.

Any sizeable role demands a well-conditioned body. Nora, in *A Doll's House,* is not required to perform with excessive physicality aside from her grueling Tarantella dance. Yet she is almost always on stage for the approximately three hours of performance. Even without the Tarantella, this is an arduous physical and emotional task. Farces such as *A Comedy of Errors* or *Les Fourberies de Scapin* require nearly acrobatic action, and Scapin's bag scene alone requires extraordinary energy, agility, and coordination. Even small roles may demand feats of physical endurance. Jean, in Ionesco's *Rhinoceros,* is not on stage as long as Berenger, but the exercise scene that is followed by his transformation into a rhinoceros demands extraordinary physical exertion and coordination. In Shakespeare's *Titus Andronicus,* Lavinia has no dialogue after the middle of Act II, Scene 3 because her tongue has been cut out. But the physical demands of her pantomime during the rest of the play (her hands, too, have been cut off) are so exhausting that recently an actress in a famous repertory company had to give up the role—one of two she was performing, the other being Cleopatra.

The conscientious actor is aware that he must keep limber, and that all of the expressive parts of the body must be conditioned so that they may respond immediately to the demands of his imagination, thoughts, and feel-

7

ings. In general, ordinary calisthenics, practice in certain sports such as swimming, tennis, or fencing, which demand quickness and coordination, and dance will develop the physical needs of the actor. Specific exercises for the expressive parts of the body should be practiced too. Independent strengthening of the facial muscles, neck and shoulders, arms, wrists, hands and fingers, torso, hips, knees, feet and toes, will make each of these areas of expression more responsive. To cultivate the connection between stimulus and response, a fine exercise for the actor is to allow himself to respond with abandon to music or a collection of sounds.

Even when the actor has developed such flexibility, all of his work and preparation will be to little avail unless he is able to conquer physical tensions. The most supple bodies and beautiful voices become awkward and ugly without muscular freedom. Such tensions, of course, are due primarily to psychological factors, and a partial solution will be found in the actor's understanding of stage fright, and in his ability to concentrate on the appropriate stimuli, relating, and justification (all to be dealt with subsequently). The release from tension may be aided by physical means as well. Exercises that loosen the muscles of the face and jaw, neck, torso, wrists, lower back, and knees, with regular practice, will make it easier for the performer to respond to the mental processes that also make relaxation possible. Sometimes, physical action alone, as practiced by athletes in their pregame calisthenics, may be sufficient to effect the kind of loose, relaxed, and "warm" bodies that are so vital for performances and grueling rehearsals. It is during rehearsals, in fact, that relaxation is particularly important, for it is then that the actor first attempts to channel into expressive action his mental, emotional, and intuitive forces.

THE VOICE

The actor's voice, too, demands the kind of conditioning that will give it power, variety, and flexibility. How many would-be actors are frustrated because, despite their thorough understanding of, and feeling for, a role, their voices will not respond to the kind of pitch or quality demanded by it! How many actors have not been cast because, despite their many qualifications for a part, they are not equipped to project with sufficient volume and energy! Ideally, vocal aspects of characterization such as force, pitch, quality, and tempo should grow naturally out of the actor's internal realization of the role. This will not occur, however, unless the actor is endowed with, or has developed, a vocal instrument that will respond effortlessly to internal stimuli.

Vocal relaxation is as important as physical relaxation. It is, in fact, dependent upon it. Tensions invariably affect voice production. Tight vocal cords will create strain, hoarseness, and perhaps an undesired pitch. A tense torso will constrict the lungs and diaphragm, preventing sufficient air from being taken in, and making more difficult the pressure required for vocal force or volume. A tight mouth, tongue, and jaw will not only prevent good enunciation, but may suggest a character quite different from the one intended.

One final, and no less important, objective for the actor to become as physically well-conditioned as possible is the development of the endurance and strength so necessary to combat the strain invariably created by rehearsals and performances. The actor may be on his feet for hours at a time, repeating scenes that require not only the usual vocal magnitude, which is in itself demanding, but extremely violent and energetic action. Dress and technical rehearsals preceding the performance are long and arduous, yet the actor is expected to appear to be fresh and vital for the first and all subsequent performances. The actor owes it not only to himself, but to his fellow performers, to keep in shape, for all of them inevitably are affected by defects in his performance. (The discussion later in this chapter on the actor's need to relate himself to other characters will stress the importance of this aspect of acting.)

One of the most vital considerations that the actor must make and one easily forgotten in the welter of activities required of him, is rest. His strength and physical fitness will enable him to endure the exigencies of rehearsals and performances, but part of his fitness is dependent upon his ability to conserve his energies through rest and relaxation whenever possible. Too many persons who attempt to act are overly fond of the social life that the theatre so abundantly affords, and too much partying results in lethargic rehearsals and performances. The student actor, who must spend much of his day devoted to study, yet find the time to learn his lines, develop his part, rehearse, and eventually perform, must therefore be willing to sacrifice many of the usual social activities he enjoys. Many actors, believing that they have reached their goal with the first performance, celebrate and "party-it-up" to such an extent that they lose their energy and alertness for remaining performances. The rules established for athletes during their competitive seasons, which demand that they keep in top condition and properly pace themselves, might well be adopted by actors.

The actor's work in rehearsal and performance would be appreciably improved if it were preceded by a series of warming-up exercises for relaxing and toning the body and the voice. Some directors take the time before rehearsals to conduct such exercises because they realize that the efficiency of rehearsals frequently may be lessened by the inability of the actor to involve himself because of tension or a lack of physical and vocal readiness. But it is the actor himself who must assume this responsibility when directors do not include such preparations in their rehearsal time. The actor should determine for himself what he needs in order to be effective, and anticipate the appropriate time to exercise before rehearsal begins. Both directors and actors should be careful to avoid excessive prerehearsal or preperformance exercise; going into their work in a worn-out condition is as harmful, if not more so, than not exercising at all!

Vital, agile, and alert vocal and physical resources are absolute requisites for the serious actor. He must do everything in his power to fully develop the potentialities of his body and his voice. Daily exercises such as those described here are one means of achieving such ends.

EXERCISES

The following are basic exercises for the actor's control and development of his body and his voice. They are recommended for daily practice as well as for warming up. It is suggested that the serious actor supplement such exercises with some kind of regular physical activity such as swimming, tennis, jogging, fencing, or dancing.

I. PHYSICAL PREPARATION

A. *Relaxation*

   1. Lie on your back. Try to release all the tension from your body. Now mentally check your tension spots, and if they are still tight, relax them. The usual tension spots include the muscles around the eyes, lips, jaw, shoulders, wrists and fingers, shoulder blades, small of the back and buttocks, knees, ankles and toes. Concentrate on each of these areas several times until you feel that they are completely free of tension.
   2. Still on your back, with eyes shut, imagine soothing images. Visualize soft, pastel colors one by one. Imagine you are lying on the soft grass of a green field and that a tender breeze is fondling you.
   3. If you are in a group, take turns in manipulating one another's bodies by lifting an arm, a leg, a wrist, etc. These parts of the body should be raised without resistance, and drop loosely when released.

4. In group exercises, try massage. The "patient" should lie on his stomach while the masseur sits on the lower part of his back. Gently massage the lower neck, the shoulders, the shoulder blades, and work up and down the spine.

5. In a standing position, place your feet about 18 inches apart. Allow the torso to collapse forward so that your head and arms are dangling. In this position, check all tension points and relax them. When finding yourself to be completely prostrate, allow your toes to tighten, then let the tightening move slowly up the instep to the ankles, calves, knees, and thighs. Stop occasionally to make sure that the other parts of your body have remained loose. Do *not* straighten up until the following procedure is practiced: feel the tension move into the small of your back, then slowly allow it to grip your spine, one vertebra at a time. By the time you reach the neck, your torso should be upright. Your entire body should be stiff *except* for your shoulders, arms, wrists, hands, and head. Make sure that these areas are still relaxed. Now feel the tension move into your head, then out of the top, where it becomes a string pulling at the topmost part of the head. Feel the pull raise your head and spine as far as they can go. *Feel* tall and upright. Now pull the shoulders back and breathe deeply and slowly. After three or four breaths, collapse the torso again, relax the entire body, and repeat.

6. In an upright position, with the entire body relaxed, begin a head roll. Try to create the illusion that your head is completely loose where it connects to the neck, and let it drop forward. Do not pull it forward—let it drop as if by gravity. Your eyes should be closed. Now very, very slowly, allow the head to roll to your right shoulder. Let your mouth drop open. Very, very slowly, allow the head to drop backward. Very, very slowly, allow it to drop to the left shoulder. Finally, allow it to drop forward once again very, very slowly. Repeat several times, then reverse the roll clockwise and repeat.

7. At the beginning of these exercises and intermittently as you perform them, you should loosely shake your arms and wrists, then your legs from the knee down, and finally, your feet from the ankles.

8. Conclude by playing "rag doll." This can be done individually or in pairs. If individually, allow yourself to feel completely loose and disjointed—without bones. Your head should flop forward, your arms should hang down loosely and feel completely uncontrolled by nerves or muscles, your legs should be bent at the knees. There should be no tension in *any* part of the body. When you feel completely loose "walk" across the room in a floppy, seemingly uncontrolled manner. All joints, neck, elbows, knees, etc., should feel loose and disconnected. Try to sit in this manner. Fall down. Perform an action such as eating an apple, making a phone call, or dressing yourself.

　　In pairs, let one actor be the manipulator of the other, who is the rag doll. The manipulator can stand in back of the doll and manipulate any part of his body to test whether the parts are truly loose or rigid. He may gently push the head in any direction, lift his arms or wrists, even toy with the fingers and joints. The rag doll must permit all manipulation with no resistance. The manipulator may shove the back of the doll's knees with his own, raise the doll's legs at the knees and shake them. He may take the rag doll by the shoulders and shake it vigorously. Finally, the doll can fall in a heap and the manipulator can try to put him into a prone position. (This will also require some imagination!) Reverse roles.

B. *Toning*

1. Stand in a neutral position, with the feet about one foot apart. Imagine a force inside yourself in the region of the stomach. Allow this force to move up and swell out your chest and straighten the spine. Let it move up the neck and into the head and beyond, pulling your head and spine as high as possible. Now raise your arms sideways and reach high above your head. Stretch. Rise on your toes. Continue to stretch, like starving Tantalus desperately reaching for the fruit that is just beyond his grasp. Continue to stretch for 30 seconds, then collapse the entire body and repeat.

2. In the same position, raise your arms sideways until they are straight out at shoulder position. Stretch your arms. If you are in a group, position yourself so that when you raise your arms sideways, there will be six inches between the tips of your fingers and those of the persons on each side of you. Then everyone stretch, trying to touch fingertips.

3. Do the same exercise with the arms forward.

4. Lie on your stomach, with arms resting forward beyond your head, and relax. Imagine a force at the base of your spine. Allow it to move up your spine, energizing it then flowing into your arms as far as you can. Let the force raise them from the floor via the fingertips. Do not raise your head until your arms are raised as high as they can go. Now lift your chin as high as possible. Try to see the ceiling straight above you. Hold for twenty seconds, relax, and repeat.

5. In the same position, imagine the force once again at the base of your spine. This time, allow it to move down into the legs and through the toes so that both legs become fully stretched. Allow the force to raise the legs from the toes as high as they can go. Hold, then relax.

6. In the same position, imagine the force at the base of the spine now moving in both directions toward your fingers and toes until your back is arched and your only contacts with the ground are your hips and belly. Stretch your arms and legs as high as possible and hold for ten seconds, then relax and begin again.

7. Stand up. Relax the entire body. Lift your head through the pate so that your neck stretches. Turn the head sharply to the right, then forward, then left, forward, and right. Repeat several times.

8. Turn your head at a forty-five-degree angle to the right. Force your chin to your right collarbone, pull hard and feel the stretch in your neck. Now twist your head so that it leans back over your right shoulder, and your chin extends upward toward the left. The stretch now is in the throat muscles. Now pull the chin down to the left collarbone, stretching the neck once again, then sharply roll your head back over your left shoulder, pointing the chin high to the right, stretching the throat muscles. Repeat the exercise rhythmically and without break.

9. Now perform the same exercise with the entire body. Your feet should be about eighteen inches apart. Begin by clasping the thumbs of both hands and raising your arms together high above your head. Stretch the arms and bend your body so that your fingertips touch the toes of your right foot. You should not bend your knees. Now pivot on your right hip, swinging the arms across the body and upward and back to the right. Your torso should be pulled back and to the right, the chin pulled back as far as possible, and eyes focused on the ceiling. Stretch the abdominal muscles. Lean back as far as you can. Now swing the arms forward to the left and down toward the toes of your left foot without bending your knees. Then pivot on your left hip, swinging your arms across the body and back to the left and lean back leftward, your chin pointing up and to the right. Repeat the exercise rhythmically and without break.

10. Lift your arms straight up and tilt your head back so that you are looking at the ceiling. Raise yourself on your toes, then slowly do a deep knee bend. Do not take your eyes off the ceiling, and remain on your toes. Slowly raise back into an upright position and stretch upward. Let your head and arms drop. Relax, then repeat the exercise.

   Note: Between exercises, roll your head loosely and do shake-outs with arms, wrists, and feet. Someone should provide a count to each exercise, beginning with a regular rhythm and tempo. Then the count should be repeated with:

   a) an excessively slow but regular tempo;

   b) a rapid but regular tempo;

   c) an irregular rhythm to which the exerciser must alertly respond.

II. VOCAL PREPARATION

A. *Relaxation*

1. Repeat the slow head roll exercise (A6 above).
2. Yawn several times.

3. Keeping the mouth open, breathe slowly and deliberately. Close your eyes. After doing this several times, let a sound emerge softly from a relaxed throat. Imagine something pleasantly soothing, and repeat.

4. Repeat the above, but now hum softly each time you exhale.

5. Relax the jaw muscles by letting them drop, then lightly jiggling the jaw from side to side.

6. Relax your lips. Close them lightly, then blow air between them so they flop easily. The only energy exerted should be from the diaphragm. All facial muscles should be flaccid.

7. Part your lips slightly, and using the tongue, create a gentle raspberry. Again the only energy source should be from the diaphragm. Tongue and lips should be completely relaxed.

B. *Toning*

1. Place your hands beneath your rib cage and press in. Inhale deeply. Your rib cage and diaphragm should expand, pushing out the hands. Exhale slowly. Your diaphragm and rib cage should contract. Let your hands follow, pushing in slightly. Repeat several times, exhaling slowly and evenly each time. Breathe through the mouth. Do not raise the shoulders when you breathe in.

2. Keep your hands in the same position, and utter the sound "HA," so that it projects about ten feet. Breathe in, then say "HA" as you exhale. Make sure that the diaphragm and rib cage contract when the sound is made.

3. Repeat this exercise, but now project the sound about thirty feet. There should be no physical or vocal strain.

4. Repeat the exercise, but now project the sound as forcefully as you are able—as though you are calling someone who is a long distance from you. This, too, should be performed without strain. The only moving parts of your body should be the rib cage and diaphragm.

5. Exercise your resonators. Place your index fingers at the sides of your nose. Take a deep breath and hum an "N" sound. Feel the vibrations on the bones covering the nasal cavities. Continue the nasal sound slowly and evenly until you are out of breath. Repeat, but now vary the volume by starting quietly, then increasing the nasal sound. Alternate the volume until you are out of breath.

6. Hold your hands alongside each jaw, the fingers placed just under the ears, and the base of the palms under the chin. Your thumbs should be alongside your larynx. Take a deep breath and say "AH" as you slowly exhale. Feel the vibration along the jaw and in the upper throat. Repeat and vary the volume as above.

7. Place your fingers just outside the lips, and say "OOH" continuously in one breath. Feel the resonance at the sides of the mouth. Repeat, varying the volume of the "OOH" sound.

8. Place the index fingers at the sides of the nose, and the thumbs above the larynx. Take a deep breath and hum, then halfway through your exhalation shift to the sound "AH" and extend it until you are out of breath. Be conscious of the shift in resonance from "HUM-M-M-M" to "A-----H."

9. Keep the thumbs against the voice box and shift your fingers to the sides of your mouth. Take a deep breath and begin by extending the "AH" sound. Halfway through the exhalation, shift your resonance to "OOH" and extend until out of breath.

10. Rotate your jaw energetically from left to right and right to left. Say "YOWSAH" on your rotations, opening your mouth wide and stretching the jaws on the vowel sounds.

11. Click your tongue against your upper palate several times.

12. Stick out your tongue as far as possible, touching the tip of your nose, your cheeks, and chin with it.

13. Repeat projection exercise no. 2 but with the following vowel sounds: "HA"—open mouth and jaws as wide as possible; "HEE" —stretch lips wide; "HO"—exaggerate the movement of the lips to the smaller opening; "HOO"—push lips out as far as possible.

14. Using the sound "LA," exercise your pitch range. Say "LA" five times, focusing the sound deep in the chest. Repeat, focusing in the throat. Repeat and focus at the mouth level. Repeat and focus in the eyes. Repeat and focus above your head. Reverse the procedure.

CHAPTER 2

The Actor's Experiential Being

Splendid physical endowments, a lithe and mobile body, and a magnificent voice will provide no guarantee, of course, that the possessor of all these qualities will be a gifted actor any more than a Stradivarius will ensure a virtuoso performance from an average violinist. The actor, like all true artists, must have a special vision and highly developed intuition. Does this mean that one is born with these gifts, and, if not, he or she might as well give up? Not at all! First, there is no proof that these so-called "gifts" are a result of heredity rather than experience, or that the artist's perception cannot be developed as can his physical faculties.

In reality, while "special vision" and "intuition" appear to be mystic terms, their cultivation may be easily explained: they are nothing more than a capacity to respond to the world around us with the deepest, most intense awareness. The word "sensitive" is an extremely appropriate one, if applied properly. Unfortunately, "sensitive" too often has been associated with "delicate" or "fragile," as well as "artistic," with the result that weak, pale, quiet, and introverted persons have been regarded as potential poets or artists, when these traits may actually be the symptoms of a tubercular victim, or of an individual with severe feelings of inferiority.

ARTISTIC SENSITIVITY

Artistic sensitivity implies an unusually powerful response to objects and experiences, and involves the ability to recall and express such a response when deemed necessary. Why one person reacts more fully to the shades and nuances of experience than another cannot be fully explained, but surely any normal individual, if willing, may increase his sensitivity. He can learn to be more cognizant of, and to be more fully responsive to, the ingredients of existence, until (like the supposed congenitally atuned individual) he may absorb experience without labor.

All normal human beings, even most animals, are given five senses in order to perceive the world around them. Basically, we are provided with these capacities for the purpose of survival, and the average individual rarely uses his senses for more than utilitarian purposes. The "feel" of a piece of furniture or utensil is ordinarily related to its comfort or usefulness. The chair is "to sit in"; the fork "to eat with." The average man absorbed with his own concerns from day to day, performing habitual rites and duties, senses the world about him, but with practically no awareness of anything that does not materially concern him. Spring suddenly may burst upon him with new color, fragrance, and sound, but as he leaves his house with his mind upon the routine of his daily life and occupation, he may be totally unaware of the sensual delights of the new season. Or the season may have some special significance for him: a farmer, among other things, will look for the signs of new growth that will signify a productive crop; the student may observe the changes about him, and think "only two and a half months until vacation"; the housewife recognizes that it is time for spring cleaning; the sports enthusiast realizes that track and baseball preparations will now proceed. Perception, in each of these instances, is not made in terms of the qualities of the environment for themselves, but in terms of their function.

The artist, however, while he may be aware of such functions and associations, looks sharply at the objects of nature itself. The painter observes their colors and shades, the way in which they are affected by seasonal light, their textures, their form in space, and their spatial relationships, among other things.

The actor's chief concern is with people—with the actions of men. The layman perceives other people in pretty much the same way in which he perceives nature: either indifferently or functionally. He ordinarily would not recognize some of his own neighbors, or the children and animals that play in his street. On the other hand, he may be aware of identities, but if asked to describe the people with whom he is familiar, he would be at a loss to contribute a thorough description. We tend to take the appearance and activities of our own families for granted, and many of us are unable to specify, except for certain obvious characteristics, their features, their habits, their attitudes, their responses to life itself. The actor must learn to see people and experience in terms of themselves in order to stock the storehouse of his imagination, which in turn supplies him with sources for characterization.

IMAGINATION AND INVENTION

The problem created by the use of the word "imagination" is that people are inclined to believe that it exists as a strange power acquired in some inexplicable, mystic way, and is perhaps dependent upon divine inspiration. Actors who decide to wait for this magic transmission are likely to wait a long, long time before they receive it—if they ever do. In the case of actors or artists who believe that this is precisely what has happened, the chances are far more probable that the subconscious alertness and clarity of their observation and experience have enabled them to arrive at whatever results have been achieved. Invention is almost always the result of building upon previous discoveries. Shakespeare borrowed his plots, and applied the experience of his time and tradition to create their brilliant delineation. The superior imagination is due more to the meaningful application or reordering of experience intensely perceived than to mystic flashes of revelation. The first step, then, toward the development and enrichment of the imagination must be in the direction of exercising our perception of experience. The actor must learn to really *see*, and he does this by intensifying his observation of his outer world—the world of his environment—and his inner world —the world of his senses and emotions.

OBSERVATION: THE EXTERNAL
WORLD

The Environment

It has been stated previously that the major source of observational study for the actor is people. But people exist in and are influenced by their environments. One of the elements that contributes to our conclusions about people is the way in which they respond to their surroundings. In what kind of a room is this or that person comfortable or uncomfortable? How does a genteel southern belle react to excessive heat as compared to an obese laborer? Later, in dealing with the actor's work on his imagination, we shall see how important it is for him to be aware of the character's environment as an aid to his expression of his inner life. It follows, then, that the actor must learn to be habitually aware of as many aspects of his environment as possible.

EXERCISES

1. In order to test your present capacity for awareness, close your eyes after reading each of the following questions, and determine how well you are able to answer them:
    a. What is the color and design of the jacket of this book?
    b. Can you itemize all of the furniture in the room in which you are now located?
    c. What are you sitting on? Describe its shape, color, texture, and condition.
    ·d. Is there a floor covering in the room? Describe it in terms of material, color, and pattern. If there is no floor covering, describe the floor.
    e. Can you describe the doors and windows in the room? Is there a window covering? Is it sheer or heavy and opaque? What color or colors does it contain? If there is a pattern, describe it.
    f. Can you describe the ceiling?
    g. Can you describe the wall covering? Is it painted or papered? What is its color? If there is a pattern, describe it.
    h. How many electrical switches are in the room? Where are they located? What color are the plates over the switches?
    i. How many light fixtures are in the room? Where are they located? Describe them.
    j. Are there any regular accessories in the room such as bedspreads, tablecloths, pictures, *objets d'art,* etc? Describe as many as you can.
    k. What is the shape of the room? Can you guess its approximate dimensions?
    l. Are there spots or marks on the ceiling, walls, or floor?
2. Go into any room and study one side of it carefully, then turn away and itemize everything you are able to recall about it. Include descriptions of all the objects that you recall in terms of color, texture, size, or specific characteristics. When you have finished, look again at that portion of the room selected and see how accurate you have been.
3. Ask someone to group a half-dozen objects on a table. Give yourself two or three minutes to look them over, then close your eyes and itemize the objects, describing colors, shapes, sizes, and special characteristics.

Continue this exercise regularly, adding to the number of objects on the table.

4. Select a tree in leaf that is in a part of your regular environment. Study it carefully, then turn away and answer the following questions:
    a. How tall is the tree?
    b. What is the color or colors of its trunk?
    c. Is the trunk smooth textured or rough? Describe it.
    d. How does the trunk of the tree stand on the ground? Is the ground smooth around its base, or are there gnarled roots above the surface of the ground?
    e. Is the tree perfectly upright or is it leaning? If it is inclined, which way does it lean?
    f. Do the branches of the tree form a round or triangular head?
    g. Does the head of the tree have an open appearance or one of density?
    h. What about the follage? What is its shape, size, and color?
    i. Can you ascribe some overall characteristic to the tree? Does it impress you as "Proud?" "Fat?" "Droopy?" "Stark?" "Flamboyant?"

    Look once again at the tree and determine how accurate you have been.

5. In performing your daily functions, look more closely at your surroundings, trying to discover what you have not noticed before. If you are a student living in a dormitory, for example, what natural or man-made objects on your campus lie in your path from dormitory to classroom? Have you ever really "seen" your classroom in terms of the questions asked in the first exercise in this series?

You will notice that most of these exercises have been related to your *regular* environment. How much of it have you really been prone to see? Is it apparent that you are now in essence looking at these familiar surroundings for the first time? Can you understand why many artists believe that in one sense they must observe the familiar as if they themselves were children first becoming aware of the existence of things around them?

People

The actor is especially responsible for seeing people in the same way (although the human world, of course, is much more complex), with the same eye for external detail as has been suggested for a tree or a room. Whether he does it consciously or subconsciously, in fragmentary or complete fashion, the actor will benefit by building a storehouse of character references consisting of his observations of people. Anton Chekhov was in the habit of writing most things down as he saw them, for use in his stories and plays.

The Personal Papers of Anton Chekhov is a published collection of his notebook, letters, and diary, and illustrates Chekhov's tendency to record what often appear to be the most trivial observations. Those who are familiar with his work, however, will recognize how he was able to put them to significant use. While most of the impressions he selected to record for future use consisted of fragments of incidents with an eye toward irony, Chekhov often recorded descriptions of the simplest physical characteristics, such as the following:

> She had not sufficient skin on her face; in order to open her eyes she had to shut her mouth and *vice versa.*
>
> A schoolboy with mustaches, in order to show off, limps with one leg.
>
> When he laughs, he shows his teeth and gums.
>
> A girl, when she giggles, makes noises as if she were putting her head in cold water.
>
> A man who when he fails opens his eyes wide.
>
> He picked his teeth and put the toothpick back into the glass.[1]

In Chekhov's case, part of his careful scrutiny of people was for the purpose of creating interesting characters for his plays and stories. The actor can do the same for the purpose of having the widest choice for the selection of character traits, which may eventually enhance the characters he is to bring to life.

As with the objects around us, it is not necessarily only the unusual, or the abnormal that should occupy our interest. When we really perceive, we find that the usual contains much that is *un*usual. The number of ways in which the most ordinary and undistinctive persons may differ in their actions may be infinite. It is interesting how, in describing the individual differences of such persons, we resort to the apparent distinctions of age, size, coloring, vocal traits, and obvious idiosyncrasies, and ignore innumerable details that more thoroughly and realistically distinguish one person from another.

EXERCISES

1. Select two persons of the same sex who strike you as having a great deal in common in terms of age, size, and type. Watch them closely and compare their postures and habitual stance. Notice whether both

of them distribute their weights in exactly the same way when standing still. How wide apart are their legs kept? In standing, does one seem more passive or active than the other? Are the knees bent? Are the toes pointing out, in, or straight ahead? What is the relation of elbows and wrists to the body? Are the hands and fingers of one more tense or relaxed than the other? Are their heads held erect, or tilted to one side? Is the chin held out or in, up or down? What little mannerisms appear in the facial expressions of each? Are the lips tense or relaxed? Does either tend to chew his upper or lower lip? Are the lips normally kept open or closed? Are the eyes straining or relaxed? Does one blink more than the other? Do the eyes of one look about more than the other? Watch the breathing rhythms of each. Does one take deeper breaths than the other? Apply the same observations to these persons moving and sitting. When they are speaking what characteristics do you notice? Does one gesticulate more than the other? Where and how does the gesticulation occur? Does one use his fingers, hands, wrists, lower arms, or shoulders more than the other? What are the differences in the pace, timbre, quality, and pitch of their voices? Does one hesitate and take more time to respond than the other? Is the use of "UH" or habitual voice-clearing typical of either?

2.   Ask each of the persons whom you have selected to perform an act common to most of us, such as brushing the teeth. Do they do this in exactly the same way? Even if both are familiar with the correct manner of brushing up and down, do they brush the same way? Do they hold their brushes alike? Do they brush with the same speed and pressure? On what side of the mouth do they start? How long do they take? How do they apply toothpaste to the toothbrush? Do they recap the toothpaste tube before brushing or after—or at all? How often do they rewet the brush? Do both of them allow the water tap to stay open all the while they are brushing? Or do they turn the water on only when they wish to rinse off their brushes? Do both persons study their teeth in the mirror as they brush? Or do they do this before or after? Do both rinse their mouths after brushing? How? Select other normal habitual human functions and perceive how these functions vary in terms of individual differences.

3.   Select two persons with whom you have the opportunity of fairly intimate observation. One should be around your own age, and the other considerably older. Following a general scrutiny such as the kind already indicated in which personal physical habits and characteristics are studied, observe very carefully some specific activity that you will be responsible to perform.

   Investigate such questions as the following: how does each of these individuals get up in the morning? go to bed at night? eat a meal? play cards, or some other indoor game? read a book, magazine or newspaper? Remember that no detail should be ignored in your study and subsequent imitation. Movements and variations of the movements of the face, head, neck, shoulders, elbows, arms, wrists, hands, fingers, torso, hips, legs, knees, feet, and even toes, in each of their activities should be carefully scrutinized and accurately reenacted. Out of such an exercise, not only should you achieve a distinct awareness of subtle individual differences, but of differences caused by age. Such differences probably will be less in terms of physical attributes than in how those attributes are used. You will notice, for example, that speed, rhythm, tone, and flexibility of muscular action and response will vary considerably.

Thus far, the emphasis in the observation of other people has been upon ordinary outward physical characteristics that distinguish one person from another. An additional type of external study is possible in terms of behavior, or in the observation of people under the influence of particular attitudes and emotions, for individuals vary greatly in terms of their reaction to their environments and to other people. Man often responds differently to the same stimuli. We do not all respond to hot and cold in exactly the same way. Some of us are more restrained, others more demonstrative, when it comes to expressing our feelings and attitudes. In coping with problems, some of us are more tolerant, some less, and some not tolerant at all, of frustration. Some are more influenced by reason in dealing with obstacles and goals, others by emotion, and some appear to become indifferent. In addition to these broader categories of behavior, individuals have their own distinct physical mannerisms in expressing their responses. Consequently, in studying behavior, the actor will be concerned with the way in which responses are expressed. For example, he may notice that the person he is studying has a tendency to restrain anger—to fight back his own ire when provoked. The actor must then ask how his model communicated this quality to him. He may have noticed that the character began, as he became irritated, to speak more slowly, quietly, deliberately; that the muscles in his face, particularly around the cheeks and jaws, seemed to tighten; that his lips appeared to purse; that he took deeper breaths; that he refused to make eye contact with his adversary; that there was an occasional shift of discomfort in his legs or torso; that his hands may have been clenched or occupied with some unconscious action, such as the rubbing together of finger and thumb, or palm of one hand stroking the back of the other, or palms wiping against the outside of the thighs. Perhaps he had some peculiar idiosyncrasy such as pursing his lips, or, when seated, raising one leg on its toes and jiggling the leg up and down.

EXERCISES

1. Using the two characters, one young and one old, who were selected for a previous exercise, study in particular these characters' modes of response to separate stimuli. What is the characteristic way in which each one expresses certain attitudes and emotions?
2. Select one major response for each character, study in the most complete detail the outward manifestations of each response, and demonstrate your findings to an audience.

Once the actor has begun the process of careful scrutiny of other people, he must never stop. He must continue to be receptive to impressions of the people with whom he comes in contact. Eventually, he should acquire the habit of recording his impressions automatically. In supermarkets, subways and buses, on park benches, in his own and at other people's houses, he must see people in terms of their individual traits and differences, including their responses to external stimuli. In addition, the actor must expose himself to environments other than his own: perhaps a horse show for the milieu of the wealthy, a slum area for that of poverty, or hospitals and asylums, where he may observe responses to pain, suffering, and psychotic behavior, and areas where he may perceive other nationalities and regional types. There should be a regular time, too, when he reflects over recent encounters, recalling what he considers to be the significant impressions made upon him. He might make a nightly habit, as he prepares himself for sleep, to think of two or three persons he has seen that day, and to recall as many of the details as possible that distinguished them.

Secondary Sources

Thus far our attention, in the observation of other people, has been directed toward the primary source, that is, the person himself studied by the artist firsthand. There also are secondary sources for observation that can prove to be of great value in the actor's study of the outward manifestations of human behavior.

The actor's secondary sources consist of the descriptions of individuals by other people. The previously cited notations of Chekhov observations are, for us, examples of secondary source material. Autobiography, biography, descriptions in books, periodicals, and newspapers provide secondary source material. The actor learns through these the behavior of man second-hand, which is better than not at all, and in those instances where a superior reporter is at work, the actor may receive descriptions that are potentially more perceptive than his own.

Those of us who are concerned with other people and their behavior usually, like storytellers, enjoy sharing our observations. There is no reason why the actor cannot add striking descriptions by others to his storehouse of character portraits. In fact, there are many instances when the actor is obliged to rely heavily on secondary sources. When he is to portray an actual person rather than a fictitious one, he is under some obligation to learn as much as possible of that person's physical and vocal attributes, so that he may select with some accuracy those details that he believes are pertinent to, or will enrich, the writer's point of view. In the characterization of a personality as recent and as distinctive as President Franklin Delano Roosevelt in Dore Schary's *Sunrise at Campobello,* the actor would be neglecting his duty if he were to ignore photographs, recordings, biographical materials, and motion picture clips (if available) in order to suggest the physical endowments of a man with whom audiences still may be familiar. How much richer the portrayal when the actor has access to Roosevelt's characteristic head tilt, his way of smoking a cigarette, the kind of glasses he used, the way he wore his hat, and his unique speech pattern!

BIOGRAPHY. One biographical portrayal that has been highly successful on the stage is that of Annie Sullivan, the teacher of Helen Keller, in William Gibson's *The Miracle Worker.* Gibson has selected the events in the life of his protagonist that transformed her from an ignorant savage to a civilized, reasoning human being. Unlike the character of Roosevelt, Miss Sullivan's personal physical characteristics were not familiar to the public, and there is little to help us in the way of photographs or records that might be relevant to this period in her life. In a recent biography, physical descriptions of Annie at twenty, the age during which she began to work with Helen Keller, are practically nonexistent. But several tangibles in her character have been suggested, upon which Gibson has drawn, which should stimulate the actress into finding an external image of Annie. In the aforementioned biography, *The Touch of Magic* by Lorena H. Hickok, the following scattered descriptions are made:

> Finding a home for Annie would have been difficult enough because she was going blind. She also had a very bad disposition, was subject to violent outbursts of temper and had never in her short life shown

the slightest trace of love or affection for anyone. A child psychologist would have understood that a child in her predicament would be apt to develop into a little lone wolf fighting the world.[2]

Annie, in later life, is quoted as saying, as she spoke of Alexander Graham Bell, "I never really felt at ease with anyone until I met him. I was extremely conscious of my crudeness, and because I felt this inferiority, I carried a chip on my shoulder which somebody was forever trying to snap off.[3]

William Gibson, in converting Annie into a dramatic character, suggests certain traits that are evidently based upon the behavior tendencies of the young Annie. His introduction to the character states, "The chair contains a girl of twenty, Annie Sullivan, with a face which in repose is grave and rather obstinate, and when active is impudent, combative, twinkling with all the life that is lacking in Helen's and handsome. There is a crude vitality to her."[4]

As a result of such limited physical description, the actress playing the part will have more freedom in finding the appropriate physical concept of Annie Sullivan than the actor playing Roosevelt. There is, however, in the portrayal of this great woman, an aspect of physical characterization that is perhaps more concrete and specific, requiring investigation into other areas of primary or secondary sources—or both. Annie always had eye trouble. She suffered from a disease called *trachoma,* and Gibson has included this defect as part of his depiction of the character. In such an instance, the actor is obliged to learn the nature of the disease and, what is more important, what it makes its victim do. In the Hickok biography, the disease is described as follows: "When a person has trachoma, the lumps inside the eyelids, soft and fuzzy at first, eventually become hard, like calluses. These keep scratching the eyeballs, causing ulcers and scar tissue. Gradually the scar tissue covers the eyes, and blindness results."[5]

When Annie was twenty she had had a successful operation that restored her vision, but the result was not perfect. Her eyes were tender, sensitive to light, and tired easily. She wore dark glasses to protect her eyes from glare. The responsibility of the actress playing Annie is to investigate and, if possible, observe directly, the victims of *trachoma* or of similar eye afflictions. What, the actress should determine, do these unfortunate patients do when they attempt to focus upon an object? How does their expression vary with the distances or sizes of the objects they wish to see clearly? How do they react to glare? What do they do when they feel that their eyes are strained or irritated? How does a person of uncertain vision move about?

FICTION. Helpful secondary sources of observation may also be found in the depictions of character in other art forms. In narrative literature, the writer has more freedom than does the dramatist in presenting a complete and literal description of his characters and what they do. Some writers, such as Thomas Wolfe, occasionally resort to the most minute details in their depiction of character. For example, in Wolfe's novel *You Can't Go Home Again,* the tenth chapter consists of twelve pages that describe the awakening and early morning activity of Mr. Frederick Jack, a vigorous businessman in his middle years, proud of the success and order of his life. Here are a few extracts that conceivably might be of value to an actor playing a similar character:

At seven twenty-eight Mr. Frederick Jack awoke and began to come alive with all his might. He sat up and yawned strongly, stretching his arms and at the same time bending his slumber-swollen face into the plump muscle-hammock of his right shoulder, a movement coy and cuddlesome. "Eee-a-a-a-ach!" He stretched deliciously out of thick, rubbery sleep, and for a moment he sat heavily upright rubbing at his eyes with the clenched backs of his fingers. Then he flung off the covers with one determined motion and swung to the floor. His toes groped blindly in soft grey carpet stuff, smooth as felt, for his heelless slippers of red Russian leather. These found and slipped into, he padded noiselessly across the carpet to the window and stood, yawning and stretching again, as he looked out with sleepy satisfaction at a fine, crisp morning.[6]

Thoroughly awake now, Mr. Jack closed the window and moved briskly across his chamber to the bathroom. He liked lavish plumbing, thick with creamy porcelain and polished silver fixtures. For a moment he stood before the deep wash basin with bared lips, looking at himself in the mirror, and regarding with considerable satisfaction the health and soundness of his strong front teeth. Then he brushed them earnestly with stiff, hard bristles and two inches of firm, thick paste, turning his head from side to side around the brush and glaring at his image in the glass until he foamed agreeably at the mouth with a lather that tasted of fresh mint. This done, he spat it out and let running water wash it down the drain, and then he rinsed his mouth and throat with gently biting antiseptic.

He liked the tidy, crowded array of lotions, creams, unguents, bottles, tubes, jars, brushes, and shaving implements that covered the shelf of thick blue glass above the basin. He lathered his face heavily with a large silver-handled shaving brush, rubbing the lather in with firm fingertips, brushing and stroking till his jaws were covered with a smooth, thick layer of warm shaving cream. Then he took the razor in his hand and opened it. He used a straight razor, and he always kept it in excellent condition. At the crucial moment, just before the first long downward stroke, he flourished slightly forward with his plump arms and shoulders, raising the glittering blade aloft in one firm hand, his legs widened stockily, crouching gently at the knees, his lathered face craned carefully to one side and upward, and his eyes rolled toward the ceiling, as if he were getting braced and ready beneath a heavy burden. Then, holding one cheek delicately between two arched fingers, he advanced deliberately upon it with the gleaming blade. He grunted gently, with satisfaction, at the termination of the stroke. The blade had mown smoothly, leaving a perfect swath of pink, clean flesh across his face from cheek to jowl. He exulted in the slight tug and rasping pull of wiry stubble against the deadly sharpness of the razor, and in the relentless sweep and triumph of the steel.[7]

Dickens' eccentric characters are defined inevitably in terms of external actions that clearly reveal their essential traits. Notice how the following examples from *David Copperfield* not only stimulate clear images of the characters in our imaginations, but point the way to the inner men themselves. First, observe the following descriptions of the cheerful, simple-minded Mr. Dick:

The unbroken stillness of the parlour-window leading me to infer, after a while, that she was not there, I lifted up my eyes to the window above it, where I saw a florid, pleasant-looking gentleman, with a grey head, who shut up one eye in a grotesque manner, nodded his head at me several times, shook it at me as often, laughed, and went away.[8]

Mr. Dick, as I have already said, was grey-headed and florid: I should have said all about him, in saying so, had not his head been curiously bowed—not by age; it reminded me of one of Mr. Creakle's boys' heads after a beating—and his grey eyes prominent and large, with a strange kind of watery brightness in them that made me, in combination with his vacant manner, his submission to my aunt, and his childish delight when she praised him, suspect him of being a little mad; though, if he were mad, how he came to be there, puzzled me extremely. He was dressed like any other ordinary gentleman, in a loose grey morning coat and waistcoat, and white trousers; and had his watch in his fob, and his money in his pockets: which he rattled as if he were very proud of it.[9]

"Mr. Dick. An old and intimate friend. On whose judgment," said my aunt, with emphasis, as an admonition to Mr. Dick, who was biting his forefinger and looking rather foolish, "I rely."

Mr. Dick took his finger out of his mouth, on this hint, and stood among the group, with a grave and attentive expression of face.[10]

And here are some of the outward manifestations of literature's supreme hypocrite, Uriah Heep:

As he held the door open with his hand, Uriah looked at me, and looked at Agnes, and looked at the dishes, and looked at the plates, and looked at every object in the room, I thought,—yet seemed to look at nothing; he made such an appearance all the while of keeping his red eyes dutifully on his master.[11]

But, seeing a light in the little round office, and immediately feeling myself attracted towards Uriah Heep, who had a sort of fascination for me, I went in there instead. I found Uriah reading a great fat book, with such demonstrative attention, that his lank forefinger followed up every line as he read, and made clammy tracks along the page (or so I fully believed) like a snail.

"You are working late to-night, Uriah," says I.

"Yes, Master Copperfield," says Uriah.

As I was getting on the stool opposite, to talk to him more conveniently, I observed that he had not such a thing as a smile about him, and that he could only widen his mouth and make two hard creases down his cheeks, one on each side, to stand for one.

"I am not doing office-work, Master Copperfield," said Uriah.

"What work, then?" I asked.

"I am improving my legal knowledge, Master Copperfield," said Uriah. "I am going through Tidd's Practice. Oh, what a writer Mr. Tidd is, Master Copperfield!"

My stool was such a tower of observation, that as I watched him reading on again, after this rapturous exclamation, and following up the lines with his forefinger, I observed that his nostrils, which were thin and pointed, with sharp dints in them, had a singular and most uncomfortable way of expanding and contracting themselves; that they seemed to twinkle instead of his eyes, which hardly ever twinkled at all.

"I suppose you are quite a great lawyer?" I said, after looking at him for some time.

"Me, Master Copperfield?" said Uriah. "Oh, no! I'm a very umble person."

It was no fancy of mine about his hands, I observed; for he frequently ground the palms against each other as if to squeeze them dry and warm, besides often wiping them, in a stealthy way, on his pocket-handkerchief.[12]

It would not be unwise for the aspiring actor to establish a reference file of character descriptions and states of being that have impressed him with their sharpness and insight. He might simply categorize these characters, so that as he is faced with particular roles, he could check his file, which would in turn refer him to the various characters he has recorded under specific types.

VISUAL ARTS. Another secondary source may be found in the visual arts and in photography. Illustrations in books, when executed with imagination, as they were in the nineteenth century, may be stimulating to the actor in many ways. In addition to showing how the dress of a particular period may have been worn, these illustrations often capture a frozen moment that reveals the essence of a character, a position and expression that capture a particular attitude, state of mind, or emotion. Look at the "Phiz" illustrations in *David Copperfield* for a good example of this. The illustration "Somebody turns up," between pages 260 and 261 of the New Oxford Illustrated Dickens first published in 1948, provides a marvelous view of Uriah Heep, skinny and slimy, seated on the very edge of a chair, his thin legs close together, with the toes of his left foot pressing on those of his right, his elbows close in as he puts the tips of his long bony fingers together, leaning toward David, shoulders hunched with humbly smiling face tilted to one side. "Mr. Micawber delivers some valedictory remarks," between pages 516 and 517, shows Micawber standing and pompously addressing his listeners. His egg-shaped head is tilted to one side, as he smiles with eyebrows raised, the left eyebrow slightly higher than the right. His elbows are extended, as his left hand rests, thumb up and index finger straight down, upon his paunchy stomach. The other hand is bent gracefully from the wrist in a magnanimous open gesture.

30

FIGURE 2-1. *"Somebody turns up." Dickens's* David Copperfield, *illustrated by H. K. Browne ("Phiz"). Victoria and Albert Museum, Crown Copyright.*

One does not have to play either of these roles to make use of what he finds here. These expressions clearly essentialize false humility, and ludicrous, but dignified, self-importance for all time. The same may be said for portraiture and sculpture, which may capture the single moment when a significant trait of character, or an emotion, a style of stance, the essence of youth or age is expressed. Who can embark upon a play of the eighteenth century without Hogarth? How helpful might be the character studies in Rembrandt's *Night Watch,* or Leonardo's studies of old age!

The photograph, too, whether candid or posed, may provide similar benefits. Pictures in the daily newspapers or news periodicals reveal to us the most truthful and often most unexpected expressions of grief, fear, joy, hatred, stoicism, shyness, affections, and the like. Candid shots of people of all ages from many walks of life are the materials of many of the world's great photographers. Study the fascinating pictures of Alfred Steiglitz, Edward Weston, Henri Cartier-Bresson, Edward Steichen, and Margaret Bourke-White, and notice how they observe the human scene.

31

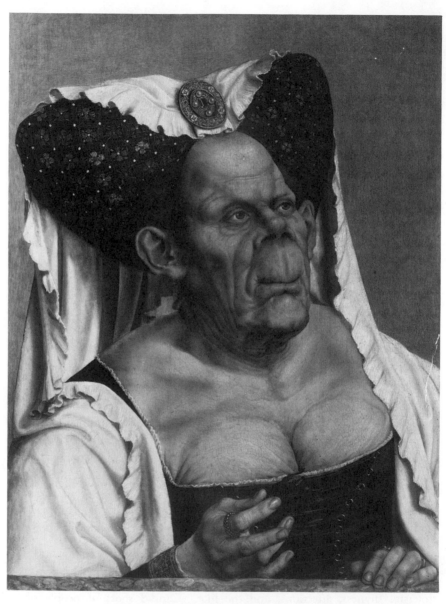

FIGURE 2-2. *"A Grotesque Old Woman," painted by Quinten Massys,
c. 1510-20. Reproduced by courtesy of the Trustees,
The National Gallery, London.*

EXERCISES

1. Think back on some of your favorite books. Can you recall authors who concentrated upon describing the external details of their characters? Go back and review some of these. Specifically relate the actions that are described to the nature of the character, and/or his various states of mind, emotion, or attitude.

2. If you are not in the habit now, begin to familiarize yourself with works of art, particularly those concerned with the depiction of people. Select one or two paintings that impress you, try and state your overall impression of them, and carefully analyze the artist's treatment so that you may determine how he succeeded in evoking your impression.

3. Do the same with photographs from newspapers, magazines, and photograph collections. Locate a copy of the Steichen collection, *The Family of Man,* published in 1955 for the Museum of Modern Art by the Maco Magazine Corporation,[13] and select pictures that represent the various ages of man from youth to old age, and those which capture the emotions, devotion, ecstasy, grief, fear, etc., and study them carefully.

4. Imitate in still life one of each of the above sources.

5. Find a single appropriate action for each of the above, and perform it sustaining the characteristics of the source imitated.

ANALOGY AND METAPHOR

While the proper study of man is, of course, man, it is not uncommon for man to understand or describe himself in terms of analogy or metaphor, where he compares himself and his fellow beings to animals and objects. When people are compared with gazelles, or with pigs, we react immediately to an image that characterizes a person more meaningfully than an objective physical description, because an attitude also is evoked. There is a difference between referring to someone as merely "graceful," and comparing him to a gazelle, which reminds us of a particular kind of grace—dignified, alert, gliding; between saying that someone is "fat and sloppy" or calling him a pig, which brings about the vision of a cumbersome, obese, habitually dirty member of the animal kingdom, with floppy ears, a snout, beady eyes, and ludicrous "oinks." Of particular value to the actor is the mental image that analogy suggests. If he is to portray a graceful or a sloppy character, how much more stimulated will he be by the image of a specific corresponding animal than by any number of adjectives!

33

The actor does not merely aid himself with metaphorical images, but through the actions that his images stimulate, he inevitably creates a similar metaphorical image for his audience. The actor should, in fact, be as adept as the poet in making analogies, and he can only do this by heightening his perception of the animal and physical world. Suppose, for example, the actor wishes to project a character with great physical strength. He has many choices for demonstrating strength, depending upon the essential nature of his character. A sympathetic or admirable character might have the steady, solid strength of an oak, or the dignified, graceful, and velvet strength of a panther, but a ludicrous or unsympathetic person might be portrayed as having the heavy, dull, and plodding strength of an ox, or the crude, dangerous, inhuman strength of a gorilla. In such instances, the selection of certain characteristics of the animal chosen will provide the actor with meaningful expression, and the audience with the kind of intensified recognition for which metaphor is so useful.

Animals

There are a number of occasions when the playwright himself deliberately will model characters upon members of the animal kingdom. Aristophanes was the first in the history of extant drama to do this. In *The Birds,* for example, his performers undoubtedly were costumed to represent various birds, and were required to imitate their external characteristics. Ben Jonson's *Volpone* is an outstanding example of the conscious use of animal analogy in the depiction of character. Jonson provided the major characters in the play with names of animals. Volpone is "an old fox . . . an old, crafty, sly, subtle companion"; Mosca is "any kind of fly"; Voltore is "a ravenous bird called a vulture"; Corbaccio is "a filthy great raven"; and Corvino is a "crow, raven."[14] The actors playing these roles must recognize and make a study of the animals they are supposed to represent, utilizing their appropriate physical and vocal mannerisms. More recently, Ionesco's *Rhinoceros* has provided a challenge to actors, who must undergo a metamorphosis in the play from human being to rhinoceros. The actor playing Jean should spend considerable time observing the rhinoceros firsthand at the zoo, in photographs, and in films.

Most plays do not specifically designate a metaphorical object, but the perceptive and creative actor will be aware of the potential connection between characters and animals, and make use of such a connection to essentialize certain facets of his character's personality. Examples of such processes are included under "Imagination and Observation," in Chapter Three.

FIGURE 2-3. *Corbaccio in Ben Jonson's* Volpone, *in the Santa Barbara Repertory Theatre production.*

Objects

Objects, too, may provide useful keys to the portrayal of certain types. People are not infrequently compared with living objects such as trees, flowers, or vegetables, and nonliving objects such as furniture, machines, bowls, jars, or pitchers. For example, trees may give the impression of great dignity and strength, stretching straight and tall, or they may be squat and deformed; some trees droop sadly, some are thin and delicate, some are old and gnarled. Note that all of these characteristics may be applied to people. In fact, some of these descriptions really consist of the projection of human traits upon nonhuman objects so that the analogy is reversed and the objects remind us of people. Inanimate objects, like animals, often may provide excellent mental images. The furniture of different periods or cultures may tell us a great deal about the people who made and used them, and provide us with a sense of character. A chair, for example, may be crude or refined, heavy and solid, or light, delicate and airy, extremely ornate, or simple and practical. Chairs, like humans, have legs and often arms. They have characteristic postures: some stand upright, some are curved, some tilt back, some seem to wish to embrace you.

One of the most delightful examples of the use of an object as an aid to characterization is told by David Itkin, once a member of the Moscow Art Theatre, and a former teacher and director at the Goodman Theatre in

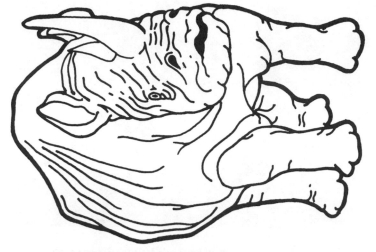

b) the result.

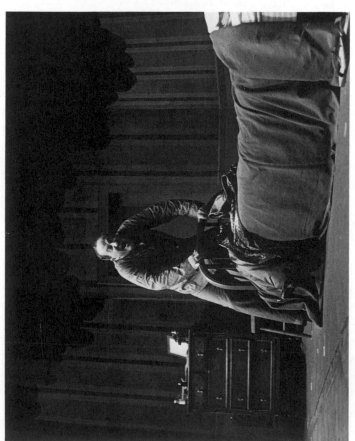

FIGURE 2.4. "Man into Rhinoceros": a) the "turning" scene,
Scene from Ionesco's Rhinoceros, as performed at the
University of California at Santa Barbara.

FIGURE 2-5. *A Victorian style chair. Victoria and Albert Museum,
Crown Copyright.*

FIGURE 2-6. *A samovar style chair. Victoria and Albert Museum, Crown Copyright.*

Chicago. In the following extract from a letter to this writer, he describes how, in portraying a character, he was inspired by his observation of a samovar:

> The Samovar, per se, is utilized to indicate the external image of a character. By that I mean, the object itself by the very nature of its shape reminds one of a very pompous and stuffy person. Also, I might add, one who displays great dignity with a penchant for exhibitionism. (As opposed, of course, to the lowly, everyday tea or coffeepot.) The handles are to me the individual's hands, and again denote a pompous strength and solidity. I can see this character lowering them and rubbing them over his protruding abdomen.

Notice how Itkin describes the evolution of the object from its inanimate state into movement. Frequently by first absorbing the physical characteristics of the still object, the actor is stimulated into imagining how the object might move and even sound.

FIGURE 2-7. *"Samovar into Man."*

EXERCISES

Select a member of the bird family and some other animal that feasibly may be observed by you.

1. Describe the features of the bird and the animal respectively: are the eyes large or small, close together or far apart? is the forehead large or small? is the nose or beak prominent? straight? curving? flat? what are the shape and size of the mouth? does it bare teeth or fangs? what is the relationship between eyes, nose, and mouth? Describe the body and legs of each. Do they stand straight? Do they hold their heads up or down? Are their legs tall or short, bowed or straight?

2. Describe the bird and the animal in motion: do they have distinctive characteristics when moving? do they appear to be coordinated? do they move rapidly or slowly? Describe the movement and positions of all parts of the body of each when in motion.

3. Describe the bird and animal in terms of activity: how do they eat? how do they react to other animals? to people? If they play, describe their movements, rhythms, and habits.

4. Create pantomimes involving the bird and the animal. Begin each pantomime by imitating their features only, then imitate their movement, and finally imitate an activity that you believe is most characteristic of your selections.

5. Select another animal, study it carefully, and create a pantomime as above.

Select a living but inanimate object, and a man-made object.

1. Study the material of which the objects are made. Are they hard or soft? Smooth, rough, or lumpy? Bright or dull?

2. Study their structure. Are they upright or bent? Wide or narrow? High or low? Heavy or light? Ornate or simple? Do they appear to open out or be closed in on themselves? Can you compare the parts of the object to parts of the human body?

3. Are they perfectly static or do they move under certain influences? For example, if you have selected a tree, notice how it is affected by wind, rain, or snow. If a rocking chair, how does it rock?

4. Imitate as closely as you can your objects of study. Begin with a static portrait based on a mental image, then depending upon your selection, demonstrate how it is affected by external forces. Finally, whether your objects move or not, move as you think they *might* move if they could.

The primary purpose of any artist is to intensify and illuminate the vision of his audience. To succeed in this, he must develop a superawareness of the world about him. As he develops his perception he decreases the need to resort to clichés and stereotypes. He must, of course, develop the techniques and skills to project his vision, but these can only be vacuous and wasteful when they serve trivia.

OBSERVATION: THE INNER
WORLD

The actor, in the final analysis, can rely, for his understanding and expression of character, upon the extent and manner in which he absorbs experience. We have thus far been concerned with what has been referred to as the "external world," or the world viewed through the senses. There are certain experiences, however, that are personal and subjective, which the actor must explore as closely as the things outside himself. He must develop an awareness of his *own* responses to stimuli, since these responses are usually more meaningful to the individual experiencing them than when they are derived secondhand. The chief purpose of such self-exploration is not to be self-indulgent or therapeutic, but to broaden and develop the actor's capacity to become more aware of truthful internal experience and its manifestations.

Just as the average person lives from one day to the next negligent of his environment, he also is inclined to ignore his own sensory and emotional reactions. There is, after all, no reason for him to reflect upon the way he had felt during certain circumstances. Why should he analyze his sensory or emotional responses to such conditions as freezing, burning, being angry with his best friend, or mourning a close relative? For the actor, however, the recollection of such states is absolutely vital to his art. Just as he must be ultrasensitive to the world about him, so also he must be ultrasensitive to his inner responses.

One of the reasons why it is most important for actors, or any artist for that matter, to learn how to explore their inner world is that it will help them to avoid easy clichés, or stereotyped ways of expressing specific sensory and emotional reactions. There was a time, indeed, when those involved in dramatic art sought for universal ways of expression so that audiences might easily and unmistakably recognize a given emotional state. The result was facile recognition, but little insight into the potential variety of emotional experience, and little belief in the actor's conviction concerning the emotion expressed. Acting with such theories could only become stale and repetitious. The fallacy of such an approach lies in the belief that an audience needs to be supplied with the least common denominator of an emotion in order to be able to recognize it, whereas in reality, the audience will respond to and accept unusual responses if they are truthful and in proper context. In addition, the least common denominator of an emotion may be completely false or incongruous with that emotion as expressed in a particular individual in a particular situation. The fact is that most of the time people do not react in terms of a least common denominator. On the stage, Miss Julie and Argan will not exhibit their fears in the same way, and several actors and actresses may achieve correct though distinctly different expressions of fear when playing the same character.

One of the functions of the artist, as has been previously emphasized, is to awaken the spectator to aspects of experience of which the latter has not been sufficiently aware, and often these aspects of experience prove to be the simplest and (after we have been reminded) the most obvious ones, so that frequently the observer will say, with great surprise, "Of course!" For example, in many of our sensory responses we normally use senses that are not directly related to a stimulus. Sometimes when we want to hear better what a person is saying, we *look* at him more intently, rather than hold a hand to one of our ears. In a dark, unfamiliar room, we rely upon touch, of course, to move safely about, but frequently we *listen* more acutely too. In such a situation, touch would not necessarily be limited to the fingers and hands, but would also include explorations of the feet.

On the stage the actor moves about in a world of make-believe. He must appear to be cold when the theatre is hot; he must appear to be groping about in a darkened room, when the light that illuminates him for the audience is bright enough for him actually to see; he must appear to hate an actor whom he really likes, or to love one to whom he is indifferent; he must eat lustily when he has no appetite, or appear to be starving when he has had a full meal just a few hours ago; he must drink colored water and convince an audience it is wine, or drink ice-cold coffee and appear to have scalded his mouth. Through such appearances, he must convince his observers of the imagined reality of the stimuli to which he responds, and to do this successfully—that is, believably—he must find the most truthful way to respond to the imagined stimuli. In turn, his capacity to produce the most significant kinds of honest response depends upon his own sharpened awareness of the world of sense and emotion.

The Senses

During rehearsals for a college production of a play, one of the actors was responsible for making an entrance which demanded the illusion that the character had come a long distance on foot, and was in a desperate hurry. The actor's first tendency was to pant and heave his shoulders. The result was unbelievable because he had little belief in the action he was attempting to perform. He was relying upon the easily recalled cliché, and was concentrating upon the *effect* of breathlessness instead of his own perception of the actual response.

In order to solve the problem, during rehearsals the actor ran back and forth behind the setting just before his entrance. The result was that he was unable to utter a line until he could catch his breath, and when he spoke, he lacked the breath control to project his lines. An audience might believe in the character's condition now, but at the expense of being able to follow the action of the play. Absolute reality on the stage will not, in many cases, succeed; often it simply is not possible. It has been indicated previously that conditions of light, sound, or temperature must be illusory. The theatre is not real life, and no one expects it to be, but often it is necessary that it create a satisfactory illusion of real life, so that while the actor's stimulus may begin in reality, on the stage he presents the illusion or the representation of that reality. In the case of the running actor, the performer had, in essence, the correct idea. He attempted to discover the actual condition of breathlessness by putting himself through a real experience involving the cause and effect of breathlessness. He failed to realize, however, that this is only the first step, and that the stage realization of his experience is dependent upon the controlled re-creation of that experience. The step between experience and performance is the analysis of the experience and its reenactment by recollection rather than by reproduction.

The actor was aware of the cause of his breathlessness: considerable running without rest. He became aware that when he was out of breath, more was involved than panting and heaving. He learned that his mouth was dry, and that his tongue was swollen; that the need of his body for air caused him to breathe more rapidly than usual. In fact, it did not seem possible that he could satisfy that need, so he tried to breathe more deeply, to suck in as much oxygen as he could. He found that such circumstances made facile speech impossible, and that he had to slow down his speech and get in sufficient air to support it. He had to suck in even more air in order to speak with adequate strength. In order to supply himself with the necessary amount of oxygen, he had to breathe through his mouth, and expand his chest and rib cage. This meant that he could get out only a few words at a time, so that normal phrasing became difficult. He had to wet his tongue and lips in order to enunciate, otherwise the words would stick painfully in his mouth. He understood that it took him quite a while to recover; that while his breathing became more normal and his speech easier, the process was gradual rather than abrupt, and that when he had had his say, he continued to gasp and breathe deeply, and desired something moist for his dried-up mouth.

Note that in describing the recalled circumstances, we have emphasized the *cause* of the condition, *how* it made the victim *feel,* and *what* it made him *do.* While it is this last aspect, the effect, that will convey the necessary ideas to the audience, such effects are thoroughly dependent upon the actor's awareness of their causes. The actor has, for example, licked his lips and tried to induce more saliva (the effect) *because* he was aware of the tendency to dehydrate (the sensation), which occurred when he ran vigorously without pause over a certain period of time (the cause). Ideally, during the performance, the actor must never concentrate upon how he feels or upon effects, but upon the stimulus, which if sufficiently strong and vivid, should set off the appropriate responses. Of course, should the actor's stimulus produce no sense of truth in the actor's response, he will *automatically* respond with the action he has rehearsed. The value of relying primarily upon stimuli is that, as in real life, they produce sensations and actions that have the illusion of spontaneity. When the actor concentrates upon effect, the reaction is liable to appear studied and mechanical. As undesirable as a mechanical reaction might be, however, it is preferable to no reaction at all, or to one based upon a cliché. What is important is that the actor should rely, whenever possible, upon his own experience, recalling details that will enable him to produce actions which might otherwise be unrealized.

In many instances, the performer will be unable to test an actual sensory experience, such as was possible in the incident of breathlessness, in order to realize the consequent sensations and responses. For example, one of the situations in *The Would-Be Invalid* requires that Argan react to scalding water on his feet. No actor in his right mind would insist on pouring scalding water on his own feet even for the sake of his art—especially when such action might result in incapacitating him for the role!

There are several alternatives to finding honest solutions for such problems, and most of them involve the *recollection* of previous similar sensory experiences. In the anecdote concerning the actor who needed to create the illusion of breathlessness, the actor tested the actual experience, then instead of running every night, he relied upon his recall of cause, sensation, and response. In situations where the actual experience cannot reasonably be experimented with, the actor must seek similar or parallel experiences in his past. To illustrate, let us try and solve the problem of the scalded feet. The beginning of the episode in which Argan prepares to soak his feet may be solved simply. Most of us have had the experience of testing a hot bath, or a hot foot soak with our toes. We can recall that we gingerly pointed our toes toward the steaming water, planning to expose as little of our skin as possible. We quickly dipped the tips of the toes in and out, but not so quickly that we did not get an actual sense of the water's temperature. If the water was truly scalding hot, we withdrew sharply and flicked the smarting toes; perhaps, upon contact with the water, we had to take in a quick breath, possibly hissing between our teeth at the same time. We would recognize too that our entire body tensed, particularly the foot and calf, with the sensation of heat.

The actor might be able to experiment with all of this. But what about the actual scalding? Most of us, at one time or another, have burned ourselves. For some, it is not difficult at all to relive that time and to respond almost instinctively to the memory. It would be too easy, however, to generalize that response—that is, to recall our most obvious reactions to that sensation. In order to explore our specific reactions, some of which might actually have been rather unusual, we must find ways of sharpening the memory process through the following questions:

1. *When* did it happen?
2. *Why* did it happen?
3. *Under what conditions* did it happen?
4. *Where* did it happen? Describe as many sensory associations with the environment as you can.
5. What did you *do* when it happened?

The more vivid your recollection of the environment and all associated incidents, the more likely the possibility of a kind of self-hypnosis in which you can reexperience the event.

EXERCISES

Have four members of the group who have experienced a scalding try the procedure outlined above.
1. In reenacting the incident, each actor should concentrate upon the occasion, the environment, and the stimulus.
2. Observers should scrutinize the entire body of each performer as he acts out the experience.
3. Discuss the differences. Whom did you believe or disbelieve? Why? Did anyone do something unexpected but astonishingly correct?

On many occasions the actor will be confronted with the problem of producing certain sensory responses with which he will, in all probability, not have had direct experience. Desdemona suffocates to death. Most actresses playing the role probably never have had the experience of being nearly suffocated to death. Most Desdemonas just flail helplessly. The actress' task in such a situation is, first, to learn something about the experience of suffocation so that she may be able to liken it to comparable experiences that she may have undergone. Suffocation occurs when the lungs fail to receive sufficient air to sustain life. Breathing is impaired and finally stops altogether. The process is not unlike our previously discussed sensation of breathlessness. The individual who exerts himself to the point of being almost literally out of breath undergoes an act of partial suffocation. His organs are simply not receiving an adequate amount of oxygen. When this occurs, his lungs ache; he must breathe deeply; he depends upon the proper expansion of the chest and rib cage, and an uninterrupted flow of air from his nostrils and mouth. The objective of a person who is suffocating or is very much out of breath would be, "I must get air into my body at all costs!" Other parallels may be found in drowning, in trying to breathe in excessively humid heat, and in using lungs congested from respiratory infections. The performer may draw on any one of these, depending upon which of them provided her with the most severity, and which of them she is able to recall with the most clarity. This example shows how the actor, once the particular sensation has been investigated, attempts to find parallel experiences, then abstracts from them those characteristics which most nearly resemble those of the sensation desired.

A task that will facilitate the actor's job of sensory recall is one that parallels the recommendation made concerning observation of the external world. By becoming more aware of his own sensory responses immediately during or after their occurrence, the actor increases his ability to remember and utilize those responses. Extreme reactions to the experiences of sight, sound, touch, taste, and smell, as well as to experiences that enhance or inhibit them, should be studied and recorded mentally for future use. With many actors this is a habit performed almost instinctively.

EXERCISES

1. Perform a simple pantomime in which you express honest reactions to the following sensory stimuli:
   a. Glare
   b. Darkness

    c. Loud explosion

    d. Almost inaudible sound

    e. Rough texture

    f. Smooth texture

    g. Hot objects

    h. Hot atmosphere

    i. Cold

    j. Lifting a heavy weight

    k. Sweet food or liquid

    l. Sour edibles

    m. Bitter or hot taste

    n. Acrid odor

    o. Suspicious or subtle odors

2. Create pantomimes for each of the following fragments. In the process be sure to recognize, first, what senses are to be utilized. Look to your own experience to aid you, and follow the procedure described above to provide you with stimulus, sensation, and response. No actual properties should be used except tables or chairs, if necessary:

    a. You are a fugitive in a mountain cave. It is midnight and the temperature is near freezing.

    b. You are a King's taster. You are to test all five courses of the meal that he is about to eat. The fifth course is poisoned.

    c. You have just walked ten miles without resting. You finally stop and rest from extreme fatigue and discomfort.

    d. A bullet is being removed from your leg without anesthesia.

    e. You are living in a country at war. You are writing a letter by candlelight. Soon you detect poison gas. As the room fills with fumes, you search for a gas mask that you have misplaced.

    f. You are in a crowded but air-conditioned train. You get off into wet heat and glare. There is no shelter to protect you as you wait impatiently for transportation.

    g. You are alone in an isolated house. It is two o'clock in the morning, and you have had difficulty in going to sleep. You hear a strange noise. Eventually, you try to determine the source of the strange sound.

    h. You are reading a magazine and smoking a cigarette. (If you do not smoke, use observation of others to determine the habits of a smoker.) You read an article dealing with cigarettes as a major cause of lung cancer. You discard the cigarette, but begin to feel the urge for a substitute as you continue reading.

    i. You must trudge through mud to get to your back door. When you get there, you remove your shoes (in pantomime), and try to avoid getting your socks muddy. You then try the door. It is locked. You look for your key. It is gone. You put your shoes back on and wade to the front of the house.

3. Concentrating upon the senses, find the appropriate action for the following scenes (pantomime all objects):
   a. Start with Jean's line, early in the play, "Now have you got something good for me, Christine?" and conclude with Christine's line, "Some damn mess that Miss Julie wants for her dog."
   b. Pantomime Christine's actions when she washes the dishes.
   c. Pantomime Miss Julie removing the cinder from Jean's eye.
   d. Pantomime Argan's sudden need to go to the toilet.
   e. Work on Argan's opening monologue, pantomiming all properties.
   f. Perform the scene where Toinette and Angelique make the bed, again pantomiming all properties.

The Emotions

In the history of acting, many theories have evolved concerning the "correct" way of creating emotion, or the illusion of emotion, on the stage. These theories generally have fallen into two categories: working from the "outside in," and working from the "inside out." Both share the opinion that emotions on the stage must be communicated—that is, they must, in some way, move the audience with recognizable manifestations of emotion. Where they differ is in the methods used to create the desired response in the audience. In the famous late-nineteenth century controversy between Constant Coquelin, the great French actor, and the well-known English actor Henry Irving, the Frenchman appeared to favor an external approach and the Englishman an internal one. Coquelin stated,

> The actor ought never to let his part "run away" with him. It is false and ridiculous to think that it is a proof of the highest art for the actor to forget that he is before the public. If you identify yourself with your part to the point of asking yourself, as you look at the audience, "What are all those people doing here?"—if you have no more consciousness where you are and what you are doing—you have ceased to be an actor: you are a madman. And a dangerous madman too. Conceive Harpagon climbing the balustrade and seizing the orchestra by the throats, loudly demanding the restoration of his casket!

> Art is, I repeat, not identification, but representation.

> The famous maxim, "If you wish to make me cry, you must cry yourself," is therefore not applicable to the actor. If he has really to cry, he would, more likely than not, make his audience laugh; for

tragedy often becomes comedy to the spectators, and sorrow frequently expresses itself in a grimace.[15]

to which Irving replied,

When M. Coquelin maintains that an actor should never exhibit real emotion, he is treading old and disputed ground. It matters little whether the player shed tears or not, so long as he can make his audience shed them; but if tears can be summoned at his will and subject to his control, it is true art to utilize such a power, and happy is the actor whose sensibility has at once so great a delicacy and discipline. In this respect the actor is like the orator. Eloquence is all the more moving when it is animated and directed by a fine and subtle sympathy which affects the speaker though it does not master him. It is futile to deny absolutely to the actor such impulses as touch the heart by the sudden appeal of passion or pathos. Kean was not a player who left anything to hazard, and yet he had inspired moments, which anyone holding M. Coquelin's views might ascribe to insanity.[16]

Both men, however, were not entirely in disagreement, for Coquelin clearly indicated that the actor begins with the character and the self when he said, "If you have assimilated the essence of your personage, his exterior will follow quite naturally. . . ."[17] Then, in a subsequent reply to Irving's article, he stated, ". . . the actor must first become penetrated with the essence of his personage, that he must in a way swallow and digest it, and when once he has assimilated it, the exterior will follow of itself quite naturally."[18]

But some of Irving's objections might validly be directed toward certain practices that clearly did exist during his time. Many actors tended to depend upon, or to have thrust upon them in their training, traditional interpretations and techniques. "An actor," said Irving, "must either think for himself or imitate someone else. Such imitation produces a reverence for certain stage traditions that is sometimes mischievous, because an actor is tempted to school himself too closely to traditional interpretation, instead of giving fair play to his own insight."[19]

Another kind of external approach to the emotions that prevailed may be related to our previous use of the term "least common denominator." Attempts were made to develop a scientific method, notably in the school of Delsarte, which led to cliché, stereotyped, and uninspired emotional expression.

One of the few modern theorists who placed some value on an external approach was the late Michael Chekhov, who, in a very stimulating book called *To the Actor,* spoke of the "psychological gesture," whose aim it is to "influence, stir, mold, and attune your whole inner life to its artistic aims and purposes."[20] The psychological gesture is a physical movement that expresses, in a broad, idealized way ("the archetypal gesture"), certain emotions and attitudes. The movement, if performed freely and uninhibitedly, according to the author, "will awaken and animate in you a definite desire, want or wish."[21] (This technique will be utilized later in exercises on style.)

On the other hand, the internalists, if so they may be called, believe that the only truthfully expressed emotions are those which are stimulated by the actor's inner life. Unfortunately, some of the practitioners of this approach exhibit faults that are as comparable in their harm as some of the practices of the external method. During the nineteenth century, under the influence of the Romantic concepts of man's nature, the qualities the artist sought were freedom of expression, the capacity for unrestrained emotion, and the elimination of all rules and restrictions that might inhibit the artist's free imagination or the stamp of his individuality. For tragedians under this influence, the more intense and violent the emotions, the better. Many of these actors believed that the expression of emotion should be unimpeded by rational concerns, that the genius of the artist was often the result of inspiration or sudden revelation. Testimony that such attitudes resulted in many exciting and awesome performances is plentiful. But there is evidence, too, that numerous problems were caused by "inspirational" acting techniques. What if the actor failed to receive his mystic stimulus? Suppose he did not *feel* either inspired or responsive? And, when inspired, how was he always to be sure that his remarkable surges of emotion were appropriately and coherently expressed? What happens to the ensemble when each actor is permitted freely to submit to his emotional impulses? Under such conditions, actors sometimes set fire to the stage, and seriously wounded other performers with knives or swords. Under such conditions, actors either cut or slighted those portions of the play that did not call for virtuoso displays of the grand emotions.

It was against the excesses of both internal and external approaches to acting and emotion on the nineteenth century stage that Constantin Stanislavski, unquestionably the most influential acting teacher of our time, rebelled. The purely external approach was termed "mechanical acting" by him.

In mechanical acting there is no call for a living process, and it appears only accidentally.

You will understand this better when you come to recognize the origins and methods of mechanical acting, which we characterize as "rubber stamps." To reproduce feelings you must be able to identify them out of your own experience. But as mechanical actors do not experience feelings they cannot reproduce their external results.

With the aid of his face, mimicry, voice, and gestures, the mechanical actor offers the public nothing but the dead mask of nonexistent feeling. For this there has been worked out a large assortment of picturesque effects which pretend to portray all sorts of feelings through external means.

Some of these established clichés have become traditional, and are passed down from generation to generation; as for instance spreading your hand over heart to express love, or opening your mouth wide to give the idea of death. Others are taken ready-made, from talented contemporaries (such as rubbing the brow with the back of the hand, as Vera Komissarzhevskaya used to do in moments of tragedy). Still others are invented by actors for themselves.

There are special ways of reciting a role, methods of diction and speech. (For instance, exaggeratedly high or low tones at critical moments in the role, done with specifically theatrical "tremolo," or with special declamatory vocal embellishments.) There are also methods of physical movement (mechanical actors do not walk, they "progress" on the stage), for gestures and action, for plastic motion. There are methods for expressing all human feelings and passions (showing your teeth and rolling the whites of your eyes when you are jealous, or covering up the eyes and face with the hands instead of weeping; tearing your hair when in despair). There are ways of imitating all kinds of types of people, various classes in society (peasants spit on the floor, wipe their noses with the skirts of their coats, military men click their spurs, aristocrats play with their lorgnettes). Certain others characterize epochs (operatic gestures for the Middle Ages, mincing steps for the eighteenth century). These ready-made mechanical methods are easily acquired through constant exercise, so that they become second nature.

Time and constant habit make even deformed and senseless things near and dear. As for instance, the time-honoured shoulder-shrugging of Opéra Comique, old ladies trying to look young, the doors that open and close by themselves as the hero of the play comes in or goes out. The ballet, opera, and especially the pseudo-classic tragedies are full of these conventions. By means of these forever-unchanging methods they expect to reproduce the most complicated and elevated experiences

51

of heroes. For example: tearing one's heart out of one's bosom in moments of despair, shaking one's fists in revenge, or raising one's hand to heaven in prayer.

According to the mechanical actor the object of theatrical speech and plastic movements—as exaggerated sweetness in lyric moments, dull monotone in reading epic poetry, hissing sounds to express hatred, false tears in the voice to represent grief—is to enhance voice, diction, and movements, to make actors more beautiful and give more power to their theatrical effectiveness.

Unfortunately, there is far more bad taste in the world than good. In the place of nobility a sort of showiness has been created, prettiness in place of beauty, theatrical effect in the place of expressiveness.[22]

Of the inspirational actor of the internal school, he claimed,

One cannot always create subconsciously and with inspiration. No such genius exists in the world. Therefore our art teaches us first of all to create consciously and rightly, because that will best prepare the way for the blossoming of the subconscious, which is inspiration. The more you have of conscious creative moments in your role the more chance you will have of a flow of inspiration.[23]

One must call Stanislavski an internalist because his method emphasized that the actor, by developing his own inner resources, would bring the proper and most truthful external expression to his acting.

His (the actor's) job is not to present merely the external life of the character. He must fit his own human qualities to the life of this other person, and pour into it all of his own soul. The fundamental aim of our art is the creation of this inner life of a human spirit, and its expression in artistic form.

That is why we begin by thinking about the inner side of a role, and how to create its spiritual life through the help of the internal process of living the part. You must live it by actually experiencing feelings that are analogous to it, each and every time you repeat the process of creating it.[24]

But the difference between Stanislavski and the Romantic internalists was that Stanislavski believed that, instead of inspiration, careful and detailed exploration were essential to work out the most appropriate and truthful emotional states. He did not believe in leaving anything to chance.

Although the fact is often overlooked, Stanislavski also was concerned with externals. Included in a previous quotation was the statement, "The fundamental aim of our art is the creation of this inner life of a human spirit, *and its expression in artistic form.*" He says, too, a short time later, "An actor is under the obligation to live his part inwardly, and then to give to his experience an external embodiment."[25] It was Stanislavski who most successfully provided us with a body of concrete suggestions by which the actor learns to explore his inner resources, apply them to the character in given circumstances, and present his characterization with intrinsic expression and control.

As with the subjective nature of sensory responses, the actor must exercise and develop an awareness of emotional responses. He does this by learning how effectively to probe his own past experience, and, because new experience eventually becomes past experience, he must learn to exploit his emotional responses when or shortly after they occur.

When exploring emotions previously felt, certain procedures should be followed if appropriate dramatic use is to be made of them. The actor needs, first, to be warned that there is no value in trying to recall *how* he felt on particular occasions. An audience cannot see his adrenalin glands or feel his pulse rate. More important is the fact that, as in reality, when the moment of emotion occurs, one does not ask himself how he feels. Normally, a certain sequence occurs during an emotional situation. First of all, something must provoke feelings. A telegram, a phone call, or another person brings us news that makes us happy or sad. Our attention is upon the messenger and upon the nature of the news, not upon how we feel. Can you truly act or be happy just because someone orders you to be so? Much more effective a stimulus would be the thought of something that is capable of making you happy.

EXERCISES

1. Try, without thinking, to be:
   a. happy
   b. sad
   c. loathing

   This exercise probably will result in clichés, and a minimum of actual emotion.
2. Concentrate deeply upon the following images. It is important that you be completely relaxed. Do not force overt responses.

a. The faces of a group of children laughing uproariously.
b. The expression of a small child, neglected, unloved, in a catatonic state.
c. A soldier with a machine gun, posing smilingly over a heap of bodies of women and children he has just slain.
d. The face of someone in the past whom you deeply loved.

It is possible that your response to some of these images will be purely internal. Do not be concerned about this now. The important thing is to understand the efficacy of appropriate stimuli to the emotions.

While it is true that concentration upon a stimulus rather than the emotion itself is a more effective way of generating a believable response, for the actor this is merely the first step toward depicting believable emotions on the stage. Emotion in stage characters rarely exists for its own sake. It is fed by conflict, and in turn, becomes the motive for action or inaction. The stimulus itself must in most instances be more than passive in the mind of the character; it must be an object that the character is forced to do something about. Instead of such expressions as "It makes me happy," "sad," or "irate," a more suitable, because it is more active, statement would be, "It makes me want to dance with joy," "be alone with my thoughts," or "turn away with disgust," or possibly, "to control myself."

When exploring past emotional experience, then, the actor must be concerned with the stimulus and what it makes him want to *do*. Vague, filmy recollections will not work; the actual conditions of the situation must be made as vivid as possible. The techniques used in making sensory recollections sharper also may be applied to the emotions; it is, in fact, practically impossible to disassociate emotion from the senses, since the former is invariably aroused by the latter, even when the cause itself is not specifically sensory. For example, suppose that the actor confronted with the problem of expressing grief recalls an incident when his father told him that his dog had been run over and killed. His grief, he recalls, was a result of the loss of his pet. However, to more vividly recreate his response in that particular situation, it is most important to recall his father's appearance as he told him the bad news, the tone and volume of his voice, and whether or not he touched him, and if he did, how he did so. He might recall, too, the first thing that happened when he heard the news: perhaps that he pictured his pet at a moment when it way gay and lively, or how it looked, or might have looked, when struck down. It is the sensory details that give new life to the memory of past experience and provide the power to provoke not merely the feeling that the original event inspired, but the recreation of a similar response—if not the actual one.

In our previous discussion of sense memory, emotions were deliberately overlooked, but imagine the various possibilities of emotional activity that might be generated when one is scalded. The stronger your ability to re-capture sensory experience, the greater your potential to actively recapture emotional experience.

EXERCISES

1. Make a list of general emotions.
2. Perform a simple action in which you express one of them.
3. Recall a specific episode in your own experience when a similar emotion was experienced by you:
   a. What was the specific cause of the emotion?
   b. What was your response?
   c. Recall all the sensations that were associated with both the stimulus and the response. Describe the environment in detail, the nature of the stimulus, and all sensations connected with it. Describe your-self in terms of age, size, clothing, and state of mind at the time the stimulus occurred.
4. Perform a simple action based upon this experience to express the emotion.
   How does your first attempt to project the emotion compare to the second?

Just as was the case with sensory experience, there will be numerous occasions when you will be called upon in the theatre to create emotions that you have never experienced. How can you understand Juliet's emotion in the potion scene if you have never had to drink a solution of unknown quality that might kill you; or, if it works as expected, might be responsible for your being buried alive in a tomb filled with corpses? How can you deal with Othello's emotion—or Desdemona's—when he murders her? You have never killed anyone (and perhaps you are not even married). Not every capable young actress will be able to refer to her own experience to find a duplication for Miss Julie's condition following the seduction. How can an actor who has never been a part of a class system understand Jean's fear of his aristocrat-employer? How many women will be able to refer to an actual experience in their own lives when they were reduced to a puppet-like trance such as Miss Julie's at the end of the play? How many persons have experienced the confused and ambivalent experience of love-hatred, dominance-submission, pride and self-pity, that Miss Julie undergoes? Not every woman can claim that she has experienced a discovery such as the one Béline suffers when she learns that her dead husband is really alive, and is now aware of her hypocrisy.

Obviously, if every actor or actress had to have had experiences that duplicated those of the characters he portrays, not only would most roles be impossible to cast, but the appropriate actors would have to be selected from unskilled persons of all walks of life in the real world. And how would it be possible to cast individuals who have experienced dying, or who are condemned murderers? Must we go to kings, queens, and princes in order to properly cast characters who must understand what it feels like to be royal?

The fact is that we do not, and usually cannot, have had the same total experience as the characters we portray, but as human beings, we all have had our share of the gamut of possible emotional responses. In some capacity we have all loved, hated, feared, envied, been sad, despondent, anguished, or cheerful. We do not have to be killers to have experienced, on a lesser scale perhaps, a desire to inflict harm, or the kinds of emotion that may lead to such a desire. A sense of power and dignity may be as much the property of the nonaristocrat as of those of royal blood. The actress playing Juliet may not have been confronted with a situation such as that in the potion scene, but she will no doubt have experienced some of the emotions clearly connected with such a situation: fear and anxiety of the unknown, desperately wanting to avoid an unwanted experience, and weighing the risk of danger to achieve something strongly desired.

In dealing with the emotional behavior of a character in a play, true understanding is the result of the actor's ability to find parallels in his own experience. In order to do this, he must first abstract into universal terms the emotions to be portrayed. The actor may never have been confronted with the possibility of imminent death, but he has, in all probability, experienced the fears and anxieties of danger or of facing the unknown. His next step will be to find the specific incident in his own experience that may be related to the universalized emotion. When he succeeds in finding such an incident, he then proceeds to bring it alive through associations, in much the same way as he has done with reviving sensory responses. Out of his re-creation of as many of the details of the experience as possible, he concentrates upon the stimulus, the sensation, and the response, although his primary concern is in making the stimulus sufficiently vivid to cause sensation and response to become virtually automatic.

56

The final moments in *Miss Julie* contain material that should serve well to exemplify the application of the procedures recommended for emotion memory. As the play nears its conclusion, both of the principal characters undergo a series of emotional shifts. *Remorse* over what to them is a hopeless situation, and *fear* of being found out are the emotional foundations to be abstracted from the situation. Both basic emotions, however, require further elaboration. The characters' remorse is the result of an act that cannot be undone and for which there seems to be no solution. The actor might use as a stimulus the phrase, "There is no way out." The characters' fear is based upon the threat of discovery by someone who holds power over them. In Jean's case, he fears the reaction of the man who can destroy his security; in Julie's case, she fears the shame of discovery. For both actors, a stimulus phrase might be, "I am going to be found out."

Taking the phrases, "There is no way out," and "I am going to be found out," the actor seeks experiences of his own where these phrases might have been pertinent. He will ask himself whether or not he was confronted with the futility and frustration of not finding a satisfactory solution to a serious problem, and on what occasions his own security or honor were threatened. Ideally, the actor would seek situations in which a parallel stimulus existed: a dominant figure whom one either feared or held in such esteem that exposure of some deed to him would be intolerable. For some, it might be their image of God; for others, a severe or highly principled parent or teacher. The situation, of course, need not be as overwhelming in reality as the one in the play, but at the time of its occurrence, it must have seemed so. In retrospect, an incident where the actor may have feared that he has been discovered cheating by a favorite teacher whose esteem he desired may not be as shattering or humiliating an experience as the one in which Jean and Julie find themselves, but at the time of the occurrence, perhaps nothing could have seemed as catastrophic! It is the sense of *that* time that the actor wishes to recall. With the discovery of the appropriate occasion, the actor then proceeds to re-live it in his imagination as vividly as possible. He attempts to detail the event as specifically as he can, probing for as many associations of facts and sensations as possible. *When, where, how, why* did it occur? Precisely *what* happened, and in *what sequence?* He explores every possible sense in connection with the event: the smells, sights, sounds, tactile effects, even tastes that might be associated with the incident. Finally, he attempts to determine what was *done* and how was it done. During or after the process of such investigation, the actor suddenly may be stricken with a sensation similar to the one that occurred. He must then ask himself what it makes him want to do. How does his present reaction compare to the one he experienced originally? What did he do, or want to do, at the time? He may recall, for example, that the sense of shame made him restless—he could not sit or stand still because of the sense of the impossibility of escaping the consequences—he felt trapped, hemmed in. A number of other sensations and consequent actions may have occurred at the same time, some of which he may be re-experiencing during recall. He may have been extremely tense. The tension probably exerted itself in different parts of his body. As a result he probably responded with a series of perhaps unconscious nervous actions to relieve or rechannel the tensions. His mouth may have dried up, his heart and pulses may have been pounding at an unbearably rapid pace. What did these uncomfortable sensations make him do? Thinking about an old shame now makes one cringe, shut his eyes tightly, and perhaps bite his lower lip, in order to block it out.

At this point a perfectly valid question might be asked. In a play, the responses or actions of a character already are dictated by the playwright. How can the actor's exploration into his own past experience be of any value, when his own specific responses may not be precisely amenable to those of the character or action demanded by the play? There are many actors who make the mistake of substituting their own exact responses for those of the character, just as there are those who believe that they must go out and undergo the exact experience of their character. The impracticality and inevitable distortion that invariably occurs are unnecessary. The essential value of emotion memory is that it may enable an actor to better *understand* and *believe* in the emotional situation of the character, and that it will aid him in finding a way of *executing* the action demanded by the script without resorting to vague, generalized, and cliché-ridden responses.

Much of the second half of *Miss Julie* finds the two principals acting in various ways as a result of their fears and anxieties. They do specific things required by the plot of the play. Jean ultimately chooses a cowardly solution in order to protect himself, and Julie attempts to employ his will in effecting her own solution, suicide. There are even more specific actions within this framework. For example, both characters must react to the speaking tube when it rings insistently, and Jean must answer it. The playwright does not, and cannot, tell us in terms of total physical action (facial expression, gesture, movement, sound) how these things are done. The actor, by "mating" the demands of the script with his own understanding—his own personally explored stimuli—will better perform his duty, for he will execute the requirements of the play with the richness of his own belief and conviction.

In applying the procedures outlined for emotion memory, certain precautions should be observed. First, it is best, during early rehearsals, not to force emotional reactions too soon. The actor must take time to get to know his character and its relation to other characters. During early rehearsals, it is advisable for the actor to "neutralize" himself by avoiding the enactment of emotion and by preventing himself from being burdened with preconceived ideas. This is not always easy. The eager actor too often wants to experiment immediately, or give vent to his instinctive reactions. The result is usually superficial, and because it has not been sufficiently worked out or properly adapted (a procedure that often is slow in developing), the results may be little more than clichés or hackneyed responses.

Neither should the actor try to make himself "feel" something inside. "Squeezing out" emotions can only result in vague and generalized behavior, and most often creates muscular tensions that reduce rather than enhance honest and believable responses.

EXERCISES

---

1. Select one or more of the following situations. Abstract the emotions that you believe are involved in each situation, and create emotional objectives. Find parallels to these objectives in your own experience, and, using the processes described, submit yourself to as complete a recollection as possible of the event and its details. Finally, work out a pantomime in which the selected situations are acted out with the aid of your own experience.

    Note: The same problem should be explored by two or more students. This should demonstrate the variety of possibilities regarding the same emotion that can truthfully be projected.

    a. You have just discovered that your best friend has betrayed you.
    b. You have just been told that your mate has been killed in an automobile accident.
    c. You are locked in a room with a person who is intolerable to you.
    d. This is your last hour of life.
    e. Your entire future depends upon this horse race.
    f. This is the hour before your wedding.
    g. The war has just ended.
    h. The person who most threatens you is now in your power.
    i. You are caught in a lie on the witness stand.
    j. Your painting has just won first prize.

2. Analyze the kinds of emotions suggested in the following scenes. Using the procedures suggested, play the scenes with the action you have discovered:

   a. Start with the moment in *Miss Julie* when Jean catches a cinder in his eye. Conclude with Jean's response to Miss Julie's statement, "You are proud," with "In some ways. Not in others."

   b. Start with Jean and Miss Julie's return to the kitchen following the ballet, and conclude with Miss Julie's remark, "How wonderful, wonderful."

   c. Start with the entrance of Dr. Purgon in *The Would-Be Invalid,* and conclude with his exit.

   d. Start with Béline's entrance when Argan pretends to be deceased, and conclude with Angélique's plea that Argan permit her to marry Cléante.

Some actors rely upon stereotyped responses to stimuli. Others respond intuitively, sometimes but not always, with interesting and exciting results. The actor who consciously explores his inner life is more likely to discover responses that are sometimes unique, but always will truthfully parallel the sensory or emotional experience of the character he is to portray. Honesty in such responses depends on the actor's concentration on appropriate stimuli rather than on feeling or effect. As important as the exercises that develop the actor's voice and body are, so are the exercises that explore experience in terms of the senses, the emotions, and the spirit.

CHAPTER 3

Imagination

Just as the possession of a superbly trained voice and body without sensitivity falls short in the art of acting, the sensitive individual will miss the mark unless he is capable of creatively ordering or making imaginative use of his heightened perception. We have seen already that by exercising our awareness of experience, both sensory and emotional, we feed our imaginations. We have sought ways in which we might make truthful for ourselves (and consequently for the audience) the illusions of the stage. Through the power of imagination, supplied by the perceptive processes, we make non-existent suns, moons, and stars exist; we persuade audiences that we are what we are not, and we move them with simulated passions. But to conjure up visions and make them seem real does not in itself constitute the artistic imagination. It is only when we use our powers to control, channel, or adapt experience toward an ordered and significant goal that we may be considered to possess a truly artistic imagination. We have observed already that the actor must probe his own experience and adapt it in a purposeful way—that is, to the exigencies of plot, character, and dialogue—if he is to succeed in bringing a character honestly to life.

The actor's use of his imagination, however, must be developed for more than the realistic representation of the sensory and emotional processes of characters on the stage. Imagination becomes a guide to meaningful behavior for every moment that the actor occupies the stage. Neither the actor nor the audience must ever question the significance of any action during the course of a play. Even the act of doing *nothing* must be deliberate. But action cannot be arbitrarily selected, nor must it be selected with a consciousness of effect (that is, seeking effect without relevant cause, or effect in the sense of a demonstration of virtuosity). The creation of appropriate action is a result of imaginative justification. The more thorough the actor's search for *stimuli* in character, given circumstances, and atmosphere, the more he will find to do.

Of course, some of the most important sources for justifiable action already have been suggested. In the preceding chapters, we found an approach to the utilization of personal experience that provided provocative stimuli and truthful responses, i.e., meaningful action. We are concerned with the actor's use of his imagination to explore the possibilities for additional stimuli, but first the actor should learn to develop and train a constantly functioning imagination.

IMAGINATION AND OBSERVATION

We have stressed the necessity for the actor to learn how to see and absorb his environment. His goal in doing so is to provide himself with a rich source from which he may draw material for characterization. We have observed, too, that the material of life is never transferred to the stage without some alteration. Instead, the actor makes imaginative use of his experience and observation. In order to train this kind of imaginative function, the actor must make as much a habit of imaginative perception as he does of perceiving itself. In the study of observation, three areas were emphasized: people, animals, and objects. Each of these areas may also be exploited for the exercise of the imagination.

People

It is not uncommon for even the most unimaginative person to make certain guesses or judgments about another on the basis of the most casual encounter. We see a woman who is obese and we say, "Too bad she can't control her appetite," or, "It must be glands. I pity her—and at her age, too. She must be miserable." We see an old, ragged, dirty tramp hitchhiking on the highway, and it suddenly strikes us that he was young once like ourselves, with aspirations and hopes for the future. We wonder what happened to make him this way. On the basis of facial expression, we conclude that "He is surly," "She always looks so happy," "I don't trust him," "She seems so vain," "He is pampered," and so on. It is normal to imagine things about people. This normal kind of guessing game, however, merely scratches the surface in terms of a deeper use of the imagination. It is based too often upon stereotype and prejudice, and rarely is deeper than a hasty, impersonal, and trivial reflection.

The actor, like a detective, must probe more deeply. We know already that his initial observation must be thorough. The more careful and studied the perusal, the greater the stimulus to imagination. Instead of the mere color of someone's skin, facial expression, height, weight, or physical defect leading to a quick conclusion, it must be a combination of these things and more: the clothes he is wearing, how he wears them, his gestures and apparent habits, the way in which he looks, or does not look, at other people. Is he animated or sluggish? What does he have with him—a cane, a newspaper, a suitcase, a candy bar, a package? Before reaching his conclusions, the actor should reflect upon as many details as possible. It could be that a very small, ordinarily indistinguishable or casual item such as a frayed collar, or a wedding band on a finger of the left hand, might lead the imagination in a particular direction. The observer then asks himself to determine, on the basis of his impressions, what kind of person this might be. After creating as full a sense of the character as possible, he asks himself, "Why is he here? Where is he going? Where did he come from?" He tries to create an imaginary life for the character that will help him justify his answers to these questions. Finally, he places this character in an imaginary situation and asks, "What might this person do under certain circumstances?"

EXERCISES

1. Observe a person whom you do not know personally, and do the following:
   a. Make a thorough list of his characteristics.
   b. Determine why your character is where he is, where he might be going afterward, where he came from.
   c. Create a pertinent imaginary life for this character.
   d. Place the character in an imaginary situation and determine what he might do.
2. Do the same as the above, using a person in a photograph.
3. Repeat the above with a person in a painting.

4. Using the two characters whom you carefully studied in an earlier observation exercise, create an imaginary situation for each one and work out reactions that you imagine would be appropriate. Act them out in pantomime.

Animals

The art of metaphor surely is dependent upon the imaginative use of perception. Making meaningful connections between the activity of people and that of animals, or recalling observations from animal life that are applicable to the portrayal of humans, depends upon the actor's ability to do something with observation that goes beyond mere imitation. The connection between animals and people does not have to be exact. When we think of someone as "birdlike," for example, we do not have to imagine him with wings, although we may picture him with flapping elbows. Birdlike characters do not have to fly, but they may walk with short, quick steps like some birds; their gestures may be small and quick, they may "peck" at food, they may turn their heads quickly from side to side, or they may even move their heads back and forth as they walk.

EXERCISES

---

1. Using the animal you selected and studied for your earlier observation exercise, do the following:
   a. Abstract its chief characteristics and apply them to an imagined human character, so that he becomes "catlike," "bearlike," or whatever the case may be.
   b. Place your human character with his animal-like characteristics into a situation that will emphasize these characteristics.
2. With the assistance of other members of your class, work out a dramatization of one of Aesop's fables.

Objects

In terms of metaphor, what has been said about animals also applies to objects. It is interesting to investigate some of the well-known figures of speech that most of us take for granted. For example, how many of us have even really checked up on such expressions as "He is like a stick of wood," "She reminds me of a vegetable," "Steady as a rock." In the case of the stick of wood, we would find that sticks of wood vary, but what usually is intended is a piece of wood lacking in character or life, one that is dull in color, texture, and shape. Suppose we asked ourselves, "If that piece of wood could walk and talk, what would it move and sound like?" By such a process, we are led to a deeper understanding of the comparison, and then are able to make more imaginative use of it. Notice, however, that the process demands more than a cursory acceptance of the metaphor. The object of comparison must be investigated and carefully observed before it can be utilized imaginatively.

There is an additional, and no less important, stimulus that objects may provide for the actor's imagination on the stage. We have seen already that the actor reacts sensorily to objects: to texture, size, weight, or other qualities that provoke particular sensations. Objects frequently have another quality —that of *association*. They very often symbolize something for us—something that goes beyond the actual physical or sensory aspect of the object itself. For example, when an actor plays a king, his crown may actually be a prop made of papier-mâché with cheap stones glued onto it. The actor, relying upon his sense memory, will imagine that it is as heavy as gold, and that the jewels have the same deep and dazzling colors as the gems of an actual crown. In addition to this illusion, however, he will recognize the crown as a symbol of his kingship. It may, depending upon the play, represent power, ambition, awe—or the character may detest the responsibilities that it suggests. In Shakespeare's *Richard II,* the protagonist undergoes a significant change concerning his attitude toward kingship. This attitude may be reinforced by the actor's way of handling or wearing his crown. Within one scene, Richard's attitude toward kingship includes two different references to the crown. Upon his return from Ireland in Act III, Scene 2, he learns that a rebellion is taking place, but confidently states,

> *Not all the water in the rough rude sea*
> *Can wash the balm off from an anointed king;*
> *The breath of worldly men cannot depose*
> *The deputy elected by the Lord:*
> *For every man that Bolingbroke hath press'd*
> *To lift shrewd steel against our golden crown,*
> *God for his Richard hath in heavenly pay*
> *A glorious angel: then, if angels fight,*
> *Weak men must fall, for heaven still guards the right.*

But not too long afterward, as the news gets worse and worse, he comments,

> *... for within the hollow crown*
> *That rounds the mortal temples of a king*
> *Keeps Death his court, and there the antic sits,*
> *Scoffing his state and grinning at his pomp,*
> *Allowing him a breath, a little scene,*
> *To monarchize, he fear'd and kill with looks,*
> *Infusing him with self and vain conceit,*
> *As if this flesh which walls about our life*
> *Were brass impregnable, and humour'd thus*
> *Comes at the last and with a little pin*
> *Bores through his castle wall, and farewell king!*

In this scene and elsewhere, Shakespeare endows Richard with varying imaginative responses to the same object. Actors must have something of Richard's imagination, and supply the objects they use on the stage with similar significant associations. Providing objects with such attributes will invariably lead to actions that convey to audiences the inner workings of the character's mind and emotions.

In order to sharpen his ability to perceive and use objects symbolically, the actor should allow his imagination to operate in a manner similar to that of perceiving unknown or unusual individuals for the first time.

EXERCISES

---

1. Using the two objects you selected for earlier observation exercises, do the following:
    a. Abstract the distinctive qualities of each and create characters who are "like" the objects.
    b. Place these characters in situations that will best draw out their object-like qualities.
2. The teacher hands each student an object. The student then has five minutes to create a pantomimic situation in which the object becomes central.
3. a. WOMEN. You have a pot of geraniums, a broom, and a Bible. Create a character and a situation in which these objects have symbolic or associational value.

b. MEN. You have a letter, an old pocket watch, and a harmonica. Create a character and a situation in which these objects have symbolic or associational value.

We have seen that an effective imagination relies upon all of the actor's observational resources that have been enumerated. But while the imagination is fed by awareness, it requires expertise to develop action beyond that which was observed literally. This is why the actor not only must observe, but also must explore the territories into which his observation of people, animals, and objects may lead him.

IMAGINATION AND CHARACTERIZATION

When dealing with character analysis, the physical aspects of character will be avoided because it is more appropriate and significant, perhaps, to discuss a character's external traits on the basis of a combined knowledge of what the character *is,* and the contribution that observation and imagination may make toward character physicalization. To an extent, of course, certain physical aspects of character have been touched upon in the areas of sense and emotion memory. Those aspects, however, are related to the sensory or emotional expression of the moment, and further discussion is necessary to show how all expressions and actions in a play must be permeated physically with the identity or individuality of the character.

In the animal world, various breeds of the same species are characterized by certain differences. Two different breeds of dogs, for example, performing somewhat similar actions such as barking, running, sitting, eating, sleeping, and reacting to stimuli will have their own distinct ways of doing all these things—depending upon size, physical proportions, breeding, or temperament. Among human beings, people performing similar actions will differ from one another as a result of differences in sex, age, size, conditioning, temperament, or need.

As individuals, each of us is endowed with a distinct physical personality, part of which is alterable and part of which is not. You found, for example, in your pantomimes of other persons, animals, and objects, that you could adjust your physical being only to a certain extent. On the stage, actors vary in terms of the degree to which they disguise their own physical character-istics. Some will channel the play's characters into their own physical mold and make no effort to alter their own voices, features, postures, movements, tempos, or even personal mannerisms. When casting is appropriate in such instances, or when a part is written to exploit the distinctive personality of a star, such techniques work, but there have been numerous instances when actors have portrayed biographical characters and still retained, without an iota of alteration, their own physical personalities. This seems to be partic-ularly true in motion pictures, with the result that when thousands of people think of Alexander Graham Bell they picture Don Ameche; Cole Porter is Cary Grant, and Thomas Edison is Spencer Tracy.

On the other hand, there are actors who seem to thrive on physical alteration. While such splendid actors as the late Paul Muni and Charles Laughton, Lord Laurence Olivier, Alec Guinness, and Glenda Jackson often have played roles without much physical alteration, they have proved on numerous occasions that they can believably distort their own features and bodies to suggest the characters they wish to project as quite different from themselves. Of course, it takes much talent to play such a variety of roles well, and the result for the actor may be an almost unlimited range of widely different stage roles.

The process of physicalization, whether it be broad or subtle, must begin with the play. Some actors, enamored of their physical virtuosity, will start too soon to conjure up a few extreme physical distortions. Others, anxious to utilize some recent observation of a real life "character" or animal, will try to find ways of imposing their discoveries incongruously upon their character. It is wrong, too, for the actor to determine, previous to careful study, that he will look and sound exactly like a biographical character he is to portray. It is far better for the actor to probe, to study the part slowly, to feel his way cautiously, intuitively, into understanding and identification with the character. On the basis of the playwright's suggestions and the actor's own analytical process, the actor will begin to develop images of his character. He may, during rehearsals, find himself altering his body, his tempo, his characteristic way of doing things. Eventually he may reach a point where he finds it necessary to consciously explore primary and secondary source materials for assistance. But he does this on the basis of the sug-gestions, hints, and ideas that exist in the play itself.

In the play, suggestions concerning the appearance of characters will appear with more or less frequency, depending upon the playwright, in stage directions and/or in the dialogue. In *The Would-Be Invalid,* we learn from both a description in the cast of characters and a line spoken by Béralde

FIGURE 3-1. *Lord Laurence Olivier as Justice Shallow in* Henry IV, Part II.
Photo by John Vickers, London.

that Argan is fit and vigorous despite his protestations of physical suffering. In *Miss Julie,* the stage directions inform us that Miss Julie is twenty-five years old, and in various other places she is described as "coquettish," having behaved "tartly," "nervously," "apathetically."   In the dialogue we are told

FIGURE 3-2.   *Lord Laurence Olivier as Mr. Puff in* The Critic.
Photo by John Vickers, London.

by Jean that she is splendid to look at, by Christine that she is proud, and by Julie near the end of the play, "Oh, I am so tired. I can't bring myself to do anything."

In addition to such direct statements, conclusions can be drawn from

FIGURE 3-3. *Lord Laurence Olivier as Richard III. Photo by
John Vickers, London.*

behavioral patterns discovered in analysis (see Part II), which may be developed into physical patterns.

Miss Julie, for example, is young, and at the opening of the play almost overly energetic. She is all over the place, dancing with the servants, checking on the medicine for her dog, teasing Jean, and anxious to keep up the pace all night long. Physically, then, she appears to be a highly charged

71

young woman. We learn that her parents raised her like a boy. Although there is little doubt concerning her femininity, might there not be a suggestion of mannishness about her? In her early scenes, Julie is vain and coquettish. She teases Jean. At the same time she is in command. She has proud and haughty tendencies. We know from her objectives that honor and position are important to her and she defends herself against external threats to them. As more and more obstacles confront her, she changes from early impulsiveness to humility, and finally, to helplessness. (Indeed, one of the difficulties in playing Miss Julie is due to her changeableness—the consequence of her confused desires.)

Argan's age is not specified, but because he is the head of a family, including a daughter of marriageable age, and is in robust health, we can assume that he is middle-aged, perhaps between forty-five and fifty years old. He is spoiled, wants to be pampered and babied, and reacts to obstacles with great energy and violence. Argan is stubborn and unreasonable, and a tyrant with his daughter. At the same time, he makes innumerable efforts to present to others the picture of a weak, sick old man.

Equipped with such descriptions, the actress and actor playing these parts are now ready to try to match the imagined characters with their own real life observations. It is naive, however, to assume that one will be able to find people in real life who share exactly the same characteristics as those to be portrayed upon the stage. An actress may be acquainted with someone like Miss Julie in age and temperament, and the actor may be familiar with a hypochondriac. Such contacts may be helpful, but the chances of finding the *complete* character outside the world of the play itself are very small indeed. The actor should not feel that he is bound to find a duplicate. Characters share numerous traits each of which we may discover in *various* sources. We may find Miss Julie's pride in one woman, and her impulsiveness in another; Argan's temper in one man, and his self-indulgence in another. If the actor wishes, he may follow a very methodical technique of listing the characteristics he is to portray and matching them with all the possible sources of his experience.

JULIE

Characteristic	*Source*
25 years old and "highly charged"	Energetic acquaintance of this age, frisky animal
Coquettish	Flirt at a party
Mannish	Male tendencies in movement as opposed to female; mannish women

Haughty, superior	Paintings or photographs of queen or princess; ballet dancer
Impulsive	(Combined with energy and carriage) a young mare
Helpless	Puppet; feather; a weak, drained invalid

ARGAN

45-50 years old, robust, and energetic	Father, uncle, teacher
Wants to be pampered	A little boy, 4-8 years old
Hot-tempered, tyrannical	A hungry bear; spoiled brat who has temper tantrums
Pretends illness	Child who does not want to go to school; self-pitying acquaintance; poseur.

Once observational sources have been located, they must be developed in terms of their specific manner of suggesting the sought-for characteristics. For example, what is the action of a young mare that may help to convey Miss Julie's energy, impulsiveness, and dignified carriage? What specific actions did the flirt at the party perform that stamped her as a coquette? In what parts of the body do the masculine tendencies in mannish women assert themselves? How did the ballet dancer hold her head, shoulders, and body that conveyed pride in her bearing? For Argan, what do little boys who want to be pampered *do?* What are some of their attention-getting devices? What physical motions and gestures are used by brats with temper tantrums? How is their loss of control physicalized?

EXERCISES

1. List the characteristics of Jean or Christine in *Miss Julie,* using the procedure described above. Find sources in your observations whereby these characteristics may be matched in people, animals, and/or objects. Consider the possibility of Christine as a vegetable.

2. Justify the following analogies made of characters in *The Would-Be Invalid.* How would you physicalize these characters on the basis of such analogies?

    a. M. de Bonnefoi: a snake
    b. M. Fleurant: a butterfly
    c. Thomas Diafoirus: a kangaroo with the head of a chipmunk
    d. M. Purgon: an eagle

3. Improvise circumstances and situations for some of the above characters, retaining their vocal, physical, and behavioral qualities. Determine what they might do in the following situations:
    a. A neutral party interviews each character for a position.
    b. A neutral party accuses each character of stealing.
    c. Pair off characters in both plays and have them interview one another.
    d. Place the paired-off couple in unique circumstances: at a dance; at an auction; in a traveling compartment on a train or carriage, etc.

Just as the imagination is fed by observation, then proceeds to enrich and amplify its source, the process of characterization works in much the same way. The text provides the initial stimulus providing the direction in which the actor must explore his experience and observation. The results of the marriage between clues in the play and appropriate materials from life are imaginatively developed in the choices made by the actor as he fleshes out and determines the character's response to the circumstances of the play. Essentially, imagination is the force behind everything that an actor *does* on stage because he is providing his own unique embodiment and physicalization for characters who exist only in the form of printed dialogue.

CHAPTER 4

Justification of Action

It was stated earlier that the actor's art is the art of action. We have learned that acting is *doing,* but that in order to do what is believable and richly creative, the actor must search for justifiable stimuli for everything he does. Thus far, the stimuli that have been explored included the action results of sense and emotion memory, and methods of physicalizing characters through analysis and observation. These stimuli provide a solid foundation for characters in action, but there are several additional ways of using the imagination that will expand the actor's capacity to involve himself more deeply in the role, thereby enabling him to find shades and nuances that will make the character more interesting and vivid. All of these additional ways of stimulating the imagination depend primarily upon a single principle: the actor's ability to *relate* himself to the given circumstances of the play. Given circumstances include the situation and the setting of each scene, the character's attitude—as ruled by his motivating forces toward situation, setting, and other characters—and his own mental and emotional processes.

RELATING TO SITUATION
AND SETTING

The actor should look upon every scene in which he is involved as possessing a situation in a particular environment. The situation may be very simple, as is the case in the opening of both *The Would-Be Invalid* and *Miss Julie.*

In the former, the situation consists of Argan figuring out his medical expenses, and in the latter, it consists of Jean's relating his reaction to Miss Julie's offstage activities and his interest in being served supper by Christine. Or it may be complex, as when Beline is trapped by the ensemble into revealing her true nature, or when Jean and Julie reenter the world of reality after the seduction. In these situations, each of the characters involved must be aware of his intrinsic association with the situation. Later we shall see that such associations become more complex, but for a starting point, the first questions asked by the actor are, "What is the situation?" and "What part do I play in it?" (In Part II, the principles of beats and objectives will enlarge upon this.)

The actor's next concern is the setting in which the situation takes place. One of the major mistakes made by actors during rehearsals is their oblivion to the environment, because it is not literally there. Ordinarily, rehearsals take place on a bare stage with a chalked or taped ground plan and a few objects of furniture. The lights are work lights with no illusion suggesting place or time of day. Properties are either nonexistent or are mere substitutes for the real thing. The "realities" of setting and properties often do not appear until later rehearsals that occur quite close to the opening performance. Actors oblivious to environmental conditions until such a late date neglect one of the basic stimuli to meaningful action. Entrances, exits, windows, fireplaces, set pieces, and the true size and style of furniture and properties are all important not merely for the storytelling "business" of a play, but for their associational values to the characters. It is important, too, to discover whether the setting will be light or dark, whether it will suggest heat or cold, elegance or shabbiness. An awareness of such conditions provides the actor with something to respond to, causing the relationship between character and environment to become a meaningful one.

In *Miss Julie,* the setting is the well-equipped kitchen of the Count's estate. It contains an entrance to the exterior, and also to one of the servant's bedrooms. It contains a window facing out-of-doors. In the room there are tables, benches, and chairs for the preparation of meals and the dining of servants, plus the kind of paraphernalia one expects to find in a kitchen. The room is neat and clean at the opening of the day but becomes badly disordered after the wild dance of the servants. Important properties in the play include the bell and speaking tube by means of which the servants are summoned, the count's riding boots that Jean brings in on his entrance, and the bottles of beer and wine. The time is Midsummer's Eve, a time of year in Scandinavia when daylight persists throughout the night, and which is the occasion for a Bacchanalian type of revelry.

As with situation, there is a basic relationship between character and setting. Each of the characters relates sensorily to time, place, and object: one may be tired or cold; he may find objects heavy or light, rough or smooth, sweet or sour. Relationships become more complex, however, when the nature and attitudes of the characters toward situation and setting are considered. Argan is first discovered figuring out his medical expenses. He is alone, so he does not have to impress anyone with his illness. Occasionally, he remembers how "sick" he is as he coughs, wheezes, or gargles self-pityingly. Essentially, however, he is concerned with his bills, toward which his attitude varies. He enjoys his task because it gives him a sense of the importance and seriousness of the remedies, but he becomes angry at the outlandish fees that have been charged. The setting is the bedroom of a wealthy bourgeois with an ornate bed and occasional pieces of furniture, but perhaps more important is the fact that it suggests, with all of its bottles and basins, the room of a presumably sick man. Argan, of course, is happy and comfortable in this room, in the sense that it establishes proof that he really is sick. In the opening situation the bills assume particular symbolic values, when Argan addresses them as though they were actually the doctors and druggists who sent them. His attitudes in the situation are directed toward the bills, as he is first pleased by them and then angered, and are manifested in the manner in which he handles the markers, which are put down, now agreeably, now angrily, now spitefully.

In the opening situation of *Miss Julie,* Jean is provided with a great deal of expository material. The playwright, through Jean's narrative, lets us know where Jean has been and what Miss Julie is up to. But the actor is not a narrator. He avoids being a mere expository device by recognizing his relationship to situation and setting. Jean, it is true, is reporting to Christine, but his report is dramatically justified when he relates it to attitude and objective. He wants to express his *reaction* to Miss Julie's behavior, and this, in turn, is influenced by his desire to appear superior. There is malice in his report to Christine. When he tells Christine how Julie insisted on dancing with him, Jean not only suggests that he believes Julie to be "wild," but he is, without being fully aware of it of course, boasting about being "chosen."

The actor playing Jean relates in the following ways to situation and setting:

1. The excitement of the revelry. Before entering, he has been waltzing continuously at Miss Julie's insistence.
2. He enters his domain. The estate belongs to the Count, but in the

kitchen Jean is the master. He is comfortable and at home in this room, although he often feels that it is not good enough for him. He is superior to it. On the other hand, when Julie first enters, up until the seduction, he is "in his place." The result is that, alone with Christine, he may flaunt the kitchen and its furnishings by sitting on the table, putting his feet on the chairs, helping himself to the accommodations as though they actually belonged to him. When Miss Julie is on the scene, however, he is in control of the kitchen, but in the manner of one who is responsible for it to someone else. After the seduction, of course, Jean will feel free to resort, even in front of Miss Julie, to his free and careless attitude.

3. The door through which Jean has entered and the window look out upon the area in which the festivities are taking place. While Jean describes what has happened offstage to Christine, he may associate the direction of the outside door and window with those activities. Jean might even look out the window to be sure no one is coming before he describes to Christine the scene that he witnessed between Julie and her fiancé.

4. Jean enters with the Count's boots. Consistently in the play, Jean is awed and frightened by the thought of his employer and superior. The boots, onstage throughout the play, are a constant reminder to Jean of his basic inferiority.

5. The phone and the speaking tube have the same connotations for Jean. Its ring alerts him to his duty and to his servitude.

EXERCISES

1. The following pantomime, with its step-by-step development, is intended to show how the actor may find justifications for action that will make a scene more meaningful for himself and his audience:

   a. Perform a simple pantomime of setting a table. Make sure that the visualization and handling of objects is believable.

   b. Set the table again, but under the influence of the following conditions:

      1) The set is a neat combination dining room-living room in a low-priced second floor apartment house.

      2) The door to the kitchen is upstage center. There is a door to other rooms in the house at left stage. The entrance from outside is at downstage right, and a window to the street is upstage of it.

      3) The furniture in the room consists of a buffet upstage left of the kitchen door, with dishes, silverware, and napkins. A dining table with four chairs is left of center. Upstage of the entry door and under the window is a cheap sofa and an end table with a

lamp upon it. There is a bookcase upstage right of the kitchen door with a clock-radio and a photograph of a newly-married couple. A coffee table with a telephone and a few magazines on it sits in front of the sofa. Upstage of the coffee table, in front of the bookcase, is a modern armchair.

    4) The character setting the table is a young bride. The dishes and crystal are expensive wedding presents, and are irreplaceable.

  c. Set the table again, adding the following conditions:

    1) It is five minutes to six. At six o'clock, the bride's husband is bringing his boss to dinner.

    2) It is extremely important that the boss be impressed, like her, and admire her domestic skill.

    3) She has had a terrible day. She is not organized, and there has not been sufficient time to get things ready. Now the table must be set before they arrive, but her hair is still in curlers, and the roast, potatoes, vegetable, and pie are in the oven. A salad has not yet been made.

  d. Set the table again, but in the process, another student should interrupt the action with the following:

    1) The telephone rings. It is mother.

    2) A car stops out front.

    3) A timer rings in the kitchen.

  e. Perform the pantomime once again with a time limit of sixty seconds.

2. Three actors are given the same situation. They are to enter a room, pour a glass of wine, and drink it. Each actor, however, has the following given circumstances:

  a. The first actor has just had his proposal of marriage accepted.

  b. The second actor has just returned from his wife's funeral.

  c. The third actor drinks the wine because he has a cold. He hates wine.

3. Describe both Christine and Julie's relationship to the setting in *Miss Julie*. Improvise actions that reveal their attitude toward the kitchen and its objects.

4. In Act I of *The Would-Be Invalid,* when Argan says, "Come now, quick my chair, and seats for everybody," all of the characters in the scene except Toinette are seated. Describe how each of the characters "relates" to the chair in which he or she is sitting.

RELATING TO OTHER
CHARACTERS

It is extraordinary, when one stops to think about it, how many different attitudes each of us has toward his circle of acquaintances. We like, we love, we dislike, or we are indifferent to persons we know. To some, we feel superior; to others, inferior; some people are always enigmas to us, while others seem too transparent; we respect a few and disrespect a few; we have opinions about the feelings of others toward us: "I think he likes me," or "I honestly believe she hates me!" In life we are always playing roles. Ask yourself who you really are: the student as you relate to your teachers? the child of your parents? the sister or brother? the character you want your friends to believe you are?

Since the drama essentially is concerned in a highly concentrated way with the relations of men, every character in a play, almost without exception, has very decided attitudes toward every other character with whom he comes in contact. The most minor characters in the most minor scenes will be out of place and undramatic, unless they are endowed with a sense of their relationship to other persons in the scene. There are often complaints that Ibsen's expository scenes are dull. They must be if they are played simply for the sake of disseminating information about antecedent events, or providing the audience with preparation for characters who have not yet appeared. But give the expository characters an objective, relate them in some way to one another and to those about whom they speak, and they come alive. The opening scene in *Miss Julie* is essentially expository in nature. But in Part II we shall learn that, at the same time, Jean's and Christine's objectives are in play, and that the characters can relate to setting and situation while revealing expository material. Add to this the fact that the characters' relationship to one another is being firmly established, and you have a scene that has many more functions than appear on the surface. Jean is in the same "class" as Christine, but has aspirations to raise himself, while she is content with things as they are. He is "comfortable" with her because she is of his class, but she is his inferior because 1) he has already bettered himself by learning French and aping aristocratic manners, and 2) he considers himself her sexual superior because he is a man, and he has "conquered" her. He enjoys her attentions and wants to impress her with his superiority. Christine is quite accepting, both of her status in life and of her relationship to Jean. She is quite willing to indulge his pretensions because she feels a genuine affection toward him. He is of her class, but she recognizes his supremacy over her and accepts it.

One of the elements of character that will be discussed in the character analysis concerns the question of characters undergoing change in the course of the play. Generally speaking, such changes, often the result of discoveries, are accompanied by changes in attitude. Jean and Julie's attitudes toward one another fluctuate constantly before the seduction. She shifts from an authoritarian position to one of equality and tenderness, then back again to the role of haughty mistress. Jean keeps himself in check but occasionally attempts to assert himself as Julie's equal. After the seduction, the pattern changes: their roles are reversed, and Julie ends up taking orders from Jean. Even within that pattern, however, there are constant shifts on the parts of both characters from physical attraction to repulsion, and from self-humiliation to scornful superiority. There is also a significant change in attitude on the parts of both Christine and Julie toward each other.

Attitudes toward other characters must find their way into expression. It is not enough to know how you feel about other characters on the stage. Knowing how you feel about others becomes a stimulus for *doing* something about it. What must Christine do to show her affection for Jean and her desire to cater to him? It must affect her tone of voice, the way she looks at him, the fact that she listens to his every word. She can put his things away, she can serve him his food with great care—choosing the best piece of meat and making sure that it is sufficiently heated. She can be tempted to touch him whenever they are close together, or to fondle his clothes or possessions.

EXERCISES

1. You are a waiter (waitress) in a fashionable restaurant. Perform a pantomime in which you take a customer's order and serve him. Do this pantomime three times, varying it each time by the application of the following attitudes:
   a. You are a new employee and are anxious to please.
   b. Your customer is pretentious and overly particular and you find him ludicrous.
   c. Your customer is dirty, sloppy, and repulsive. It becomes intolerable for you to serve him.
2. Perform the first scene in *Miss Julie* as you think it should be done. Then try it again, but change the attitudes of Jean and Christine toward each other in the following way:
   a. Christine is secretly amused by Jean. She exaggeratedly plays up to him, but really does not care for him at all.
   b. Jean is uncertain of Christine.

The employment of attitudes and relationships toward others may be extended to stimulate action and response in another way. There are times when we wish to activate our attitudes—that is, to impose them upon other people in such a way as to evoke some kind of response. There are times when we attempt to influence the attitude of others: we want them to love us, to get angry with us, to pay attention to us. During such times we do everything we can to "budge" the other person. This "budging" process, the deliberate attempt to evoke a response, has been termed "communion" by Stanislavski. One of its chief values on the stage is that it creates a process whereby we recognize the living presence of other actors and are forced to actually engage ourselves with them. Too often, the actor is involved only with himself. He performs with others and reacts to them with a set of clichés, which simply suggest that the actor wishes to impress others with the fact that he is listening or paying attention. Normally, when we are engaged in an activity with other people, we do not consciously say to ourselves, or deliberately suggest to them, the fact that we are aware of their presence. We take this for granted, and are more concerned with a give-and-take whereby we respond to and evoke responses. Too often, the actor fails to recognize that his fellow players are real human beings. They either remain actors "acting," or become nonexistent as a result of the actor never really seeing them. The actor learns his part and his cues, his objectives and his attitudes, and enacts them all with little need of a spontaneous, live exchange between real people.

Recall that when dealing with the emotions, it was emphasized that we react *directly* to a stimulus; we do not say to ourselves, "I am angry," or "I am joyous." Instead, something makes us angry or happy and we respond accordingly. In the same way, we act upon other people or are acted upon by them. A sneer may be directly responsible for our fury. The important thing for the actor to remember is that he does not let his anger come from simply thinking, "At this point I am supposed to be mad," but from the expression on the face of the character who makes him angry. Of course, the success of communion will depend upon the convincing efforts of both actors. If the sneer is not there and the other actor does not commune, to what can the actor respond? ". . . without absorbing from others or giving of yourself to others there can be no intercourse on the stage."[26]

The process of communion is affected by "adaptation," or the manner in which one person adjusts himself to another. Suppose you wish to persuade an acquaintance to go out for a walk, when he really wants to remain indoors. Your methods of persuasion will probably depend upon the kind of person you are attempting to convince. If he is intellectual, you might appeal to his reason; if he is emotional, to his feelings. You might try to flatter him or shame him into doing what you want, depending on the kind of person he is.

EXERCISES

---

1. You are at a dance. Ask the following persons to dance with you:
   a. Your sister
   b. Your teacher
   c. The girl with a shady reputation
   d. The campus queen
2. Repeat the above but instead of playing yourself, be the following characters:
   a. An arrogant football star
   b. A shy, introverted person
3. You have just discovered that you have not been cast in a play for which you tried out. Report the news to:
   a. Your father, who used to be a fine actor
   b. Your boyfriend (or girlfriend), who idolizes you
   c. The person who received the role you coveted
   d. Someone with whom you can honestly "let down your hair"
4. Repeat the above as the following type of person:
   a. A hypocrite
   b. A martyr
   c. A pollyanna
5. Try the same exercise as the person who got the part.

A good example of communion and adaptation occurs in *Miss Julie,* when Jean tells Julie about his childhood. Now there are several ways in which his tale might be told. It might be presented as something objectively biographical, or it might be presented with self-pity, or it might be presented lightly, with Jean viewing his youthful predicament with amusement and irony. Each one of these attitudes toward a previous event will evoke different ways of expressing them. But Jean is not telling the story simply for Julie's pleasure or his own; nor is it mere reflection. Jean has just been rebuffed by Julie after she erotically has led him on. Later, Jean admits that his story was an exaggeration. He has "adapted" to the sensitive side of her nature, with the intent of provoking a sense of pity and tenderness from her. His action is very deliberate, calculating, and convincing. How different will the actor's delivery be from mere narrative when his entire tale is stimulated by such an objective!

Miss Julie, in the meantime, is not passive, even though she listens more than she speaks. If Jean's efforts are convincing, and the actress *sees* and *listens* to what appears to be a brave and rather flattering confession, then she will adapt in terms of the character. Her readjustment from the superior mistress to the compassionate woman must depend for its truth and honesty upon her communion and adaptation with Jean.

EXERCISES

1. Pair yourself with another member of the class. Using one of the real-life characters of which you made a careful study, and applying the principles of communion and adaptation, create an improvisation in which the two characters are involved with each other in a simple situation. They may be playing cards, eating a meal, shopping, bidding against one another at an auction, discussing how to spend the evening, etc.

2. Pairing off once again, take turns in forcing your wills upon one another. The person to be convinced should *secretly* determine what kind of a person he is, in terms of what he can and cannot resist. The person attempting to persuade should attempt to discover the other's "soft spots" so that he may work upon them. Choose from the following situations:

   a. An employee has a meeting with his employer in order to get a raise.
   b. A student tries to get his teacher to change his grade.
   c. A salesman tries to sell a housewife some beauty lotions.
   d. A motorist tries to avoid being given a citation by a traffic officer.

3. The teacher provides two students with specific characters and objectives. Neither student is aware of the information given the other, except possibly some pertinent information concerning their immediate relationship and the basic situation. Specific settings and properties should be suggested. The following should serve as examples:

   a. The scene involves a husband and a wife. The actor playing the husband is told that he loves his wife, but knows that she is insane and could be dangerous. He has locked all of the doors to their apartment, and has to keep her safe until the attendants from the sanatorium arrive. The actress playing the wife is told that due to her husband's recent behavior, she is convinced that he wishes to harm her in some way.
   b. A wealthy, fashionable, and vacuous lady goes to the beauty parlor. She wants a pompadour. She always gets her own way. Her hairdresser is vain and egotistical. He has a mania for the latest fad, which he insists upon giving to her.
   c. In the following situations, the actors should *not* be informed about their relationship to one another. The setting is a dimly-lit bar. One of the characters is a drunken man (or woman) who is completely alone in the world. He just wants to be left alone. The second

character believes she (he) is the drunk's sister (or brother).   She
(he) is very tired after a full day's work and tries to get the drunk
to leave the bar and go home.

4.   a.   In a line-by-line analysis, discuss Christine's relationship to Miss
Julie in terms of communion and adaptation after Christine learns
of the seduction.

b.   Discuss M. de Bonnefoi in terms of communion and adaptation during his only scene in *The Would-Be Invalid*.

RELATING TO MENTAL OR
EMOTIONAL PROCESSES

Often in a play, a character has occasion to speak of, describe, or reflect upon
a previous occurrence. He may be doing this, as does Jean in his boyhood
narrative, in order to affect another person on stage, but he is, at the same
time, recreating a reality toward which he adapts his attitudes and emotions.
When Julie tells Jean about the manner in which she was raised, her purpose
ostensibly is to share the secrets of her early life, perhaps because she wants
him to understand her better. At the same time, however, she evokes vivid
images of real people and real events. Furthermore, she has developed
attitudes toward each of those people and each of the events.

In order to stimulate the appropriate responses to memory, the actress
must create in her mind's eye real persons whose identities have the power
of evoking the correct responses; that is, persons to whom she can make the
correct adaptations. Through imagination she can place these people into
conflict with one another and visualize the events described in literal terms.
Remember that the actress is not simply telling a story, but is *engaged* with
memory. She is involved in an *action* that is the consequence of the tensions
created between vivid recollection and the character's adaptation to it.

Perhaps the most frequent and obvious examples of narrative converted
into action occur in Greek tragedy, when a messenger is usually brought in
to report a catastrophe that has taken place offstage. It would be a great
mistake, and unquestionably harmful to the play, to look upon messengers'
speeches as mere reports. If the Greek playwright had wished these scenes
to be merely expository, he could have had the information presented quickly
and briefly. Instead, the messengers invariably are given the responsibility
of describing in vivid detail the horrors they have witnessed, and in almost

all instances there are unquestionable implications about their response to what they have witnessed. Perhaps the best exercise for the actor, in dealing with the problem of relating and adapting to mental processes, is the performance of one of these scenes. In our work on style, Euripedes' *Medea* will be used for illustrative purposes. It contains an exciting messenger speech (11. 1121-1230), which will be used now for the purpose of relating to mental and emotional processes.

The messenger is a man who could be young or middle-aged, whose objective is at first urgently to report the news of the catastrophe so that Medea might escape, but who is forced to describe in detail the atrocity he has just witnessed. He is at present a servant to Jason, but Medea had been his mistress before Jason left her. Apparently, there is much loyalty in him toward Medea.

The situation to which he must relate is Medea's imminent danger, and then the description that must be made in compliance with her wishes. The setting consists of the area in front of Medea's run-down palace and the direction leading to the road the messenger has just traveled. The messenger is to relate to the characters of Medea, a female chorus, and, in memory, to Creon and his daughter.

The messenger enters, filled with the horror he has just witnessed, and out-of-breath from his long run from Creon's palace. His first exchange with Medea involves communion and adaptation in the following way: he must urge his mistress to flee because of the crime she has committed but she is his mistress and he must be respectful. He is horrified at her acts, but loyal enough to wish to preserve her safety. The chorus of women will react with shock to the initial report. At Medea's pleased response, accompanied by no signs of alarm, the messenger is amazed and, still concerned over the possible arrival of Jason's officers, attempts to make Medea aware of the consequences of her outrage.

He is commanded, however, to describe the deaths of Medea's victims. How does the messenger react to this? Seeing the face of his mistress in ecstasy over her deed, frightened by a suspicion of madness, yet obliged to obey commands, he reluctantly begins to describe the crime, and slowly adapts to the all-too-vivid memory of what he had witnessed.

The description begins with the acceptance and childlike trying-on of the gifts by the princess, followed, in language of frightful horror, by the torture and suffering of the princess and then her father. Now the actor *must see these scenes,* and visualize the actual faces of the king and princess. There are several ways for him to create a reality to which he will adapt.

He may, with an actual man and woman in mind, try to picture the gory details, and he may even substitute his memory of pertinent atrocities he has personally observed. He may attempt to recall sensory and emotional experiences of his own that relate to burning, suffocating, and the fear of imminent death. He may enact for himself the experience of the victims. Identifying himself with each one in turn, he may attempt to ask, "How would I feel and what would I do in such a predicament?" Another technique is to ask an actor and an actress to literally enact the scene, so that the actor playing the messenger is, in essence, a witness to the calamity. Whatever method is used, the messenger must be aware that what he is supposed to have seen is not merely a silent visual spectacle, but that other senses must have been gruesomely involved such as the sounds of screams and agony and the smell of burning flesh. The result should be such a clear and vivid reality to which the actor can relate, that the appropriate adaptation of revulsion, horror, and even sickness will occur without much strain.

During the speech, of course, there will be other adaptations to make. Although the messenger becomes absorbed in what he describes, he will be interrupted occasionally by a shriek of glee from Medea and the miserable groans of the chorus. He may, on occasion, be so overwhelmed himself by recollection of a specific horror that he must stop and pull himself together.

EXERCISES

1. One or two members of the class should learn the speech and deliver it.
2. Two persons, one male and one female, should be asked to enact the scene that the messenger describes. All action should be pantomimed, with sense and emotion memory scrupulously applied. Vocal sounds should be made whenever necessary. The class should be involved in making suggestions and criticizing actions that lack belief.
3. The persons who learned the speech should now report *in their own words* the enactment they have witnessed.
4. Finally, they should repeat the scene with the original language.
5. Other members of the class should select one of the Greek messenger speeches listed at the end of Part III, and using the same process, prepare to perform it for the class.

   (*Note:* When working on this exercise, no emphasis should be placed upon style. Concentrate, rather, upon relating to mental and emotional processes.)

With this type of approach to this speech, the audience will receive more than a journalistic announcement of an atrocity. Depending on the imagination of the actor playing the messenger, the audience can be stimulated to picture the scene as vividly as he. Then the full import of Medea's act becomes more meaningful. The audience will be exposed also to the contrast of the normal compassion and horror shared by messenger and chorus to Medea's demoniacal joy. But the audience can get none of this without the fullest employment by the actor of his imaginative capacities.

EXERCISES

Apply the above methodology to the following speeches from *Miss Julie:*
1. WOMEN: Julie's description of her parents' relationship, beginning with ". . . everybody knows my secrets," and ending with ". . . I swore to her that I'd never be slave to any man." (Someone should provide Jean's cues.)
2. MEN: Jean's description of the day at the Turkish pavilion, beginning with "One day I went with my mother . . . ," and concluding with "But you were a symbol of the absolute hopelessness of my ever getting out of the circle I was born in." (Someone should provide Julie's cues.)

Every action (or inaction) on the stage must be meaningful and consequently justified. The more the actor can discover regarding his relationship to situation, locale, characters, objects, and mental or emotional processes, the richer will be his imaginative action. The actor is the creator of the action by means of which the character emerges into vital physical life. At the same time, the actor must be reminded that the justification for everything he does onstage must emanate from the text if his action is to be relevant to the play. The actor, consequently, is responsible for finding the clues in the text that will spur his imagination to appropriate action. Finding the appropriate clues is what interpretation is all about, and this is the concern of the following chapters.

PART I

NOTES

1. *The Personal Papers of Anton Chekhov* (New York: Lear Publishers, Inc., 1948), pp. 57, 68, 74, 77, 85, 97.
2. Lorena A. Hickok, *The Touch of Magic* (New York: Dodd, Mead, & Co., 1962), p. 4.
3. *Ibid.*, p. 115.
4. William Gibson, *The Miracle Worker* (New York: Samuel French and Co., 1957), p. 15.
5. Hickok, *op. cit.*, p. 3.
6. Thomas Wolfe, *You Can't Go Home Again* (New York: Harper & Bros., n.d.), p. 149.
7. *Ibid.*, pp. 153-154.
8. Charles Dickens, *The Personal History of David Copperfield* (London: Oxford University Press, 1960), p. 190.
9. *Ibid.*, p. 194.
10. *Ibid.*, p. 209.
11. *Ibid.*, p. 230.
12. *Ibid.*, p. 234.
13. If this book is not available, select other books dealing with photography. There is a plentiful supply of photography magazines, whose annual editions are filled with rewarding studies of humanity.
14. Quoted from Florio's *World of Words*, 1598, in Hazelton Spencer, *Elizabethan Plays* (Boston: D. C. Heath and Co., 1933), p. 301.
15. Constant Coquelin, "Actors and Acting," in *The Art of Acting* (New York: Columbia University Press, 1926), p. 30.
16. Henry Irving, "M. Coquelin on Actors and Acting," *ibid.*, pp. 47-48.
17. Coquelin, *op. cit.*, p. 11.
18. Coquelin, "A Reply to Mr. Henry Irving," *op. cit.*, p. 74.
19. Irving, *op. cit.*, p. 51.
20. Michael Chekhov, *To the Actor* (New York: Harper and Bros., 1953), p. 51.
21. *Ibid.*, p. 65. More will be said about the archetypal gesture in the sections of this book dealing with style.

22. Constantin Stanislavski, *An Actor Prepares* (New York: Theatre Arts, Inc., 1946), pp. 23-25. Copyright 1936 by Theatre Arts, Inc. Copyright 1948 by Elizabeth R. Hapgood. Reprinted with the permission of the Publisher, Theatre Arts Books, New York.

23. *Ibid.*, p. 14.

24. *Ibid.*

25. *Ibid.*, p. 15.

26. *Ibid.*, p. 184.

SELECTED READINGS

Benedetti, Robert L.   *The Actor at Work*.   Englewood Cliffs, N. J.: Prentice-Hall, Inc., 1970.

Berry, Cecily.   *Voice and the Actor*.   London: George Harrap and Co., 1973.

Blunt, Jerry.   *The Composite Art of Acting*.   New York: Macmillan, 1966.

Boleslavsky, Richard.   *Acting; The First Six Lessons*.   New York: Theatre Arts Books, Inc., 1934.

Dolman, John.   *The Art of Acting*.   New York: Harper and Bros., 1949.

Grotowski, Jerzy.   *Towards a Poor Theatre*.   New York: Simon and Schuster, 1968.

Hethman, Robert H., ed.   *Strasberg at the Actor's Studio*.   New York: The Viking Press, 1965.

Hodgson, John, and Richards, Ernest.   *Improvisation*.   London: Methuen and Co., 1967.

Karlinsky, Simon, and Heim, Michael (trans.).   *Anton Chekhov's Life and Thought: Selected Letters and Commentary*.   Berkeley, Calif.: University of California Press, 1975.

McGaw, Charles.   *Acting Is Believing*.   2d ed.   New York: Holt, Rinehart and Winston, 1966.

Moore, Sonia.   *The Stanislavski Method*.   New York: The Viking Press, 1960.

Penrod, James.   *Movement for the Performing Artist*.   Palo Alto, Calif.: National Press Books, 1974.

Rockwood, Jerome.   *The Craftsmen of Dionysus*.   Glenview, Ill.: Scott, Foresman and Co., 1966.

Selden, Samuel.   *First Steps in Acting*.   2d ed.   New York: Appleton-Century-Crofts, 1964.

Spolin, Viola.   *Improvisation for the Theatre*.   Evanston, Ill.: Northwestern Univ. Press, 1963.

Stanislavski, Constantin.   *An Actor Prepares*.   New York: Theatre Arts Books, Inc., 1946.

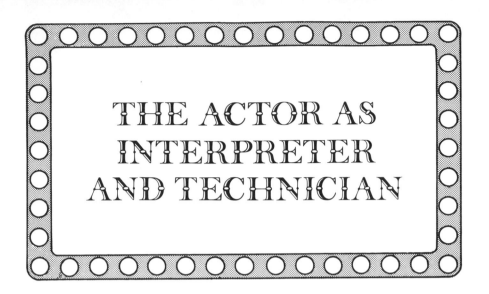

THE ACTOR AS INTERPRETER AND TECHNICIAN

PART II

INTRODUCTION

One of the practices of the early stock companies in America, and one that continues still in many theatre organizations today, consists of providing the actor with "sides" rather than a full script of the play. "Sides" are half-sheets of paper, usually stapled together and placed between cardboard strips. They contain all of the lines of a single character in the play and his "cues"—the last few words of the speeches preceding his lines. The use of the "side" rather than a full script probably was due originally to economic factors, since plays often existed only in manuscript form and the duplication of entire scripts for each member of the cast would have been too costly. In addition, the "side" was easier for the actor to handle during rehearsals, and might contain extra margin space in which he could write his stage directions and comments. Today, despite the availability of inexpensive duplication processes and the printing of successful plays in cheap editions, the use of "sides" continues, probably because of habit and ease of handling. The consequence is frequently an actor-centered

```
Queen . . . . Must we part?
Richard.    Ay, hand from hand my love, and heart from heart.
Queen . . . . thither let me go.
Richard.    So two, together weeping; make one woe.
            Weep thou for me in France, I for thee here.
            Better far off than near, be ne'er the near.
            Go, count thy way with sighs; I mine with groans.
Queen . . . . the longest moans.
Richard.    Twice for one step I'll groan, the way being short,
            And piece the way out with a heavy heart.
            Come, come, in wooing sorrow let's be brief,
            Since wedding it, there is much length in grief.
            One kiss shall stop our mouths, and dumbly part.
            Thus give I mine, and thus I take thy heart.
Queen . . . . with a groan.
Richard.    We make woe wanton with this fond delay.
            Once more adieu! The rest let sorrow say.
```

Example of "sides."

performance, because the actor is exposed only to his lines and cues rather than to the significance of the entire text.

"Side" users may argue that they become familiar with the entire play either during a read-through, when the entire cast is assembled to read and discuss the play, or when the director takes time to explain and develop the play's total meaning and values. Most experienced and conscientious actors, dedicated to the correct interpretation of a play rather than to a nonrelated virtuoso performance, will tell you that less than a half-dozen full readings of the entire play are insufficient, and that a continued study of its parts (including scenes that do not include, but that contain references to, the character he is to portray) is essential. As for the director's authority, the same actor will admit that a unifying agent is necessary and helpful, but that most directors welcome, and often demand, the creative contribution of the actor. Besides, a director's "explanations" are hardly meaningful when the actor has only a vague frame of reference to which he may apply them.

For the noncreative actor, even a full script is valueless. Many actors will underline their own lines as soon as they receive a script, and proceed to work as if they had merely "sides" in their possession, concentrating only upon their own words and cues.

The author's purpose is not to attack the use of "sides" or the method of underlining in themselves, but to warn the actor against any kind of practice that prevents him from perceiving his role in relation to the meaning of the whole play. A play, as is the case with any art form, is created with a particular kind of unity, which in turn is based upon some particular end or purpose. The effort of the dramatist, through the medium of the theatre, is to provide an experience that is made manifest by the actions of men—by what his characters do and say, rather than by narration. Characters and their actions in a really good play are not selected randomly or arbitrarily, but in terms of the nature of the experience that the play is intended to produce.

August Strindberg, in *Miss Julie,* does not bring onstage all of the occupants of the Count's castle. He chooses, rather, to present only three of them to the audience—four, if we include the revellers who, in a sense, represent a collective type of character. Why does he select just these four? Neither does Strindberg care to reveal every possible facet of his characters' personalities. Instead, he chooses to concentrate on a limited number of traits, the sum and limitation of which result in characters that surely are not like characters in real life, no matter how close to real life Strindberg wished to come in this naturalistic play.

In his preface to *Miss Julie,* Strindberg objects to a one-sided way of depicting character, because he believed that people essentially are more than some single external trait or stereotype, and are not wholly good or wholly bad. He disapproved of playwrights' "summary judgments" of men, and said that such judgments "should not pass unchallenged by the naturalists who know how complicated the soul is and who realize that vice has a reverse side very much like virtue."[1] Note, however, that Strindberg speaks about what character should be in terms of specific objectives. In his play, we are made to see characters whose complexity forces our attitudes and impressions to shift and vary, but this very complexity is the result of a fixed purpose on the part of a playwright who wishes to make his audience aware of the vacillating nature of the human personality. Note also that Strindberg's characters, as complex as they may be, are not random snapshots of the man in the street, but belong to certain classes, are of a certain age, are related consistently to the process of rising and falling, and so on. In the preface, Miss Julie is referred to as "half-woman," "man-hater," "remnant of the old war nobility," and as a person who "cannot go on living once she has lost her honor." Ultimately, Strindberg proves to be as severe as Molière, whom he criticizes, in relating his characters to a higher purpose—even if that purpose be to reveal the complexity of human behavior. The difference between the two writers is that because Strindberg's ends are, in part, a concern for the influence of heredity, environment, and chance upon character, he places greater stress on psychological motivation than does Molière. "Our inveterately curious souls are no longer content to see a thing happen; we want to see how it happens," claims Strindberg.

One of the major problems in interpretation for the contemporary actor is that, because he lives in a period and culture that stress psychological causes of human behavior, and because he has grown up with a drama that emphasizes it, he either rejects plays whose characters are not "psychologically motivated" or believes that he must create "motives" for them. The results are Oedipal Hamlets and homosexual Iagos, because the actor or director believes it necessary to explain how these characters came to act as they do, despite the fact that such motives are irrelevant. Harpagon, Strindberg complains, "is nothing but a miser although Harpagon might have been not only a miser but an exceptional financier, a fine father, and a good citizen." Strindberg is referring to the protagonist in Molière's *The Miser,* who because of his trait (practically the *only* one that Molière chooses to exhibit), is incapable of fulfilling his function as a responsible parent or as a stable member of his society, and who is victimized eventually by the gullibility that his obsession has produced in him. Molière's purpose in this play is not to explore the causes of miserliness by "rounding out" his character. His aim is to depict the ludicrous *results* of miserliness rather than its causes. Had Molière done what Strindberg suggested, the result would have been a different play, probably not a comedy, and requiring an entirely different kind of performance.

Both Strindberg and Molière have similar ends, in that their plays emphasize character. They differ, however, in their means of expressing character. Molière is concerned with the effects of miserliness rather than its causes. In wishing to present as clear a picture of miserliness as possible, he avoids other characteristics, although Harpagon is also a father, is suspicious, and is susceptible to flattery. Strindberg is concerned with exploring the causes of human action and decision. He refuses to allow us to retain a constant or fixed perception of his characters because he believes in a more relative view of human behavior. In both instances, however, the playwright has a point of view, or design, upon which his play is based and upon which he has created character; he has selected and limited their characteristics in terms of that higher purpose. This means that the actor must conscientiously study the character as it was created *within the framework of the play.* Aside from such necessities as studying period or foreign manners, customs, and costumes that require the actor to go outside the play, the essentials for understanding the character are strictly within the play.

Biographical plays are no exception. Of course the actor should make some effort to determine the surface characteristics of a well-known historical personage such as Abraham Lincoln, for example, so that with the aid of makeup, posture, and dialect, he may approximate the physical qualities of the man. But each of the many plays and motion pictures concerned with the great president may be distinguished from one another by the purpose for which his character was put to use. An early Griffith film was concerned with the impact and loss of Lincoln's first love; a later John Ford film emphasized melodramatic and patriotic elements, and Robert Sherwood's play *Abe Lincoln in Illinois* depicted a series of crises designed to reveal the development of the protagonist into a man of decision. Each of these Lincolns might resemble one another physically, but the essential character of each can be determined only by what is required by their respective plays. Raymond Massey, who played Sherwood's Lincoln on the stage and in the motion picture, has this to say about the extent of the actor's study of a biographical character:

Again and again I am asked the question: how much research should an actor do in preparing his part? While getting ready for Robert Sherwood's *Abe Lincoln in Illinois,* which I have played on both stage and screen, I deliberately avoided more than a cursory research. The deep study of Lincoln which Mr. Sherwood had made supplied me with a wealth of relevant material which an author of his genius and theatrical knowledge considered sufficient—and *not more than sufficient*—for developing the character. Overembellishment—a satiety of detail—might have seriously jeopardized in performance a figure which the author had conceived in superb economy and sincerity. I think an actor should always assume that the author has purposely cut off the ragged edges of a character.[2]

Recent studies of England's Richard III have revealed that in many important respects Shakespeare's play has distorted and maligned that monarch. Does this mean that the conscientious actor must attempt to present the *real* Richard when doing Shakespeare's tragedy? Unless he plans to rewrite the text, such an effort can only lead to bewildering contradictions between language and action in performance, and a distortion of the concept of evil with which the play is concerned. Playwrights do not write biographies; instead, they create characters or *adapt* them from life in order to intensify certain aspects of the human condition.

Now that we have distinguished the general meaning of character in drama as opposed to real characters in life, and have tried to show why character understanding must be approached without preconceived ideas no matter what its origin, we must next determine how a study of a dramatic character may be made. In a play, the only source for clues to characterization exists in what characters say and do, what is said about them, and whatever information the playwright provides in his stage directions. But a mere collection of abstractions about a character cannot provide the actor or his audience with a solid, consistent, or meaningful concept of a particular personage within a play.

To say that a character such as Argan in *The Would-Be Invalid* is a male, middle-aged, fairly wealthy, a parent, French, married to a second wife to whose insincere flattery he is susceptible, selfish, a hypochondriac, and hot-tempered is to report quite a bit that is true and important, but not enough to reveal what it is that brings all of these characteristics together, fusing them into a distinctive personality. The actor may be selfish in one scene, and may depict an appropriate emotion in another, but what is it which makes us recognize that the selfishness and the emotion are Argan's? And what are we to make of Miss Julie, who vacillates between arrogance and humility, dominance and submission, love and hate? Both Julie and Argan, in their respective plays, exhibit many different emotions; their reactions to other characters and to complications and crises vary as each play develops. How can the actor avoid making his performance a mere parade of disconnected characteristics and mannerisms?

One solution is to find a pattern. First, the actor must carefully analyze, or dissect, the playwright's character in terms of his various actions, then synthesize them by recognizing repetitions and consistencies (even deliberate *in*consistencies), and then return to each scene and perceive the separate actions in terms of the overall design of the character. This would become clearer in the analysis and synthesis of *Miss Julie* and *The Would-Be Invalid* that follow. It is, of course, important that the analysis come first; otherwise, the pattern of behavior that we seek is liable to be the result of faulty intuition, or generalized and vague conclusions.

CHAPTER 5

The Analysis

Several procedures may be followed in the process of gathering the materials and evidence that will lead the actor to his ultimate conclusions about the character he is to portray. He may go through the play and itemize what is said about the character, and what the character himself says and does. Perhaps a more meaningful mode of investigation is to determine how the playwright has chosen to reveal and develop his characters in terms of how he has structured his play. Like the writer who builds his narrative out of paragraphs, each of which presents us with a separate idea or further development of an idea, or the architect whose building is a result of the manner in which brick, steel, and wood are put together, the playwright must construct his total play with the parts or materials of his own particular medium. In the course of a play, the playwright normally must acquaint his audience with a knowledge of antecedent events, relevant offstage happenings, a clear and causal development of his plot with its complications, crises, climaxes, and resolutions. He must develop his characters so that they affect or are affected by his plot, and embody his ideas or arguments, if any, in character and action.[3] The playwright accomplishes all this by developing his play with his own unique kind of paragraph—the scene, or unit, or beat, each of which is utilized to stress at least one of the necessities itemized above.

BEATS OR UNITS

In contemporary American and English drama, plays are divided into acts, which are sometimes subdivided into scenes. In such instances, these terms represent divisions in the play occasioned by a change of time or place, or simply, as is often the case with the well-made play, to provide a pause after a crisis, during which the audience anxiously awaits its outcome. Such scene divisions are too broad for our purposes. Formal scene divisions, which come closer to providing us with the finer architectonic units that we are seeking, exist in ancient Greek tragedies and in the French method of play division. Since the action in Greek drama is so strongly concentrated to begin with (each play usually is concerned with a single crisis in the life of the protagonist, contains very few characters, and employs no subplots), its clear-cut divisions into *stasimon* (choral song and dance) and *epiodeon* (dialogue and soliloquy that develop the action) reveal quite clearly the dramatist's methods and purposes in construction. Each episode usually develops a single complication, reversal, discovery, and/or delineation of a particular character trait.

French plays are usually divided by the dramatist into small scenes, whose length is determined by the entrances and exits of characters. Since the arrival and departure of characters in plays is one of the playwright's major methods of developing action and character, dividing a play into smaller units on this basis for the sake of analysis is usually valid. On occasion, however, one may come across a long scene in which the same characters remain on the stage without being interrupted by other characters, during which time the writer nevertheless changes emphasis and direction. *Miss Julie,* for example, begins with a fairly long scene between Jean and Christine before they are interrupted by Julie's arrival. During that time, however, the subject of the conversation shifts three times, and in each unit between shifts, Strindberg begins to develop certain aspects of his play. From Jean's entrance until he asks for something to eat, the stress is on his reaction to Julie's offstage activities; the next unit concentrates on Jean's culinary tastes, then shifts into a new unit when Jean smells the concoction being prepared for Julie's dog. This brings the conversation back to Julie, and shifts when Christine asks Jean for a dance. For the purpose of analysis, the length of a beat or unit should be determined by transitions brought about by the entrance or exit of a character, by a change of subject or mood, or by a change in time or place.

While it is probably a good idea for the actor to recognize the purpose of each unit, his chief task is to recognize the character development that appears in each unit. Does the unit introduce and/or develop the physical traits of a character? Or does it provide us with expository material concerning relevant events or actions in the past in order to prepare us for a better understanding of present behavior? What objectives or desires does the character wish to satisfy in each scene in which he appears? The actor should explore each unit thoroughly for all of the hints that might aid him in understanding his character.

The first few units of *Miss Julie* tell us a good deal in terms of character, and provide us with an excellent example of how much may be revealed about a character in a scene in which he does not appear. Observe the number of important details about Julie that these few small units reveal:

1. Miss Julie's engagement was broken off two weeks ago.
2. Since that time she has acted "wild."
3. The engagement had been broken because of Miss Julie's attempts to prove her dominance over her fiancé by forcing him to jump over her riding crop.
4. There is a distinct contradiction in Julie's pattern of behavior. She is Jean reports, "too stuck up in some ways and not proud enough in others." This contradiction is further emphasized in this portion of the play when her desire to avoid the mixture of classes in dogs is contrasted to her own irrepressible desire to become intimate with the servants.
5. Miss Julie is the daughter of the Count and Countess. Her mother, now dead, is described as having exhibited the same self-contradiction as Julie: The Countess felt right at home in the kitchen or down in the barn with the cows, but when she went driving, *one* horse wasn't enough for her; she had to have a pair. Her sleeves were always dirty, but her buttons had the royal crown on them."
6. According to Jean, Miss Julie is "Beautiful! Magnificent! Ah, those shoulders—those—and so forth, and so forth!"

The actor, of course, must be wary of accepting as gospel the description of one character by another. Sometimes such descriptions are deliberately deceitful, as is the case in *Othello,* where Iago poisons Othello's mind against Cassio and Desdemona. Or they may be unconsciously contrary to truth, as is the case with Othello's delusions about Iago's "honesty." In such instances, distorted attitudes are more indicative of the character

99

of the describer than of the person described.   Iago's evil is revealed in part through his willful slander, and in part through Othello's gullibility in his evaluation of Iago.

While many of the first few units of *Miss Julie* are devoted to exposition concerning Julie's character, we are provided with much, although less direct, evidence to begin forming opinions about Jean and Christine.   For example, we learn that Jean is strongly class-conscious.   He repeatedly disapproves of Julie's contamination of herself with the servants.   He looks upon the aristocracy as another breed, yet reveals an ambivalence similar to Julie's when his own pretenses come to the fore.   Note his deliberate use of French, "My special *délice*"; his insistence upon having his plate heated; his preference for a gold-sealed wine over beer, as well as a glass with a stem; and his admonition of Christine when she uses moderately coarse language.   His apparently high opinion of himself is revealed by these affectations, as well as by his allusions to Julie's personal interest in him, and is reinforced by his smug relationship to the woman who waits upon him and tries to show her affection: "You'd consider yourself lucky if you got yourself a man as good as me.   It hasn't done you any harm to have people think I am your fiancé."

Such revelations of character must not in themselves lead to final conclusions.   Each unit contributes toward the complete picture of a character, and usually does so as a link in a chain, or a single chip or color in a mosaic.   It would be erroneous to conclude that Jean is really a superior person or that he is convinced of his own superiority on the basis of his behavior in the opening units of the play.   It becomes quite apparent in the subsequent action of the play that Jean consistently attempts to disguise or compensate for his deep-rooted feelings of inferiority.   We learn this by the shifts and contradictions that appear in the actions of Jean in various units of the play, just as repetitious materials throughout the play emphasize each character's obsession with the problem of domination in both the class and the sexual struggle.

SUBTEXT AND OBJECTIVES

Just as each unit presumably satisfies an objective of the playwright in the construction and overall design of the play, each unit usually contains an underlying objective for the characters who appear in it.   In this instance,

objective is to be understood as the goal or fundamental desire of the character, rather than his various functions in the scene. The actor, in other
words, must recognize that in the well-written play, characters are more
than mere expository figures or theme conveyors. The writer must make
their actions probable and believable.[4] He achieves this by ascribing to
them a unity of motives and desires that permeates all of their actions and
provides his characters with their individuality. The actor must be reminded, however, that the motives and desires of the character must be
determined by what is in the script, and not by any external application
of contemporary psychology. Motives are important in our understanding
of character and as a causal element in plot development, but as has been
stressed previously, motives are only as complex and deeply explored as the
play demands. In each scene of a play in which he appears, the actor must
ask, as the character, "What do I want?" It is not always necessary for
him to determine or guess *why* he wants it.

In *Othello,* Shakespeare makes the fact quite clear that Iago wishes to
destroy Othello because he hates him, but critics have been arguing for
decades over why Iago hates his general. It is quite evident that Shakespeare was not overly concerned with the motives for Iago's hatred. Does
this mean that Shakespeare created an inferior character? The answer
would be "yes" if the play were intended to be an exploration into the cause
of Iago's malignant nature. It is not. The tragedy is concerned, rather,
with the Christian struggle between good and evil, represented in this play
by love and hatred, faith and distrust, and the weakness of a man who
allows himself to be conquered by hatred and distrust.

Miss Julie, on the other hand, comes as reasonably close to a case study
as a work of art is capable of doing. The play is consistently occupied
with an exploration of the motives and causes, including heredity, environment, chance, and interaction, which influence its major characters. This
does not mean, however, that the characters in *Miss Julie* are bundles of
disconnected drives, or that their past lives and present environment may
not be channeled into single powerful objectives that give the characters
their necessary cohesiveness.

Because a dramatic character's permeating desire is the synthesis of
all of his various objectives and actions throughout the play, it is necessary
to interpret his fundamental goals in each of the units in which he appears.
In the first unit of *Miss Julie,* Jean enters the kitchen. Why has he come
there? What does he want? He has come because these are his quarters.
He has returned from taking the Count to the station, and has brought the
Count's boots into the kitchen to be polished. We learn, in the second

unit, that he has come to the kitchen to eat. He also wants to tell Christine about his mistress' demand that he dance with her. When he eats, he wants a special kind of food and drink, served in a special way. At the moment, he does *not* want to fool with Christine. In the unit just before Julie's entrance, he does not appear overtly to desire anything. What do these seemingly diverse objectives tell us about Jean? What significance does wanting to eat, wanting to report an incident that has occurred, or avoiding a little petting have in terms of Jean's significance as a character? They help us recognize that he is a servant, and that he exerts a certain control over Christine, but little more. The trouble with our analysis thus far is that it has emphasized surface objectives rather than implied or suggested ones, now commonly referred to as the "subtext."

Just as humans in everyday life do not openly exhibit their real needs or purposes, characters in plays more often than not mask their desires. Sometimes we discover that they are conscious of doing so, while on other occasions they themselves are unaware of what they *really* want. It is playwright Harold Pinter's contention that words and overt behavior more frequently conceal rather than reveal the moment-to-moment truth of people's feelings and wants, and Anton Chekhov's major plays require careful exploration of what lies beneath the surface of seemingly trivial conversations and pauses. Think of the number of times in our daily existence when we find ourselves saying and doing things that we do not really mean or feel, or think of the roles that we play with people at work, at school, or at leisure. Consider the student or employee who dislikes his class or occupation, yet suppresses his dislike before his teachers, his employer, his peers—sometimes even before himself! Consider marriages that appear to be pleasant and affectionate, but ultimately prove to be a battleground.

Edward Arlington Robinson's poem *Richard Cory* provides an excellent example of the discrepancies that often exist between outward and inward behavior:

> *Whenever Richard Cory went down town,*
> *We people on the pavement looked at him:*
> *He was a gentleman from sole to crown,*
> *Clean favored, and imperially slim.*

> *And he was always quietly arrayed,*
> *And he was always human when he talked;*
> *But still he fluttered pulses when he said,*
> *"Good-morning," and he glittered when he walked.*

And he was rich—yes, richer than a king—
And admirably schooled in every grace:
In fine, we thought that he was everything
To make us wish that we were in his place.

So on we worked, and waited for the light,
And went without the meat, and cursed the bread;
And Richard Cory, one calm summer night,
Went home and put a bullet through his head.[5]

In drama, the actor *must* find what lies beneath the surface of the lines and outward demeanor of his character; he must explore the *sub*text of all that the character says or does in the play. Let us begin again with the first unit of the play, and probe more deeply into Jean's objectives. When he tells Christine that Julie danced with him, is his only concern to narrate what happened? Or does the manner in which he reports the incident reveal some deeper desire?

> I took the Count down to the station, and on my way back as I passed the barn I went in for a dance. And there was Miss Julie leading the dance with the game warden. But when she noticed me, and she came right up and chose me for the ladies' waltz. And she's been dancing ever since like—like I don't know what. She's absolutely wild!

Notice the repeated use of the personal pronoun in this speech. Is it possible that Jean has been pleased and inflated by what has happened, despite his apparent disapproval? And what about his disapproval? Miss Julie has lowered herself in his eyes, by becoming, as he puts it later on, "common." In emphasizing the fact that Julie was attracted to him, and that he disapproved of her behavior, Jean wants Christine to recognize his superiority. Of course, the speech quoted above is not sufficient evidence for such a conclusion. It is only when we proceed and recognize similar emphases in subsequent units that we can return to the opening speech and recognize its implications. In this particular instance, we do not have to go too far to observe a pattern emerging in Jean's basic needs. He confides in Christine that he witnessed the cause for the breakup of the engagement.

JEAN: Do you know what happened, Christine? I do. I saw the whole thing, even though I didn't let on.

CHRISTINE: Don't tell me you were there?
JEAN: Well, I was.

This revelation, which Christine receives with admiring awe, indicates his pride in being "in-the-know."

At this point, Strindberg has Jean change the subject by asking for something to eat. Why? Does the playwright want to show us that Jean is overly conscious of food? A glutton? Half-starved? Or is it merely a suitable device to enhance the naturalistic style of the play? Clearly it is none of these things, although eating scenes may increase the effect of naturalism. The playwright has introduced this action in order to reveal Jean's aspirations to identify himself with the aristocracy. (The wine itself later serves as a symbol of Jean's desire to raise himself above his station in contrast to Julie's request for beer, which signifies her desire to descend.) The following excerpts illustrate this point:

JEAN (*smelling it* [the food]): Wonderful! My special délice; (*feeling the plate*) They didn't warm the plate!
CHRISTINE: You're more fussy than the Count himself when you set your mind to it.

When Christine brings him beer, Jean remarks:

Beer on Midsummer eve! No thanks! I've got something much better than that. (*He opens a drawer in the table and takes out a bottle of red wine with a gold seal.*) Do you see that? Gold Seal. Now give me a glass.—No, a wine glass, of course. I'm drinking it straight.

Tasting the wine, he says:

Very good. Excellent. But warmed just a little too little. (*Warming the glass in his hands.*) We bought this in Dijon. Four francs a liter, unbottled—and the tax on top of that. . . .

So Jean eats and drinks, and what is most important about this action and this scene is his affectation about food and drink, which proves to be further evidence of his desire to be superior, or to identify himself in as many ways as possible with the upper class. Note his use of "we" in referring to the purchase of the Count's wine.

There is one more device that Strindberg utilizes in this initial establishment of Jean's desire to appear superior. In the scenes preceding Julie's entrance, the relationship between Jean and Christine is introduced. We learn that both are servants and it is suggested that some intimacy exists between them. We have noted previously that Jean tries to impress Christine with his superiority. May Jean's desire to be superior be extended to include his relations with the opposite sex? Observe how Christine waits on him and obeys his commands. Jean never says, "Please," or "Thank you," except peremptorily at the end of the scene. He dominates the conversation, during which, except for the impression he wishes to create, he ignores Christine while she caters to his demands and indulges his pretensions. When she tries to be demonstrative, Jean becomes irritable: "Cut it out! Don't muss up my hair! You know I don't like that!" When Christine tells him she is only showing him that she loves him, he ignores her and proceeds to eat the kidney she has saved for him. To her comment about his fussiness, Jean replies: "Talk, talk! You'd consider yourself lucky if you got yourself a man as good as me. It hasn't done you any harm to have people think I'm your fiancé!" Finally, just before the end of their first scene together, Christine reacts with placid jealousy to Jean's admiration of Julie, then she asks him if he is going to dance with her later in the evening.

JEAN: Certainly! Of course I am.
CHRISTINE: Promise?
JEAN: Promise! Listen if I say I'm going to do a thing, I do it. . . ."

Jean consistently is smug and condescending toward Christine, which once again demonstrates his desire to be superior—in this case, over the opposite sex as well as over one in his own class.

In this brief scene between Jean and Christine, which may be dissected into three smaller units due to changes in subject, the actor is provided with rich suggestions for character, and with the beginning of a pattern of behavior which, when related to similar analysis of later scenes, should emerge into a clear and complete whole. In terms of the objective, we have determined that in these early units, the subtextual desire that underlies Jean's actions is to impress Christine (and reassure himself) with his superiority. Whether he deserves to be considered superior, or whether this will prove to be his major objective in the play, depends upon the synthesis of Jean's objectives in his remaining scenes.

EXERCISES

---

1. Read the first unit between Jean and Christine several times, and each time emphasize one of the objectives listed below:
    a. The characters are neutral, as though there is no more to the scene than an ordinary conversation.
    b. Jean wants to impress Christine, but she is indifferent to him and his news.
    c. Jean wants Christine to believe he is amused by what happened. Christine is terribly eager to hear everything.
    d. Jean is really thinking of how uncomfortable the offstage action has made him.   Christine is suspicious of his attitude.
    e. Jean wants to make Christine jealous.   She is jealous, but wants to conceal it from Jean.
2. Go over other units in the play and find the subtext for Jean and Miss Julie.

CHAPTER 6

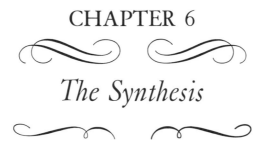

The Synthesis

The actor, in probing the play, hopes to find his clues and evidence merging into a clear pattern that will give meaning and unity to his characterization. Often, however, it is not easy for him to synthesize his evidence, for what good is his collection of clues if he does not know how to relate them? He is aided, of course, by his recognition of deliberate repetitions or contrasts, but his task can become much easier when he is made aware of certain basic questions that apply to all characterization in dramatic art.

It has been emphasized previously that drama consists of characters in action—of characters *doing*. Onstage as well as off, characters do or act because they desire, they need, they want, they crave, they covet. Even when they desire *not* to desire, need, want, crave, or covet, something must be *done,* or action must be taken, in order to avoid an *un*desired end. Action may include an inability to act, if that inability leads to conflict or struggle. But the fact that individuals want or act is not in itself dramatic. We are not particularly interested in watching a play whose protagonist gets everything he wants without some kind of resistance. In the dramatic sense, such an individual is without character. We learn something of what he is by what he wants, but he becomes more interesting and more understandable when we learn *how* he tries to achieve his ends, and he becomes even more interesting and *dramatic* when we learn how he reacts to obstacles that stand in the way of his success.

Let us assume that Jean's major objective in *Miss Julie* is "to rise above my position." Such an objective already suggests conflict, because a change in the *status quo* is desired. But Strindberg's Jean is not Jean simply because he wants to rise. He is distinctly Strindberg's Jean because he wants to rise *safely,* because he lacks the courage and will to overcome the obstacles of the class system and the possible loss of security, and because he lacks confidence in the reality of his pretended superiority. The methods of coping with the obstacles that reveal Jean as a dramatic character include petty compensations through illusion, attempts to appear superior to others, stealing the Count's wine, exploiting the weaknesses of Julie, and withdrawing from possible opportunity because of cowardice and lack of will. Such knowledge may make us want to expand Jean's objective so that it becomes "to rise above my position without loss of safety."

On the basis of this interpretation of dramatic character, certain relevant questions need to be asked:

1. What are the goals or aspirations of the character?
2. What are the obstacles to the successful achievement of these goals?
3. How does the character react to these obstacles?

Depending upon the play, additional questions related to these also may be important. How much are we obliged to know about the motives behind the goals of the character? Precisely what events in the previous life of the character have been emphasized? In *The Would-Be Invalid,* it is quite apparent that Molière is not overly concerned with Argan's origins, his early life, how he made his money, or whether he got along with his first wife. There is practically no reference to events prior to the play's opening, and there is no particular point in trying to justify the actions of the characters in terms of what may or may not have influenced their behavior outside of the play's actual time. *Miss Julie* is another matter. While the action of the play is concerned with the Midsummer Eve crisis that culminates in the suicide of Miss Julie, this action also embodies explorations into the motives and influences on the behavior and fate of its major characters. So questions concerning the lives of characters outside of the temporal framework of a play should sometimes be asked, provided the answers are relevant to the play's meaning and purpose.

Finally, the actor must observe whether or not, in the course of the play, his character has undergone changes concerning his objectives, his manner of coping with obstacles, and his relationship with other characters, with a full recognition of the causes for such changes. Here, then, are the questions (in their appropriate order) that may help the actor bring into focus the details of his analysis:

108

1. What are the drives, goals, or aspirations of the character? What is his major objective?
2. What events or conditions prior to the play's beginning are important for the comprehension of the character's motives and objectives?
3. What are the obstacles to his goals?
4. How does he cope with these obstacles? Is he consistent in his reaction to them?
5. Does the character change in the course of the play? What are the causes for change?

The balance of this chapter will be concerned with examples of how the actor might deal with these questions in preparing the roles of Argan and Miss Julie. These two examples should make apparent the variations in complexity to be found in characterization, and should illustrate the varying importance each of the questions is likely to have from play to play.

DRIVES, GOALS, OR ASPIRATIONS[6]

Argan

Argan's stubborn desire to have a doctor for his son-in-law provides Molière's comedy with its major complication—in fact, with its principal story line. Whether or not Argan will succeed in destroying his daughter's happiness is the question that gives the play some direction and suspense. Molière, however, is not overly concerned with emphasizing this story. Instead, he uses it as a framework to demonstrate comically how Argan's excesses affect himself and others, so that Argan's desire to have a doctor for a son-in-law is but one manifestation of the protagonist's objective. Wanting a doctor in the family is one of the ways in which Argan may indulge his hypochondria:

> My reason is that, sick and infirm as I am, I want to have a son-in-law and other alliances in the medical world, so that I can be assured of proper aid against illness, and so that I can have access to the necessary remedies in my own family and get full profit from consultations and prescriptions.[7]

A few lines later, he states:

> It's for me I'm giving her a doctor. A proper daughter ought to be happy to marry someone who is useful to her father's health.

Of course Argan is not sick, nor does he wish really to be sick. He wishes to feign illness, as Stanislavski, in *An Actor Prepares,* pointed out when he decided upon "I wish to be thought sick" as his main objective when he played Argan. While it is true that much of what Argan does is based upon convincing himself and others that he is an invalid, there is evidence that Argan's chief drive goes beyond (and, indeed, provides the motive for) feigned illness.

Each unit in which Argan appears reveals him as a selfish and self-indulgent man who cannot tolerate being contradicted or not having his own way. His opening monologue reveals that he enjoys being a supposed invalid dependent upon doctors for as many varied treatments as possible. Although he is not foolish enough to pay their full fees, he is foolish to pay any fees at all. When he realizes he is unattended he becomes first angry, then frantic, then self-pitying. We know that he does not *need* to be attended, but that he *wants* to be attended. The first scene with Toinette develops his characteristic of wanting to be treated as an invalid, and his hatred of being contradicted. His first scene with Angélique, and the revelation of his desire to have her marry a doctor, emphasizes less his desire to be thought sick than his desire to indulge his fancied illness. His tyranny and selfishness are made apparent when he persists in satisfying his own questionable desires even when they could result in destroying the happiness of his daughter.

It is true that his first scene with Béline further stresses his desire to be thought sick, but it clearly emphasizes too why he wants his wife to think him ill, and why Béline pleases him. He wants to be babied, to be pitied, to be petted, to be indulged. Notice how pleasant he is to Toinette and Angélique at the beginning of the second act, when they pretend to accede to his every wish, and especially when Toinette exaggerates his illness to Cleanate. Subsequent scenes concentrate upon Argan's susceptibilities to the medical profession, which has provided him with the means of indulging himself, and the working out of the problem of the lovers. At the end of the play, Argan's major objective appears to be summarized for us. As the naïve Argan prepares to become a doctor himself, Angélique chastises Béralde, who thought of the idea, when she says, "But uncle, it seems to me that you're treating my father rather too lightly," to which the *raissonneur* Béralde replies, "Well, my dear niece, we aren't so much treating him lightly as *accommodating ourselves to his fancies. . . .*" [emphasis mine]

We see now that the objective which fuses the desires of Argan, and which motivates his actions, is his wish to be indulged, to have things his way, to be the center of attention, to be pampered. Goals motivated by this chief objective include wanting to be thought sick, desiring the attendance and reassurance of so-called medical men, and acquiring a doctor in the family.

Miss Julie

More difficult than the understanding of Argan's goals, which are relatively simple and consistent, is a clear-cut conclusion concerning Miss Julie's goals, which are complex because they appear to be inconsistent—even contradictory. Miss Julie's desires appear on two levels, the conscious and the subconscious, and within each level contradictory desires appear. Strindberg tells us in his preface that he wants to portray characters true to life in the sense that there is nothing absolute about them, that they are in a constant state of flux. But we must not conclude that Strindberg's purpose in this play is merely to prove that this is so. He shows us characters who vacillate between conflicting desires, and who alter and change as circumstance and necessity force them, but these are not random, unrelated fluctuations. Careful analysis of each unit and the desires of the principal characters therein make it quite clear that all objectives are fused by the principle of dominance and submission. We have observed, in our previous analysis of the first few units in the play preceding Julie's appearance, that the issues of social and sexual superiority have been suggested in Jean's character. In those scenes, the same issues were referred to with respect to Miss Julie. Her desire to dominate in the male-female relationship had been revealed in Jean's description of Julie's efforts to "train" her fiancé. In terms of social superiority, we were offered the first suggestion of Julie's conflicting desires when Christine described the concoction her mistress had ordered her to cook—a recipe to prevent any further development of the contamination of her pure-bred dog by the gatekeeper's pugdog. It would appear from this that Julie abhors such a mixture, but we have been told before, are about to be told again, and will shortly witness, Julie's temptation to "contaminate" herself. "She's too stuck-up in some ways and not proud enough in others," says Jean.

In the ensuing scenes between Jean and Julie that precede the seduction, Julie shifts constantly in her social and sexual attitudes toward Jean. She orders him about and takes advantage of her social superiority, but her commands betray sexual desire and the temptation to lower her social position by mixing with the servants. She sensually teases Jean, then indignantly repulses his advances. She is drawn to him and to the class that he represents, but at the same time, she wishes to maintain her honor and her superiority. A desire to fall is symbolized by, among other things, her preference for beer, and by the desire revealed in her dream where "I have to get down but I don't have the courage to jump"—where she feels that "I won't have any peace until I get down; no rest until I get down, down on the ground. And if I ever got down on the ground, I'd want to go further down, right down into the earth . . ." She is discontented where she is, but if she falls, she will be lost. Notice how the social and sexual issues of dominance overlap. In her relations with Jean, Julie is torn between her mother's class and her father's, between giving in to her "weakness" (normal sexual impulses, which may result in submission), or by controlling herself, retaining a kind of masculine superiority.

As we learn in the course of the play, Julie is torn by confusion concerning her identity. What is her role? To be mistress or servant? Male or female? Her desires concerning the former are made ambivalent by parentage; the latter is made ambivalent by upbringing. Before the seduction, Julie's conscious actions favor control and a retention of status, while her subconscious desires and instincts urge her to fall. After the seduction, her conscious actions reflect a struggle to recapture some form of dominance and strength, but Jean's weakness and a maze of circumstances block her every effort, draining her will to live, whereupon she begs Jean to command her subconscious to complete its descent into death. Even as she faces the prospect of death, she is confronted by the same torments, when she repeats Christine's mouthing of the phrase "the first shall be last," and wonders where she belongs in the class system she may be about to enter.

In the first part of the play, Julie's major objective might be said to be "to mingle with the servants without loss of honor," while in that part of the play following the seduction, her objective might be "to find a way to regain some kind of honor." (We must understand that honor does not mean virtue merely, but the kind of honor associated with social status.) These objectives surely have some validity, but as was the case with Argan's "I wish to be thought sick," they are not sufficiently encompassing. How may these two objectives be joined to make a statement that may also suggest the contradictory forces which operate within Julie? Might not these opposing forces, the compulsion to retain status and the compulsion to fall, reflect the need of a confused Julie "to find her level?" The fact is that, as Strindberg has created her, Julie does not know what she wants. "Am I really myself?" she asks at one point in the play. But she is not passive. Her needs are invariably linked with the various manifestations of dominance and submission, high and low, being masculine or feminine. Out of her confusion, there emerge the actions of a character who is struggling to find out who she is and where she belongs. Just as it has been suggested that Jean's objective might be, "I wish to rise above my station with safety," Julie's might be, "I wish to risk descent with safety—i.e., without loss of honor."

EXERCISES

1. Go through each beat in which the following characters appear and find their objectives in each one:
   From *The Would-Be Invalid*
   Toinette
   Béline
   Cléante
   From *Miss Julie*
   Christine
2. Synthesize these objectives into a major objective for each of the above characters.
3. Create an improvisation for any one of these characters in which they strive for their objectives in newly created situations.

EVENTS OR CONDITIONS PRIOR TO THE PLAY'S BEGINNING

Argan

As has been previously stated, Molière provides the actor with no information that explains past events or experiences relevant to Argan's present actions. We know that Béline is his second wife, but we are told nothing about the circumstances of his first marriage. The second marriage has been created not to throw additional light on Argan's motivation, but to

reveal how his vulnerabilities cause him to neglect his domestic responsi-
bilties. Molière is more interested in ridiculing what Argan *is,* rather than
what caused him to become this way. It would be a mistake for the actor
to ask himself why people become hypochondriacs in order to better understand Argan. This would only lead him to seek ways in which these
causes might be expressed, resulting in a distortion of the playwright's purpose, or the cluttering up of scenes whose objectives would be confused by
arbitrary explanatory business. Such explanation, too, might create such a
degree of sympathy for a character as to prevent laughter.

Miss Julie

One of Strindberg's objectives in this play has been to create dramatic characters who do not appear to be figures of pasteboard. Strindberg, as indicated by his preface, is concerned with showing us that human beings can
never really be pinpointed with an adjective or an all-consuming moral
judgment.

> In the course of time the word *character* has acquired many mean-
> ings. Originally it probably meant the dominant and fundamental
> trait in the soul complex and was confused with temperament. Later
> the middle class used it to mean an automaton. An individual who
> once for all had found his own true nature or adapted himself to a
> certain role in life, who in fact had ceased to grow, was called a man
> of character, while the man who was constantly developing, who,
> like a skilled navigator on the currents of life, did not steer a straight
> course but tacked down wind, was called a man of no character—
> derogatorily, of course, since he was so difficult to keep track of, to
> pin down and pigeonhole. This middle-class conception of a fixed
> character was transferred to the stage, where the middle class has
> always ruled. A character there came to mean an actor who was al-
> ways one and the same, always drunk, always comic or always mel-
> ancholy, and who needed to be characterized only by some physical
> defect such as a club foot, a wooden leg, or a red nose, or by the
> repetition of some such phrase such as "That's capital," or "Barkis is
> willin'." . . . So I do not believe in simple stage characters. And
> the summary judgments that writers pass on people—he is stupid,
> this one is brutal, that one is jealous, this one is stingy, and so on—
> should not pass unchallenged by the naturalists who know how
> complicated the soul is and who realize that vice has a reverse side
> very much like virtue.

In order to succeed in preventing a one-sided view of human behavior, Strindberg plots his play so that the audience may observe the manner in which heredity, environment, chance, and social situations cause characters to act, react, shift, and change.

> . . . I have noticed that what interests people most nowadays is the psychological action. Our inveterately curious souls are no longer content to see a thing happen; we want to see how it happens. We want to see the strings, look at the machinery, examine the double-bottom drawer, put on the magic ring to find the hidden seam, look in the deck for the marked cards.

In *Miss Julie,* Strindberg practices his stated intent. We learn about the influences upon Miss Julie's current behavior in suggestions that are made throughout the play, but especially during her "confession" after the seduction, at which time Jean reaches as far back as Julie's first ancestor: "Do you know who the founder of your family line was? A miller who let his wife sleep with the king one night during the Danish War."

Early in the play, Julie's mixed origins are referred to by Jean when he compares her to her mother, who combined aristocratic pretences with the coarseness of her low birth: "Her sleeves were always dirty, but her buttons had the royal crown on them." We learn that Julie is the daughter of a Count and a commoner. The problem in her parents' relationship was not primarily due to their differences in class, although the mixture in Julie is significant, but in the consequences of her mother's attitude toward marriage and the battle between the sexes. (This attitude is not simply to be viewed as a particularized characteristic of Julie's mother. Strindberg's works invariably stress the inevitability of sexual warfare. Characteristic of his attitude is Jean's statement, "There's no shortage of love—even if it doesn't last very long.")

Julie's mother was a practitioner of the women's liberation movement of Strindberg's time, which like our own was concerned with the emancipation of women and their efforts to be regarded as equal, perhaps superior, to the male. Julie was raised by her mother like a boy, but also was taught to have contempt for men. Later, when her father assumed control of her upbringing, she was taught "to despise my own sex, to be half woman and half man!" She was witness to a sordid battle for superiority and dominance between her mother and her father; the father first accepting the mother despite her threat not to be a wife, then rebelling against her experiments in equalizing the sexes. Later the mother sought her revenge by burning the estate and financing its reconstruction with her own funds, but which were ostensibly provided by a lover. Her vengeance nearly drove the Count to suicide, but he once more made himself the master and found a way to punish his wife. Witnessing a marriage of hatred and cruelty, characterized by a never-ending struggle for mastery, and combined with the contradictory influences of both parents, has produced within Julie the same kind of struggle. With which parent is she to identify? She says,

> I felt sorry for my father, but I took my mother's side because I didn't know the whole story. She had taught me to distrust and hate all men—you've heard how she hated men—and I swore to her that I'd never be slave to any man.

Then later, when Jean asks her if she ever loved her father, she replies,

> Yes, enormously. But I must have hated him without knowing it. It was he who brought me up to despise my own sex, to be half woman and half man. Who's to blame for what's happened? My father, my mother, myself? Myself? I don't have a self—that's my own. I don't have a single thought I didn't get from my father, not an emotion I didn't get from my mother.

Whereas Argan's nature is clearly delineated by present action, our understanding of Miss Julie is based strongly upon the complexity of her past.

EXERCISE

Go through *Miss Julie* and list all references to events in the lives of Jean and Christine *previous* to the time of the play's beginning.

OBSTACLES TO ONE'S GOALS

Characters in plays, just as in real life, establish goals whose accomplishment will, it is presumed, bring satisfaction and happiness. In drama, as in life, the obstacles that stand between persons and their happiness may be divided into three categories. The obstacle may be another person or a group, or it may be a fault within themselves, or it may be an abstract force such as fate, social conventions, or accident, or it may be a combination of any of these. In Sophocles' *Oedipus the King,* the protagonist's doom already has been determined; King Lear's desire for a tranquil old age is prevented by his inability to properly understand the ramifications of filial love and duty; Brecht's protagonists are overwhelmed by a society that refuses to reward virtue, while Othello is victimized by both Iago and his own obsession with reputation.

Argan

In the comedy of character, the ludicrous character is usually his own worst enemy. His objective is usually based on a foible that brings him nothing but trouble or abuse. Argan's wish to be pampered makes him the foil for quacks and a deceiving wife, a dupe for the tricks of his maid, and almost succeeds in ruining the happiness of his daughter. His own faults then create obstacles to his own stability and peace of mind. But of primary consideration in terms of Argan's action are the obstacles to the various goals that he *thinks* will bring him his greatest happiness. He wishes to be thought sick, but he is perfectly healthy, and the sensible and honest people around him will not cater to his imaginary ills. He wants the services and reassurance of medical men, but they charge too much, and on one occasion, when neglecting an enema, he is threatened with dozens of diseases and the refusal of medication. He wishes to save money by marrying his daughter to a doctor, but the daughter refuses to cooperate and enlists the aid of Toinette to foil his plan.

Miss Julie

Because Strindberg was concerned with emphasizing the relativity of human behavior, the obstacles to Miss Julie's happiness include all of the categories previously itemized. She is trapped to begin with, because of the contradictions in her own desires. In wanting to find stability, she must choose between the two opposing forces that constitute her Self. The two forces cannot be reconciled, for the desire to dominate will be destroyed if she gives in to the desire to submit. Her urge to fall is countered by her urge to hold her position. If she satisfies her need to love, she gives up her need to loathe. Each force is antagonistic to the other, so ironically her desires themselves obstruct her stability.

Although Julie, because of the equal strength of these opposing forces, is destined never to be contented, there is no question that she cannot survive without her honor. While there may be some question concerning her desire to survive (for the temptation for self-destruction is strong within her), her instinct for survival is always in operation, as evidenced by her attempts at control before the seduction and by her efforts to find a way of regaining honor afterward. It is necessary, then, to consider the forces that block her survival.

1. OTHER PEOPLE. Jean, while not the sole agent of Julie's destruction, is the one human being whose actions contribute most forcefully to her fall. His sexual and social position, over which he has no control, put him into almost automatic opposition to his mistress, who has been raised with the belief that all men and servants must be her inferiors. Jean's ambition, his desire to prove his superiority, and his sexual attraction lead him to exploit Julie's weakness and the accident that brings her to his bedroom. The sexual act forces Julie into a position of submission, literally and figuratively, both in terms of her relations with the opposite sex and her social status. On the one hand, Jean has assisted Julie in achieving one of her objectives —to fall, and, on the other hand, has permanently weakened the possibility of her retaining superiority.

After the reversal, Jean thwarts Julie's attempt to regain honor through a decent life with Jean when he disillusions her by revealing the baser side of his character. His "love" for her was merely lust, and he has lost respect for her because of her submission. He is a thief, a liar, and a coward. It is this last characteristic that determines his final action with Miss Julie. His fear of the Count's reaction makes him place the razor in Julie's hand and provide her with the hypnotic order to take her own life.

Early in the play, Christine is an obstacle, though an unwitting one, to Julie's wooing of Jean. Julie is aware of their intimacy, and deliberately proceeds to "win" him from her. Later, Christine is responsible for finally closing the trap on her mistress when she announces that she will tell the stableman not to release the horses. Julie's objective in finding her identity is "aided" by the seduction, in the sense that now she may be identified with a lower class, but that class, now represented by Christine, refuses to accept her.

2. ABSTRACT FORCES, INCLUDING SOCIAL CONDITIONS, FATE, SEEMINGLY PRE-ORDAINED EVENTS, AND CHANCE. Although the previously mentioned obstacles to Miss Julie's desires include forces within the protagonist and the

obstructions created by other people, there is nothing relevant to Miss Julie's disposition throughout the play that is not the result of powers outside of her will or, for that matter, Jean's. To begin with, the characters are victims of a decaying class system that they did not create. Julie's uselessness is the condition of a class that has lost its justification and function. She is depicted as having nothing better to do than to visit relatives or flirt with the servants. She is a victim of the movement for the emancipation of women, which has influenced the marriage of her parents and produced in her the struggle between the natural woman and the then-unnatural masculine traits of the emancipated female. Miss Julie embodies Strindberg's comment in his preface that, with the new freedom she demands, the modern woman has lost her identity:

> . . . they breed and spread, producing creatures of indeterminate sex to whom life is a torture, but who fortunately are defeated eventually either by hostile reality, or by the uncontrolled breaking loose of their repressed instincts, or else by their disappointment in not being able to compete with the male sex. It is a tragic type, offering us the spectacle of a desperate fight against nature. . . .

In modern drama, the older spiritual concepts of fate based upon divine justice or predestination have been replaced by the more scientific view of *determinism*, in which the lot of a human life is determined by the genes that he has inherited and by his environmental conditioning. Strindberg, however, colors scientific inevitability with the old mystic sense of fate when he utilizes such devices as the dream of falling, the irrepressible presence of the Count symbolized by the bell on the wall and his boots on the floor, and the spirit of Julie's mother: " . . . and now my mother is getting her revenge again through me."

The influence of accident upon destiny is stressed too often to be enumerated fully here. Let it suffice to refer to the two accidents that make it possible for Jean and Julie to be locked alone in his room. First, recall that they are on their way out to return to the dance when Jean gets a cinder in his eye. Julie's attempt to get it out brings them into close physical contact, but any further intimacy is resisted despite Julie's flirting and Jean's initial effort to be intimate. The cinder incident creates a delay in leaving the kitchen and an intensification of physical desire. Then, as they are about to leave the second time, the unfortunate timing of the arrival of the revelers occurs, forcing the two to seek refuge in Jean's room. The play's major reversal has thereby been brought about as the result of two seemingly trivial accidents.

Miss Julie's obstacles then include the irreconcilable forces battling within her. These forces, in turn, are the result of heredity, environment, and social pressures, so we may say that she is struggling with them all. Finally, the actions and desires of Jean and Christine combined with a series of chance occurrences sweep into the overwhelming tide to submerge Miss Julie.

EXERCISE

Itemize the obstacles to the following characters:
  From *The Would-Be Invalid*
    Toinette
    Béline
    Cléante
  From *Miss Julie*
    Jean
    Christine

COPING WITH OBSTACLES

Human beings employ a variety of ways in trying to achieve their ends. Some behave intuitively, some with careful deliberation, some with force and violence, some apathetically, some with humor and grace, while others simply shrink from goals that appear to be too difficult to overcome. On the stage, terming a character strong or weak, rational or emotional, aware or confused, is a result of the kind of consistency with which characters struggle toward their objectives. Iago is shrewd and calculating, and reacts to difficulties with his wits, while Othello is inclined to blind passion, which obscures his judgment. Blanche du Bois, in *A Streetcar Named Desire,* bewildered and confused by a cruel, indifferent, and materialistic society, finds herself incapable of any kind of frontal attack upon it. Instead, she seeks to "find protection" (the "spine" that director Elia Kazan has applied to Blanche) by escaping into the fantasy of the genteel world for which she longs.

Argan

We have seen that Argan, in his efforts to be pampered, tries to convince everyone that he is a helpless invalid. His obstacles consist primarily of those who, knowing that he is perfectly healthy, refuse to indulge his self-centered demands. He is opposed, too, by those whose fates depend upon his selfish judgments. What are Argan's methods of coping with these obstacles? Let us trace some of his reactions to them as they occur chronologically in the play.

At the conclusion of his opening monologue, Argan becomes aware that he is unattended. Feeling slighted, he weakly rings his bell. When he gets no response, he becomes more energetically irate than his imagined condition warrants. Finally, Toinette appears, and Argan exaggerates his weakness in order to get her sympathy and attention. When she persists in ignoring his "illness" and "needs," his fury returns and he shouts angrily at her. Thus, early in the play, Molière has introduced and repeated Argan's tendency to react to frustration with ineffectual outbursts of temper.

In his next scene, Argan informs his daughter that he expects her to marry a doctor rather than the man of her choice. When Angélique and Toinette attempt to reason with him, he tyrannically insists on having his way and once again shouts and rages, resorting to physical violence in his attack on the servant. Subsequent scenes repeat with consistency Argan's hot-tempered despotism in coping with frustration. Such reactions directly contradict the condition that he wants others to believe exists, and make of Argan a foolishly naïve and unsubtle character.

Because reason is on the side of those who oppose him, Argan's stubborn refusals to accept the truth make him act unreasonably. Probably the most concentrated example of his irrational obstinacy occurs when his brother, Béralde, attempts to persuade Argan to adopt a more moderate attitude concerning both his daughter's future and his reliance upon doctors. What do we learn about Argan from the following excerpt from this scene?

ARGAN: So doctors don't know anything according to you?

BÉRALDE: Oh yes they do. Most of them have had a very good education, they know how to talk very good Latin, and how to name all the diseases in Greek, and define them and classify them; but as for curing them, that's what they don't know at all.

ARGAN: But you must still admit that on this subject the doctors know more than other people.

This is the only point during which Argan allows himself to argue about his views in a calm and orderly manner, but the same resistance, the same lack of logic exists. The only change is that instead of allowing his temper to get the best of him, he expresses his foolhardy attitudes with smug superiority.

When Argan's desire to be pampered is combined with his naïveté, his tyrannical obstinance, and his temper tantrums, he presents a total picture not unlike that of a spoiled child, incongruously embodied in a well-to-do, middle-aged male. This is epitomized, of course, in his first scene with Béline, who satisfies him with such terms as "my little pet," "baby," "dearest," "my little boy," "lambie," and "poor dear."

Miss Julie

In his preface, Strindberg states,

> Since the persons in my play are modern characters, living in a transitional era more hurried and hysterical than the previous one at least, I have depicted them as more unstable, as torn and divided, a mixture of the old and the new.

We have observed previously, in the duality of Miss Julie's character, examples of the instability of which Strindberg has spoken. It is only natural that the result of contradictory objectives in a single personality will lead to confusion, inconsistency, and vacillation when that personality is confronted by obstacles caused by these same contradictory objectives.

In the first part of the play, Miss Julie has the urge to submit, at least partially, to her subconscious desire to fall. She has refused to accompany her father to visit relatives. Instead, she has chosen to stay and mingle with the servants, participating in their festivities and flirting with the males. In choosing to do this, Julie is coping with an obstacle—her contradictory desire to retain status. How does she justify her submission to actions that are tantamount to contamination?

In answering this question, the first thing of which we must be aware is that often in the play, Julie is motivated on a subconscious level. She is not consciously or deliberately telling herself that she wants to fall. On the purely conscious level, she does not want any such thing. Instead, she impulsively obeys the forces that urge her to descend. Does she not, in the early part of the play, behave like a creature of impulse, flitting from one lackey to the next, at one moment flirting with Jean and at the next repulsing him, making sudden decisions to pick violets or to go boating on the lake to see the sunrise?

Of course there is occasional evidence that Julie is not completely unaware of what she is doing, and at these moments, she resorts to certain explanations that ironically rationalize her motives as assertions of superiority. When Jean tries to warn her about the interpretation that is likely to be made of her preference for certain domestics with whom to dance, she replies,

> Prefer! What an idea! I'm really surprised. I, the mistress of the house, am good enough to come to their dance, and when I feel like dancing, I want to dance with someone who knows how to lead. After all, I don't want to look ridiculous.

While she fraternizes with the servants, Julie frequently reminds them that she is still the mistress. She orders Jean about to remind him of this. She wants him to sit down with her, but she will order him to do so. She will drink with him, but he must kiss her foot. By ridiculing Christine, she reminds Jean that she is more desirable than the cook. She fondles Jean and teases him seductively, only to slap him when he becomes too forward. Julie's method of countering her urges to lower herself, then, is to remind herself and others that she is superior. This is the manner in which she gets her own way with Jean. She does not let him forget who the dominant person must be in their relationship.

Julie honestly believes at first that her position will keep her immune. She boldly risks her reputation and, as Jean puts it, "plays with fire," but she is able to rationalize the dangers with apparent confidence in her established rank:

JEAN: . . . Don't you know it's dangerous to play with fire?
MISS JULIE: Not for me. I'm insured!

Julie impulsively tempts destruction and tries to overcome the dangers of her game with an air of *hauteur*, with a certainty that her superiority is insulated, and she is confident that she possesses the will to put a stop to the game whenever she believes it has progressed too far. But she has not counted on other factors, including Jean's ability to provoke her pity as well as her sexual desires, the excitement and intoxication of the night and its festivities, and the accident that ultimately unites them. These are obstacles to which Julie is forced to submit.

In the second part of the play, Julie's objective is to try to adjust to her altered role without loss of dignity. Let us follow the obstacles that she encounters, one by one, and observe the manner in which she copes with them.

From the moment Jean and Julie reenter the room, Strindberg makes it apparent that their roles have been reversed. Jean enters "with bravado," while Julie places her future in his hands. But in doing so, she assumes that he loves her and will protect her. Part of this assumption is based upon her own need to justify an action that otherwise would be considered dishonorable. "Tell me you love me, Jean, or else—or else what difference does it make what I am?" But Julie can get no compensation from this illusion, for it is immediately shattered by Jean's admission of his fear of his superiors, his cold and businesslike attitude toward her, and eventually the loss of even an outward display of respect. Julie's reaction to this disillusionment is one of desperation and helplessness marked by quick shifts from wishful thinking to attempts to reestablish her authority, to humble pleas to be saved. Being authoritative is consistent with what we know of her character thus far, but the humility is new, born of her fall. Throughout the rest of the play, which is concerned with Julie's efforts to find a way out, she shifts from one extreme to the other, sometimes in quick succession; at one point, for example, she spits out, "You lackey! You shoeshine boy! Stand up when I talk to you!" Then, after a cruel retort from Jean, she crumbles with, "That's right! Hit me! Walk all over me! It's all I deserve. I'm rotten. But help me! Help me to get out of this—if there is any way out for me!"

These shifts from anger and threats to remorse and humility are the efforts of a desperate woman struggling to survive—first, with some honorable justification, and then, when this proves to be impossible, to merely survive. The important thing that we must recognize in Julie's character is the value she now places on the reestablishment of her dignity (even though she may use undignified and humiliating means to achieve it), and the fact that until she is confronted with the hopelessness and finality of the situation, she does struggle. Another important characteristic that reemerges in her struggle appears in the means she uses to save herself. They consist, as in the example above, of the same contradictions of dominance and submission that we have observed in her from the beginning.

Although the struggle persists until the play's end, and Julie, in a variety of ways, continues to shift between pride and humiliation, beginning with the drinking of the wine (no longer beer!), she moves slowly and inevitably toward complete despair and surrender. Fatigue, the effects of the wine, the hopelessness of acceptance by either class, Jean's inability to act except to give her the final command, combine to drain Miss Julie of any desire except to find peace.

One final aspect of Miss Julie's character in terms of coping with obstacles must be considered. We have seen that Miss Julie's difficulties, from the first, stem from within herself. Ultimate happiness is impossible for her because she is driven by two irreconcilable desires. The satisfaction of one will inevitably cause the destruction of the other. In this sense, her will is paralyzed by the balance of forces within her. She may temporarily give in to one or the other, but her shifts in action are prompted, for the most part, by instinctive and emotional stimuli rather than by any reasoned acts of will. These stimuli, in turn, have been caused by factors outside of Miss Julie's control. She is the victim of a fate that has been determined by the accident of birth, of domestic warfare, of a class system, of her own biological needs, and of the unpredictable circumstances of day-to-day living. Midway between the seduction and the end of the play, when she says,

> Oh, I'm so tired, I can't bring myself to do anything. Can't repent, can't run away, can't stay, can't live . . . can't die. Help me, Jean. Command me, and I'll obey like a dog. Do me this last favor. Save my honor, save his name. You know what I ought to do but can't force myself to do. Let me use *your* will power. You command me and I'll obey.

and makes her hypnotic exit with the razor in her hand, Strindberg heightens and intensifies the inertia and lack of real will that in reality have always been characteristic of Miss Julie. At the end, her behavior bears a curious resemblance to that of a puppet; it is as if her actions are manipulated by unseen strings. But that manipulation, in a more subtle fashion, has been in operation all along. It is important for the actress playing Miss Julie to recognize the analogy to puppetry, but only in relation to her lack of will. In other respects, Strindberg has made her intensely human. Unlike a puppet, her suffering is real: "What difference does it make who's to blame? I'm still the one who has to bear the guilt, suffer the consequences."

EXERCISES

1. List step-by-step the response to obstacles as they occur to Toinette, Béline, and Cléante in *The Would-Be Invalid,* and to Jean and Christine in *Miss Julie.*
2. Summarize the qualities of each of these characters on the basis of their patterns of response to obstacles.
3. Have members of the class spontaneously create new obstacles for these characters. Each actor must respond spontaneously with his character's mode of response.

CHANGES IN CHARACTER DURING THE COURSE OF THE PLAY

In his *Poetics,* Aristotle distinguishes the complex plot from the simple plot by the presence in the former and absence in the latter of *peripateia* and *anagnorisis.* *Peripateia* refers to the change of fortune of the protagonist from good fortune to bad, or bad fortune to good, while *anagnorisis* means discovery, the most artistic use of which is self-discovery. These two elements of plot usually have a causal relationship. A discovery may lead to a reversal, and vice-versa. In Sophocles' *Oedipus the King,* Oedipus' discovery of his real origin results in his downfall, but this reversal, in turn, leads him to a spiritual self-discovery that far exceeds that of his material identity. The disintegration of King Lear's fortunes brings him to a recognition of his mortality. The actor must be fully aware of changes in character as well as of the consistencies of behavior that determine the chief objective. He must also ask whether his character, as a result of the conflict, is brought to any new awareness of himself or of the world around him.

Argan

It has been noted that Argan is unaffected by reason, argument, ridicule, and even common sense. He himself does not undergo *peripateia,* but he makes a major discovery when he learns that the wife whom he has trusted has had only selfish designs upon him, while the daughter he has mistreated is truly dutiful. In a more serious play, such a thing might lead to self-discovery, where the protagonist is made to realize that the cause for all

126

misunderstanding has resided within himself. Such is not the case with Argan. He will allow his daughter to marry Cléante only if Cléante will promise to become a doctor. He remains as susceptible as ever to the designs of others when they cater to his "fancies," as is the case when he is convinced that he himself should become a doctor. While the fate of those about him has changed, Argan persists in his naïve, gullible, and egocentric fashion.

Miss Julie

There is but one reversal in the action of *Miss Julie*. The seduction is the direct cause of Julie's fall from high position to low, from the possibility of dominance to inescapable submission. Whereas Julie is characterized before the act with smugness and self-confidence, superficiality, and irresponsibility, afterward she is forced into a real and desperate struggle for survival, during which time her assurance of her "divine rights" is shattered and she undergoes terrible humiliation. From the girl who is tempted to fall but believes that she is safely protected by her position, she becomes one of the fallen, vulnerable and unprotected, futilely scrambling to climb back up again. Her final change occurs in the slow ebbing away of her spirit.

Julie's first important discovery occurs when she sees Jean in his true light and becomes aware that he can never love her, nor can she ever respect him. The entire second part of the play is concerned, of course, with Julie's gradual realization of her disgrace and its consequences, chief of which is the loss of any possible identification with either class. "I don't believe in anything anymore! (*She sinks down upon the bench, puts her head between her hands and drops her head on the table.*) Not in anything! Not in anything!" Her self-awareness becomes an awareness of her lack of self.

EXERCISES

1. Determine whether or not the following characters make significant discoveries (about themselves or their communities), and/or undergo any significant reversals:
   Toinette, Béline, and Cléante in *The Would-Be Invalid*
   Jean and Christine in *Miss Julie*

2. Do these discoveries and reversals lead to a change in any of these characters? Explain.

We have studied the protagonists of two separate plays and found that each play makes different demands upon both the scope and degree of our responses to the questions that help us determine dramatic characterization. Because Argan required less "explanation" and proved to be less complex than Miss Julie, does not mean that the characterization of Argan is inferior to or less effective than that of Miss Julie. Each is a definite and specific character with the power to successfully affect the response of audiences. The nature of that response, however, varies with each playwright's intention, and it is that intention with which the actor must be concerned in order to perform his interpretative function. The character exists *in and for the play only,* and it is there that the actor will find all there is to know about him.

CHAPTER 7

The Technical Aspects

Every activity involving skillful performance employs techniques that have proven to contribute to the mastery of those skills. In sports, for example, the player is expected to learn the fundamentals of his position in order to execute effectively. Tennis requires appropriate grips for the forehand and backhand, and the player learns the best position for his body for all types of shots as well as for the service. The baseball batter learns how and where to grip the bat, and how to vary that grip for bunts and hits to the opposite field. He must know how close to stand to the plate, and how high and how far back to hold his bat.

In the arts, technique evolves from demands and limitations imposed by the medium of expression, particularly its materials and its relation to the viewer. The painter's materials consist of various kinds of paint, a flat surface of limited space and a variety of shapes, and the tools of application (brush, spray, spatula, etc.). He must therefore learn the technique of wielding the appropriate tools and of applying the paint to the flat surface, a process dictated by the material of the surface. The painter must be concerned with the clarity of his design in terms of the proximity and direction of the viewer.

Theatre art is a three-dimensional medium using live actors in variously defined spaces. Like painting, it is a strongly visual form of expression, but unless it is pure mime, it also is aural. The art of the actor is strongly dependent upon the effective use of his materials—the voice and the body—within a prescribed space, and the clarity with which he expresses himself to an audience. A theatre audience wants to see the actor's face

129

most of the time, and to hear and understand everything spoken by him. We have already discussed the importance of an actor's attention to the tools of his profession; our concern here is the techniques by which he may further facilitate visibility and audibility. Specialized techniques in any field involve specialized vocabularies that must be learned, especially in an art such as theatre where communication between several actors and a director is vital.

STAGE SPACE

The geographical terminology used for stage areas depends upon which stage-audience convention is employed. Most theatres today separate stage and audience by the use of a *proscenium* arch or frame. The audience faces the stage directly and all of its members ideally share the same view of the scenery and action.

The proscenium stage is divided into planes and areas, and is defined in terms of its relationship to the audience. The planes are imaginary lines parallel to the rows of seats in the auditorium. Those planes closest to the audience are called the *downstage* planes, and those farthest from the audience are called the *upstage* planes. These designations were coined for

FIGURE 7-1. *Proscenium stage.*

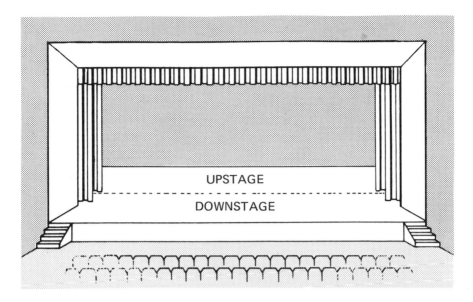

FIGURE 7-2. *Stage planes.*

the tradition of the raked stage, which sloped upward away from the audience. Today, *downstage* and *upstage* have nothing to do with height, and apply only to stage areas.

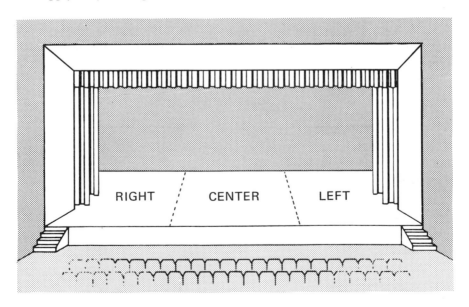

FIGURE 7-3. *General stage areas.*

131

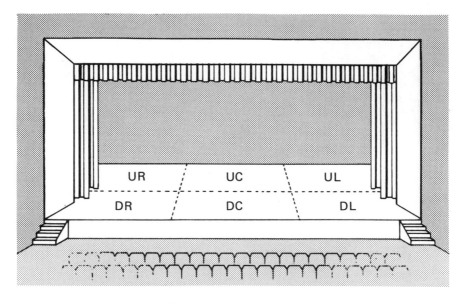

FIGURE 7-4. *More explicit stage areas.*

A second areal division is created by three equidistant lines perpendicular to the audience, creating three areas across the stage. These areas are given directional terms, stage *right, center,* and *left,* which are determined by their relationship to the actor as he faces his audience.

With the imaginary line that creates the downstage and upstage planes, the perpendicular planes create six stage areas: *down right, down center, down left, up right, up center,* and *up left.*

EXERCISES

Students should drill each other using stage area terminology until they are thoroughly familiar with it:

1. Stand *up right*
2. Move *downstage*
3. Move *up left*
4. Move to *center*
5. Move *down left*
6. Move *up center*
7. Move *down right*
8. Move *upstage*

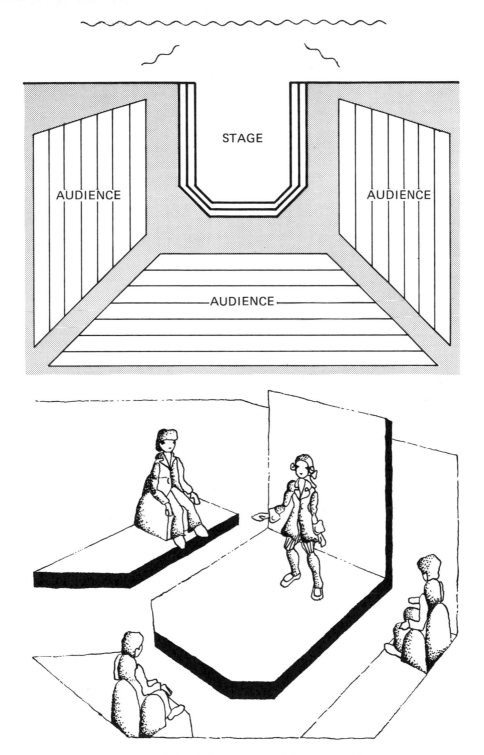

FIGURE 7-5. *Thrust stage: a) diagrammed;*
b) with people in place.

133

There are two additional types of stage that are prevalent in today's theatre. The *thrust* stage, which is modeled on the Elizabethan public theatre, consists of an acting area surrounded on three sides by the audience. The fourth side may contain scenery or may be draped. For practical purposes, stage areas may remain the same as for the proscenium stage, since there is a rear wall to orient the actor's sense of direction.

The *arena* stage, however, contains no architectural structure for *right,* *left, up,* or *down* designations. In this type of spatial arrangement, the audience surrounds the stage on four sides or in a circle. Under such conditions, the director usually devises a different terminology for stage areas. A certain circumference in the middle of the acting area might be called

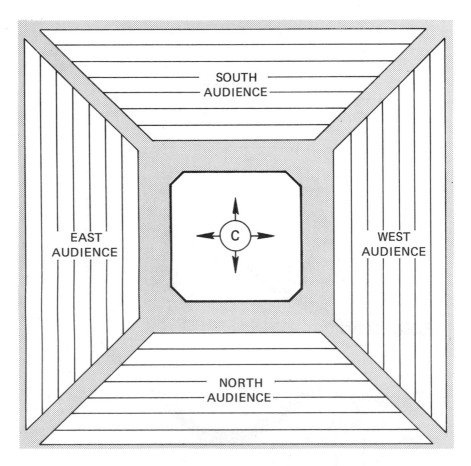

FIGURE 7-6. *Arena stage.*

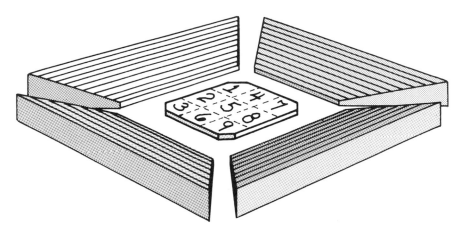

FIGURE 7-7. *Arena stage: numbered area designations.*

center stage and the four sides might be called *north, south, east,* and *west.* Another method would be to divide the stage into nine imaginary squares and number each square.

BODY POSITIONS

On the proscenium stage, the direction toward which the actor faces is ideally the same for all members of the audience. The terminology of body positions is based upon stage areas, the actor's physical relationship to the audience within each stage area, and the degree of the exposure of the front of his body to the audience. When he faces the audience directly (downstage), he is in a *full-front* position; when he faces upstage directly, he is in a *full-back* position. When he faces directly right stage, he is in a *right profile* position, and when he faces stage left, he is in a *left profile* position. Between *front* and *right profile* is *quarter right;* between *right profile* and *full-back* is *three-quarter right;* between *front* and *profile left* is *quarter left;* and between *profile left* and *full-back* is *three-quarter left.*

135

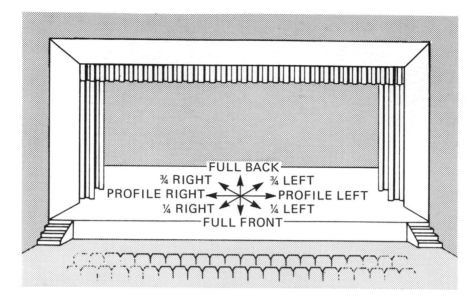

FIGURE 7-8. *Body positions.*

EXERCISES

1. Students should take turns in drilling each other in the eight body positions.
2. Take turns giving directions combining body position and stage area as illustrated by the following examples:
   a. Stand *up center* facing *full-front.*
   b. Move *down left* and assume a *one-quarter right* position.
   c. Move *up right* and assume a *three-quarter* position *right.*
   d. Move *downstage* and assume a *profile* position *left.*
   e. Move *up center* and assume a *full-back* position.

Included in the vocabulary of body positions are the more general but frequently used stage directions: *open, close, turn out, turn in.* When a director suggests that the actor *open up,* he means that he should reveal more of his face and the front of his body to the audience. For example, if the actor is standing in a *three-quarter* position and is asked to *open up,* he will adjust to the one-quarter position or possibly *full-front.* Conversely, a director may suggest that an actor assume a more *closed* position, in which

136

case the actor will adjust his body so that his front is less visible to the audience. To *turn out* is to turn away from *center* stage, while to *turn in* means to turn toward *center* stage.

While it is the director's task to be certain that what the audience must see is clearly visible and what they must not see is obscured, the actor who is truly aware should be sensitive to the process of revealing and concealing. It is a tendency of the beginning actor subconsciously to resist facing the audience, and to favor the *profile* or *three-quarter* position. The result is frustration and ultimately a loss of interest on the part of the viewer, who not only cannot see the actor's expressions but probably will lose some of his words, since they will be directed *upstage* or into the wings. Ninety percent of the time the actor should be in as *open* a position as possible when he is speaking; otherwise, he is *covering* himself. He also is covering himself when he is gesturing or performing a piece of pantomimic business, or handling a property in such a way that all members of the audience cannot see exactly what he is doing. If the actor must point, or extend his arm in a *profile* or *one-quarter* position, he should do it with his *upstage* arm; otherwise, he is covering his body or may appear awkward.

The actor also should be cautious about covering another actor when such a situation is not called for. For example, when he must move closer to another character in order to address him, he will cover both himself

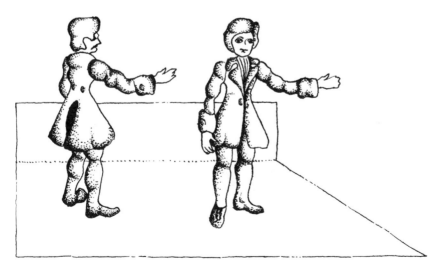

FIGURE 7-9. *Gesturing and visibility: at left, the wrong way; at right, the right way.*

and the other character if he stands *downstage* of him. *Sight lines* are the angles of vision from various parts of the audience. The actor should be aware when another actor is standing between himself and part of the audience, or when he himself is standing between another actor and part of the audience.

FIGURE 7-10. *Covering.*

FIGURE 7-11.   *Covering, at closer contact.*

If the actor is standing at a *downstage* corner of the stage and has an important speech or vital pantomimic business, he should *turn in* so that the entire audience may see and hear him clearly.

The actor can *cover* himself and others when he is seated. Generally speaking, chairs and sofas onstage are placed in either a *full-front* position or a *one-quarter* position so that the seated actor will be as *open* as possible. But when two characters are seated on a diagonally placed sofa, the *downstage* actor must sit well back and *open up,* while the upstage character should sit forward.

Finally, the actor should be familiar with *shared* position. Two actors must *share* the stage when they require equal emphasis. This means that they should be seen equally as well by all members of the audience. Nor-

FIGURE 7-12. *Position in downstage corner: top) the wrong way; bottom) the right way.*

mally the *shared* position suggests that each actor maintain a similar body position and be on the same plane.

EXERCISES

Create a series of drills for two actors such as the following:
1. Place a sofa *down left* in a diagonal position angled *upstage*. Place a chair *down right* on the same plane as the sofa and angle it in a *profile* position facing *in.*
2. Actor "A" sits in a chair *right* in a *closed* position, while actor "B" stands *up center* in a *one-quarter* position *right.*
3. "B" moves *down center* and faces *full-front.*
4. "A" rises and moves as close to "B" as possible without *covering* himself or "B."
5. "A" and "B" assume a *one-quarter shared* position.
6. Actor "B" *turns out.*
7. Actor "A" moves *left* behind sofa.
8. Actor "B" moves to sofa and sits *up right,* assuming a *one-quarter* position *left.*
9. Actor "A" moves to *down left* of sofa and sits on sofa.
10. Both actors adjust to a *shared* position on sofa.

Many of the principles and virtually all of the vocabulary of body positions are meaningless when the thrust or arena stages are used. On the thrust stage, with the audience on three sides and more than one actor on stage, the only way in which an actor will not be *covered* is when the other performer(s) are well upstage of him. And even then, the actor must stand well upstage himself if he is to be visible to all three sides of the audience. Standard body position designations are meaningless because a single position of the actor will have three different perspectives. For example, if the actor is in a *profile* position at the center of the thrust for those seated in the middle of the auditorium, he will be *full-front* to those on one side and *full-back* to those on the other. Essentially, the actor must attempt not to remain in one body position for too long a period of time for fear of alienating that portion of the audience from which he is covered. He must find justifications for more frequent adjustments of body positions and stage areas than in a proscenium production. (See pp. 211-212 for an example of solving sight line problems on a thrust stage.)

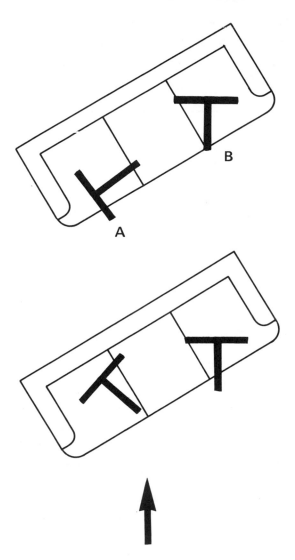

FIGURE 7-13.   *Covering in seated position: top) the wrong way;*
bottom) the right way;

The problems of body position are intensified in an arena production, where there is no *upstage* area to retreat to for a particularly emphatic scene.   Indeed, the only area where the actor in the round may achieve nearly total visibility is at the front of one of the aisles.   Here too the actor must find justifications for the use of as many areas and body positions as possible.

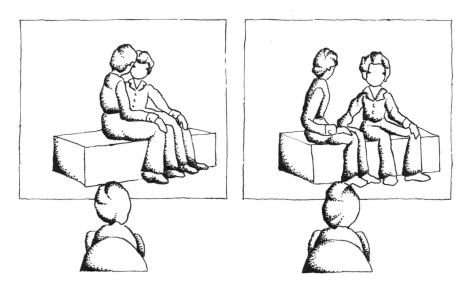

left) with actors, wrong way;   right) with actors in correct adjustment.

MOVEMENT

When an actor moves from one area to another onstage, it is called a *cross*. Since economy is one of the basic rules of acting, and a straight line is the shortest distance between two points, *crosses* normally should be straight. Often, however, the straight line cross can prove to be less efficient and even clumsy. For example, when an actor is *upstage* of another actor and must *cross* to him, he should use the straight line because he will end up in an *open* position. When an actor moves to another actor or object up-stage of him on a straight line, he will have to stop and make a turn to *open up*. When he reaches his objective, the whole procedure will look mechanical. The solution to this problem is to use a *curved cross* so that the moving actor will conclude his *cross* in the correct body position.
If the object is almost directly *upstage* of him, then he will have to make an *S-cross* rather than moving straight *upstage* and making an angular turn.

The actor should practice economy in the direction he chooses to turn when having to start a *cross* by selecting the *shortest* turn.
However, when a turn is the same length no matter in which direction it is made, it is advisable to take the turn that is most *open*.

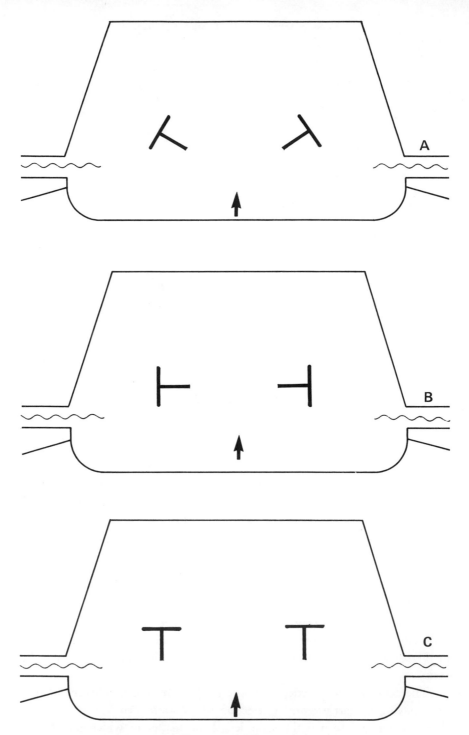

FIGURE 7-14. *Three examples of shared position.*

144

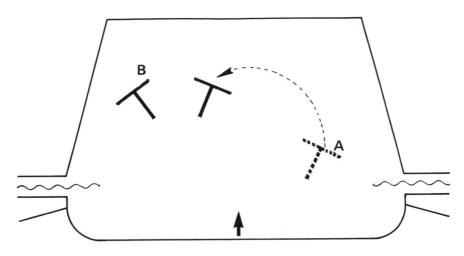

FIGURE 7-15. *Curved cross.*

For the purpose of the *open* principle, it is generally a good idea for the actor to begin a *cross* from *left* to *right* or *right* to *left* by leading with his *upstage* foot and to end his cross with his *upstage* foot forward. When an actor is standing very close to another actor or object and must *cross* in front or in back of him, he should first step back with the *downstage* foot, then leading with his *upstage* foot, make a *curved cross* past the other in order to avoid brushing up too close or bumping into him.

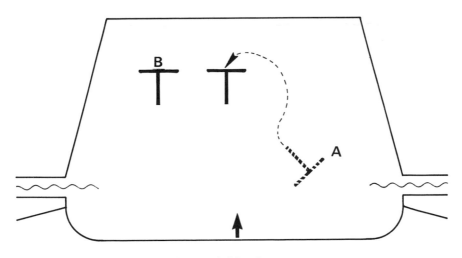

FIGURE 7-16. *S-cross.*

145

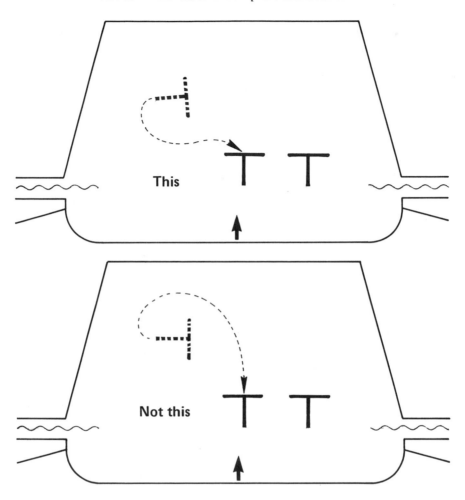

Figure 7-17. *Economy of turn: top*) *the right way;*
bottom) *the wrong way.*

When one must *cross* the stage while speaking, it is mandatory to move *in front of* the other actor; otherwise, the moment you pass in back of the other actor you are *covered*. There are plenty of exceptions to this rule, however. The emphasis may be directed toward the reaction of the listening actor, or you may be manipulating him, in which case you should work *upstage* of him. Since a moving character will in most cases achieve emphasis, it is wrong for an actor to move when another character is supposed to have the focus. This is not to say that actors cannot move while

146

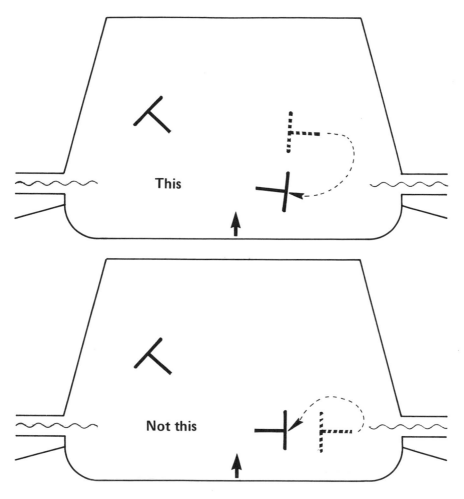

FIGURE 7-18. *Open turn: top) the right way;*
bottom) the wrong way.

somcone else is speaking or executing a bit of business; there are plenty of occasions when this is necessary. But if the movement *distracts* from the required center of interest, it must be avoided.

Sometimes an actor *must* adjust his stage position without distracting. He may be asked by the director to move in order to balance the stage, to get out of the way of an entrance, or to maneuver to a position in anticipation of a bit of business. Such maneuvers are called *cheating,* and must always be executed as unobtrusively as possible.

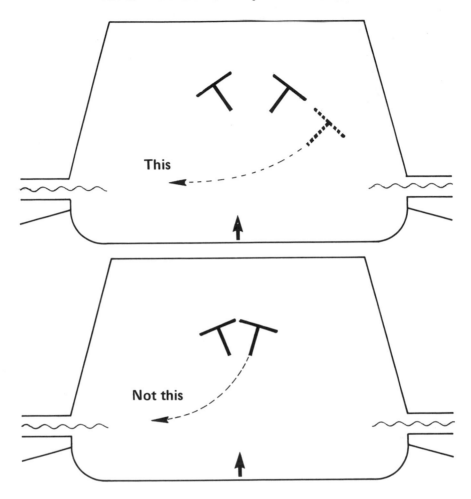

This

Not this

FIGURE 7-19.   *Front cross: top) the right way;*
bottom) the wrong way.

EXERCISES

Students should drill each other on *crosses* and turns.   Use the following stage directions, then make up your own.   Use the same ground plan as in the last exercise.

1.   Stand *down left* at the edge of the sofa, facing *right* stage.

2.   *Cross right* in front of the sofa to the chair *down right.*

3.   Circle the chair to the *right,* and end up facing it in a *one-quarter* position *left.*

4. *Cross up* left to a *shared* position with an imaginary person who is in a *profile right* position.
5. *Turn* and *cross* right.
6. *Cross* down center and assume a *full-front* position.
7. The imaginary person has moved upstage of you. *Turn* and cross to his *left* and end up in a *one-quarter* position *right*, slightly *upstage* of him.

An important aspect of the technique of stage movement is *timing*. You must decide whether to move before, during, or after a line. Your decision will be the result of emphasis. If you wish to stress the line, you will *cross* first, then speak; if you wish to stress the *cross,* you will speak first, then move. Walking and talking at the same time balances the weight of each action.

Normally, when the actor has a line during a *cross,* he should start his speech *as soon as* he takes the first step and time the *cross* so that he completes it at the same time he stops speaking. If the speech is a long one, the actor will, of course, continue to speak after reaching his objective. It is particularly important to stop the *cross* at the end of a line when a after the other character has started to speak, the moving actor will distract dialogue is taking place. If the actor who has *crossed* continues to move from the other.

EXERCISES

Perform the following four speeches from the last scene in *Miss Julie* according to the following stage directions:

1. Miss Julie stands *center* stage, *full-front,* "ecstatic." Jean stands *down right* facing her, *profile.*
2. On his line, "There's the broom. Go now, when the sun is up—out into the barn—and— (*He whispers in her ear*)," try the following stage directions and determine how the timing influences meaning and clarity:
    a. *Cross* first, then speak the entire line.
    b. Speak the entire line, then *cross* to Miss Julie.
    c. Start the line, then *cross* on "when the sun is up," and take two or three steps after completing the line.
3. On Miss Julie's lines, "That's true! I'm away the very last. I am the last!—Oh! Now I can't go! Tell me just once more, tell me to go!",

assume that Jean is about four feet away from Miss Julie in a *shared* position, *full-front*. Experiment with the following stage directions:

a.   *Cross* to Jean on "Tell me just once more, tell me to go!"

b.   *Cross* to Jean after "Oh! Now I can't go!", and do not begin the next line until you reach him.

c.   *Cross* to Jean after the last word of the speech.

d.   Have Jean begin his next line *while* Julie *crosses* to him.

4.   On Miss Julie's last line, "And the first shall be the last," experiment with the following:

a.   Start from a *one-quarter* position *right,* then move without speaking to the door *up left, turn full front,* then say the line.

b.   Using the same movement and body positions, say the entire line first, then *cross* to the door.

c.   Start the line after taking two steps to the door and complete it before reaching the door, but continue to the door and turn after completing the line.

A type of movement that exists sometimes for aesthetic purposes and sometimes for functional ones is the *counter cross,* or *dressing the stage.* This movement is made by an actor when another actor *crosses* in front of him. He is expected to take several steps in the opposite direction, and must time his *counter cross* so that it begins as the other actor passes in front of him, and end *before* the other actor's cross has been completed. Such timing assures that the *counter cross* does not distract from the major *cross.* For this reason, too, the *counter cross* must be made unobtrusively.

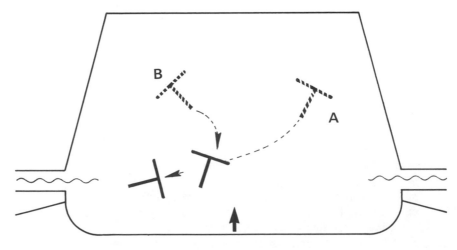

Figure 7-20. *The counter cross.*

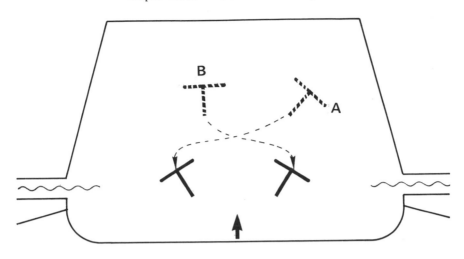

FIGURE 7-21. *Counter cross to share.*

Directors like the *counter cross* because it is pleasing as a balancing movement, but there are at least two situations that functionally demand the *counter cross.* First, if the major *cross* is to end up fairly close to the other actor, the *counter cross* will effect a more comfortable space between the actors and prevent the crossing actor from *covering* the other actor.

Second, if the moving actor must turn and address the other actor after he completes his *cross,* it may be advantageous for the other actor to *counter* into a *shared* position, so that the first actor will not have to address him *upstage.*

EXERCISES

Actors should drill each other with the following exercises, then apply their own variations:
1. Actor "A" is in a *shared* position at *center* stage with actor "B." "B" is to the *left* of "A."
2. "B" *crosses down right.* "A" *counter crosses* a few steps *left.*
3. "A" *crosses* to "B."
4. "B" *crosses* in front of "A" about four steps. "A" *counters right.*
5. "B" *crosses up center.*
6. "A" *crosses* up right.
7. "A" *crosses down left,* and "B" *counters* to a *share.*

The techniques that have been described are necessary for the craft of acting, but they must never be performed *mechanically*—that is, without the principles of *justification*. For example, when an actor makes a *counter cross,* he must not appear to be doing it because it is aesthetic or functional, but because the character *needs* to take those steps. The *counter cross* may be made to suggest some kind of reaction to the other actor, or a thoughtful quality while listening. In executing all technical demands, the actor must always remain *in character,* and move, turn, and *cheat* as the character would. The actor should know his technique so well that it becomes second nature to him. During a performance, he should never have to be thinking about the appropriateness of his stage positions, movement, sitting, turning, and timing. When the professional baseball player comes to the plate, he must not have to think about his arms, wrists, feet, and head position; he must be aware, instead, of where the fielders are playing him, whether he must bunt, "take," or hit away, and when the pitcher starts his motion, he must keep his eye on the ball. He must integrate his techniques, because the most important thing in the game is his reflexes, and they will not be sharp if he is concentrating upon technique. The same thing is true of the actor in performance.

Rules were meant to be broken, and the suggestions made here for technique are no exception. Acting is a very complicated art in which instinct and spontaneity both play important roles. Different actors do things differently and each may be fully justified. Plays and styles vary and sometimes create their own rules for stage action. If there is one unbreakable rule, it is that the actor must do what *will work* for himself and for the play. Experience has demonstrated that the techniques discussed are useful; familiarity with them should be mandatory, but ultimately their use or their rejection must be pragmatic.

PART II

NOTES

1. All quotes from the preface and the play are from the translation by E. M. Sprinchorn in the Chandler edition of *Miss Julie* (San Francisco: Chandler Publishing Co., 1961), pp. xv-xxiv.

2. Raymond Massey, "My Delineation of Lincoln." Taken from *Actors on Acting*, edited by Toby Cole and Helen Krich Chinoy. (New York: Crown Publishers, 1949), p. 534. © 1970 by Toby Cole and Helen Chinoy. Used by permission of Crown Publishers, Inc.

3. This is the structure of traditional drama and does not precisely apply, of course, to absurdist plays or other plays that reject coherence as a criterion for structure or character. It would be as wrong for the actor to force a traditional structure or interpretation upon such plays as it would be to make Shakespeare's *Richard III* sympathetic. In such seemingly incoherent forms, the actor still must attempt to find a pattern (the way in which the character has been developed or put together) in order to contribute to the playwright's purpose in creating the character.

4. Once again the reader is reminded of the exceptions in modern drama, when patterns of improbability and deliberate lack of continuity and logic are developed.

5. "Richard Cory" is reprinted by permission of Charles Scribner's Sons from *The Children of the Night* by Edwin Arlington Robinson.

6. A popular term for the unifying objective of the dramatic character is "spine."

7. Molière, *The Would-Be Invalid,* translated and edited by Morris Bishop, copyright © 1950 by AHM Publishing Corporation. Reprinted by permission of AHM Publishing Corporation, Arlington Heights, Ill. All quotations are from this edition.

SELECTED READINGS

Albright, H. D. *Working Up a Part*. Boston: Houghton Mifflin Co., 1959.

Ben Avram, Rachmael. *The Act and the Image*. New York: The Odyssey Press, 1969.

Benedetti, Robert L. *The Actor at Work*. Englewood Cliffs, N. J.: Prentice-Hall, Inc., 1970.

Blunt, Jerry. *The Composite Art of Acting*. New York: Macmillan, 1966.

Boleslavski, Richard. *Acting, the First Six Lessons*. New York: Theatre Arts Books, Inc., 1934.

Chekhov, Michael. *To the Actor*. New York: Harper & Bros., 1953.

Dolman, John. *The Art of Acting*. New York: Harper & Bros., 1949.

Glenn, Stanley. *A Director Prepares*. Encino, Calif.: Dickenson and Co., 1973.

McGaw, Charles. *Acting Is Believing*. 2d ed. New York: Holt, Rinehart and Winston, 1966.

Moore, Sonia. *The Stanislavski Method*. New York: The Viking Press, 1960.

Rockwood, Jerome. *The Craftsmen of Dionysus*. Glenview, Ill.: Scott, Foresman and Co., 1966.

Selden, Samuel. *First Steps in Acting*. 2d ed. New York: Appleton-Century-Crofts, 1964.

Stanislavski, Constantin. *An Actor Prepares*. New York: Theatre Arts Books, Inc., 1946.

——. *Building a Character*. New York: Theatre Arts Books, Inc., 1949.

——. *Creating a Role*. London: Geoffrey Bles, 1963.

THE ACTOR AND STYLE: THE GREEK THEATRE

PART III

Up to this point our emphasis has been on the universal concerns of acting: understanding a character and discovering the most truthful and correct actions with which to express it. It is certain, however, that acting techniques have varied from Greek times to the present, and that different skills are required to perform in a Greek or Elizabethan tragedy than in a naturalistic one such as *Miss Julie.* Actors who achieve success in plays by Ibsen, Chekhov, and Williams often find themselves at a loss with Sophocles and Shakespeare. Other actors, trained in the classics, have been known to feel insecure with realistic plays. In most instances, such actors are limited by their inability to respond to certain stylistic demands.

Essentially, style refers to the *manner* in which an action is expressed. We have learned that actors may differ from one another in depicting the same roles because of the combination of different physical and vocal qualities and the subjective aspects of interpretation. Such individualism in an actor defines his personal style. There is, however, a broader concept of style to which even the actor's personal style must be subordinate, which is dictated directly or indirectly by the conventions of the theatre for which a play has been written, and by certain conventions in the text of the play itself. These conventions include such factors as the theatrical environment, language, and clothing, each of which is expressive of a concept of reality and the sum of which is a presentation of that concept. Let us then consider style as employed in the classic Greek theatre.

CHAPTER 8

The Theatrical Environment

SIZE AND SPACE

We have learned that action (or expression) is influenced by imaginatively relating to various sources, and that one of the objects to which the actor relates is his environment. We have explored ways in which environment may stimulate action, but not how it may influence the mode of action. The following exercises are intended to allow you to discover how environment has the capacity to modify the expression of emotion.

EXERCISES

1. Find a justification to enter the stage in a rage, such as having just been fired from your job; receiving an unfair grade in a course; losing a role you coveted; discovering that your fiancé has been cheating on you, etc.

   Create an interior environment that is familiar to you, such as a living room in a house or apartment. Fill your space with the furniture and objects of everyday life.

   Now enter through a door and vent your fury by relating to the environment you have created. You are encouraged to use vocal expression.

2. Change the environment so that there are no doors and no objects, but simply an open, undefined space.

   As the same person, with the same justification, enter and vent your fury.

Analyze the differences in the two scenes that were caused by the environmental changes.

3. Repeat the same scene with the first environment, but enlarge your space. Make the size of the room twice the size of the original, and adjust all objects, including doors, windows, and furniture, correspondingly (they will have to be much farther apart). Perform the same action as before, but allow your body and voice to respond to the larger space. (If your laboratory space is small, play the second scene out-of-doors.)

    Analyze the differences created by the enlargement of space.

4. Repeat the scene of exercise 2, which employed an open, objectless environment, and adapt it to the larger space of exercise 3.

    Analyze the differences created by this environmental change.

5. Now work with the emotion of despair or utter futility. Find a justification, then an action to express this emotion in the normal room of exercise 1, with the audience as close to your setting as possible. Use vocal sound and minimal speech.

    Repeat the despair scene, but in the larger space and with your audience seated as far away as possible.

    What did you have to do to maintain physical and vocal clarity when you performed in the larger space and were further removed from the audience?

6. Narrate, in a small space with your audience close to you, a fairy tale or a highly descriptive tale.

    Narrate the same material out-of-doors, with your audience grouped at least forty feet away.

    What adjustments were necessary in terms of voice? Speech? Gesture? Facial expression?

QUALITY

Architectural style and decor are both products of certain life styles and in turn tend to impose certain life styles. Monarchs and industrial titans require palaces or mansions that symbolize their status, but which in turn require that the tenants behave like monarchs and titans. Elegant homes normally belong to elegant, well-bred people, while cramped abodes of squalor will provoke more casual, perhaps even slothful behavior. These are broad generalizations, of course, and in drama (and sometimes in life) are not applicable to situations in which behavior and environment are contradictory. Our concern is with what happens when a character's decorum is suited to his environment.

EXERCISES

1. Find some photographs of elegant dining rooms. Imagine your setting to be like one of them, with lace tablecloths, crystal and silver place settings, and candlelight. Your character is accustomed to this environment. Play a scene in which you dine and chat with others as you are being served wine by the servants.

2. Create a dining area of utmost squalor. Use your imagination to create conditions that are almost bestial in which to "enjoy" a meal. Imagine you are a natural product of such an environment as you share your meal with others.

Furniture, rich or poor, is shaped according to fashion and "informs" us how it is to be used. The furniture of different periods varies in shape, size, and comfort, and we must adapt ourselves to its qualities when we use it.

EXERCISES

1. Study chairs of different periods such as the Jacobean, Georgian, Victorian, and contemporary (try a "sling" chair). As with the exercises in Part I that dealt with your observation of objects, "become" two contrasting chairs. Assume a posture and stance that resemble them. Move about as you believe they might move if they were animated.

2. If there are available to you several chairs of widely divergent period styles, practice sitting on them suitably. For example, a stiff, relatively unpadded upright chair demands that one sit rather rigidly, while a deep, down-cushioned chair encourages one to lean back and relax. If you do not have adequate period pieces, use available chairs that serve different purposes; i.e., bentwood chairs as contrasted to upholstered furniture.

3. Study paintings of the periods mentioned in exercise 1 that portray people sitting in chairs. Imitate these portraits. Have someone check your posture, the position of your head, arms, and legs, and your position in the chair itself.

LANGUAGE AND SOUND

There are several aspects of language that influence the way in which we speak it. In turn, our mode of speech demands physical expression that is congruous to it. First, the *nature* of words and phrases themselves frequently requires a prescribed way of speaking and physicalizing (stance, movement, gesture, facial expression). One of the clearest examples is the difference created by formal versus informal language.

EXERCISES

Speak the following phrases with passion and honesty:
1. "Gee, I feel lousy," then "Woe is me!"
2. "Just get out of here and leave me alone!", then "Out, varlet, and never darken my door again!"
3. "Gosh, I feel . . . well, great!", then "O joy! O rapture!"

Analyze what happens to your voice and diction as you alternate between informal and formal speech. What physical changes occur?

As a rule, educated persons will speak more precisely than noneducated ones. The aristocrat will reveal his breeding in his easy choice of words and manner of speaking, while the uneducated peasant will use a simpler vocabulary and enunciate poorly. Life styles will be manifested in language and, consequently, in speech. An age of reason such as that of seventeenth and eighteenth century France emphasized precision, clarity, and wit in conversation and writing. Contemporary speech tends to stress a more casual, "unaffected" manner of delivery, and recent trends based upon a mistrust of language and intellect have resulted in minimalizing the importance of conversation and articulateness. Much of our speech intercourse consists almost solely of brief and simple colloquialisms such as "great!", "right on!", and "cool!". Low-keyed sounds and frequent mumbling appear to be favored, as though the only true communication consists of "vibes" rather than language.

In drama, style may be influenced by modes of speech that normally do not have the characteristics of common speech. Realistic plays attempt to create an illusion of everyday life. *Miss Julie* is written entirely in prose; its language is conversational and designed to sound the way people normally express themselves. But there are other plays in which the characters speak in rhymed couplets or in iambic pentameter. Such artificial conventions of language will demand a mode of utterance that is consistent with their poetic qualities.

EXERCISES

1. Read the following selections with honesty and conviction:
   a. Jack and Jill went up the hill
      To fetch a pail of water.
      Jack fell down and broke his crown
      And Jill came tumbling after.
   b. Jack and Jill climbed up a steep slope in order to get some water.
      Jack tripped and fell, breaking his head, and so did Jill.
   Note that the poem unlike its prose paraphrasing, has an insistent and regular meter, and its repetition of sounds (rhyme) creates an artificial pattern of expression.
2. Reread the poem, ignoring the metrical pattern and deemphasizing its rhyme patterns. Try to make it sound like a casual news item.
3. Reread the prose version and attempt to regularize its meter.

Trying to ignore the meter and rhyme will make a poem sound dishonest and unnatural, just as forcing poetic meter upon prose will distort it. The speaker must never ignore or try to conceal deliberate language conventions.

Language has the capacity to assume musical qualities. Regulated meter, as we have observed, is one of the musical qualities speech can effect, and in both music and speech, *patterns* of meter and tempo can create distinctive rhythms. The rhythm of a Bach fugue may easily be distinguished from that of a Mozart sonata. Resonance—the variations in the fullness and richness of sound, which distinguish a Berlioz symphony from a Haydn quartet or a jazz combo—is another quality of music that is utilized in speech utterance. Preaching and orating in prose will be more resonant than casual conversation, and the sonnets of Shakespeare will be more resonant than the ditties of Ogden Nash.

Life styles are mirrored in these abstract qualities of sound. A life of elegance and luxury produces different rhythms than the life of a riveter in an airplane factory in a bustling metropolis like New York. Different nationalities speak and move with different rhythms and tempos, as do youth and age.

Musical styles correspond to styles in the other arts that developed out of the same life styles. "Neoclassic," "romantic," and "impressionistic" are some of the names given to art and literature that share similar philosophies and characteristics. But because music is more abstract than the literary arts, it has the capacity to make us more aware of the qualities of pure sound and of how those qualities combine to produce modes of movement and speech.

EXERCISES

The following improvisations are intended to help the actor become more vitally aware of how rhythms, tempos, and resonances combine to produce feelings and sensations about style that may be channeled into stylistic action.

1. Lie on your back on the floor. Thoroughly relax, using some of the relaxation exercises described in Part I. Close your eyes. Free your mind. Check your tension spots and mentally ease them. A musical recording will be played. It will be an orchestral selection by Bach, Handel, Purcell, or another seventeenth century composer. Direct your entire attention to the music.

2. Allow the music to fill you. Absorb it—not just in your ears and mind, but in your entire body. *Sense* the music completely.

3. Filled with the music and concentrating solely upon it, rise to a standing position. *How* you get up must be stimulated solely by your experience of the music.

4. Walk around the room. Allow your manner, your tempo, and your rhythm to be determined by the music alone.

5. Now begin relating to objects in the room: chairs, tables, cups, mirrors, combs, jewelry, books, etc. All of this should be done in a manner inspired by the music.

6. Repeat the exercise to a portion of a symphony by Tchaikovsky or Beethoven.

7. Repeat the exercise to Ravel's *Introduction and Allegro* or Debussy's *La Mer*.

Discuss the manner in which each musical selection affected you. Find adjectives to describe the quality of each experience, and analyze the characteristics of the movement and relating processes that each selection provoked.

8. Develop the following pantomimic action in pairs: You are strolling down the street. Be natural—be yourself. Select a mood, justify it, and sustain it throughout the scene. You meet a friend. Greet him or her. Respond to each other's manner of greeting. Walk together a short distance, stop, and express farewells. Leave in opposite directions.

9. Perform the same series of actions, but allow your mood and manner to be influenced by one of the musical selections listed previously.

10. Repeat the actions *without* the music.

The performance of these exercises, if done with relaxation and freedom, allowing the musical styles to dominate you completely, should provide you with a "sense" of style. You will have experienced the relationship of patterns of sound to physical action, and will have prepared yourself for response to the "sounds" of a play.

CLOTHING

Clothes, it is correctly proclaimed, do not make the man, but it is also true that clothing and the manner in which it is worn may tell us a great deal about the man. Aside from its purely utilitarian functions of maintaining comfortable body temperatures and protecting vital parts of the body, clothing generally is designed to give the wearer a calculated appearance. Garments are selected on the basis of the kind of impression we wish to create about ourselves. Even when an individual is not fashion-conscious, he normally will conform to the current mode of dress, which is determined by a society's attitude toward the human body. A puritan society rejects all signs of sensuality, of "unnecessary" fleshly display, of vanity; the austerity of its moral code results in an austere code of dress. The ancient Greeks, on the other hand, took pride in the human body and, in their mild climate, took no shame in clothes which exposed most of it. During the period of the Restoration in England (1660-1700), the nobility was convinced that the distinction between man and beast was the capacity of the former to beautify itself by decorating the body with clothing that would be as elegant, rich, statuesque, and graceful as possible, even if it created discomfort or proved to be impractical for certain functions. The tendency of youth nowadays is to appear comfortable, casual, seemingly unconcerned and unaffected about dress, and to wear clothes that seem to be well-worn. Fashion, then, is not determined merely by a hunger for novelty (although often it may be), but by society's concepts of what a human being is supposed to be.

Such concepts are not restricted solely to how the garments look, but to what their qualities impose upon the human body—how they affect posture, movement, and the performance of daily activities. One of the major complaints of theatre costumers is that actors often do not understand that in certain periods clothes were not meant to be comfortable or to conform to our present generation's concept of beauty or practicality. Rather than complain about tight corsets or restrictive upper arm fittings, the actor must *exploit* such restrictions and discover the modes of physical behavior they encourage.

The effect of clothing upon us is both physical and psychological: physical in the sense that they provide the body with more or less freedom, and force us by their design to stand, sit, move, and gesture in certain ways; psychological in the sense that the quality of fabrics, the cut of the design, and the portions of the body that are emphasized cause us to *feel* a certain way. One may prefer, for example, to be unassuming and casual in his daily wear, but on certain occasions he may wish to dress up—to not only look more elegant, but to feel more elegant. Such feelings manifest themselves in the way we move—and even in the way we speak. Uniforms and the characteristic apparel of certain professions produce certain psychological effects. Nurses, theatre ushers, soldiers, hotel doormen, skin divers, surgeons, English lawyers and judges—all of these types must feel differently in uniform because of the roles they suggest, as contrasted to their nonoccupational garb. In a variety of ways, then, these costumes and the attitudes they provoke in the wearers will affect their external behavior.

EXERCISES

1. Walk, sit, climb stairs, read a newspaper, and drink tea in the following modes of dress. Adapt to the clothing, rather than struggling with it. Analyze what each combination makes you do:
    a. Casual and comfortable. Women in long trousers. Men without ties or tight collars. Bare feet or sandals.
    b. Wear corsets, high heels, tight collars, and cuffs that extend to the knuckles.
    c. MEN ONLY: wear a caftan, or a full, loose robe.
    d. WOMEN ONLY: wear men's clothing, including a hat, tie, oxford-type shoes, and sport jacket.

    e. From head to toe, put on the heaviest, coarsest materials you can find.

2. The following improvisation is for three persons representing both sexes: two women and one man or one woman and two men.

    a. You are a young married couple who enjoy a casual, informal life style. It is a relaxful Sunday and you are helping each other prepare the evening meal. You are joined by an equally casual friend. Choose clothing appropriate to the characters and the occasion, and pay attention to the details of the meal and the table setting.

    b. You are a young married couple preparing a dinner for a visiting dignitary. It is to be a formal occasion, but without servants. You must prepare and serve the food. The woman should wear an evening gown and jewelry; the man must be garbed in a tuxedo. The visitor is also dressed formally. Again, be attentive to the details of the meal and the table setting.

CONCEPTS OF REALITY

We have observed that architecture and clothing styles evolve not only from function, but from the way in which human beings interpret themselves. One aspect of such interpretation not dealt with thus far is the interpretation of reality. Since humans first began to contemplate the nature of existence, their values have been determined by their choice between a "subjective" or "objective" interpretation of the cosmos. "Subjective" implies a way of seeing that is determined by the irrational part of man's nature and deals with the immaterial world, including the supernatural, the spiritual, the emotional, and the world of dreams. "Objective" alludes broadly to a rational view of existence, which is based upon sensory perception, logic, and scientifically tested experience. In art, the subjective reality is termed "presentational," and the objective reality is referred to as "representational."

The first part of this book included some examples of different views of reality. In the section on observation, we noted the varying perceptions of the same piano by the housewife, the cabinet maker, the painter, and the musician. In the observation exercises (p. 20, #4), the first eight are objective and the ninth is subjective. Descriptions that make use of metaphor are subjective, as are the symbolic or associational values of objects such as the crown in *Richard II*.

In seeking to express deeper truths, artists often distort the reality of immediate sensory perception. Sculptors such as Praxiteles or Michelangelo stress the beauty, strength, and dignity of the human form by means of subtle distortion and exaggeration that idealize rather than merely reproduce it. Painters such as Hieronymus Bosch and George Grosz, on the other hand, distort nature and the human form in order to stress the grotesque, ugly, and perverse qualities they perceive in humanity.

In the theatre, the ancient Greeks and Shakespeare styled characters that often were larger than life, while naturalists such as Zola, Strindberg (whose work was not all naturalistic), and Chekhov depicted men speaking and behaving as they seem to do in ordinary life, and expressionists such as Kaiser, O'Neill (in *The Hairy Ape*), and Rice (in *The Adding Machine*) distorted life in order to present truths about the mechanization of man, his dream world, his alter ego, and social archetypes.

The actor, then, has the additional responsibility of expressing in characterization the kind of reality with which the playwright is concerned. He (the actor) not only must find appropriate actions but he also must be concerned with finding the proper mode of action.

EXERCISES

---

1. Improvise a short scene based upon some kind of simple daily activity such as eating breakfast, brushing your teeth, exercising your body, or walking the dog. Pantomime the action, but use vocal sounds when necessary.
   a. Perform the action in a representational manner. Everything done should conform and contribute to objective reality.
   b. Redo the same action in terms of two kinds of dreams:
      i) Hallucinatory, slow-motion dream
      ii) Nightmare
   c. Act out the same scene in an automated fashion. Have someone tap out a regular, mechanical rhythm for you to follow.
   d. Recreate the same action as a ritual celebration. Make a dance out of it, and employ ritualistic vocal sounds.
2. Try the same exercise again, but with an emphasis upon emotion. Create a specific situation and environment in which your chosen emotion may be justified. Make use of both body and voice.

Style in the theatre is the result of conventions with which each of the elements just discussed are manipulated. For example, *Miss Julie* is, for the most part, a realistic play because all of its theatrical conventions are geared toward creating the illusion of a recognizable masterial environment in which characters speak, dress, and behave as they would do in everyday life. The theatre for which it was conceived was an intimate one (see Strindberg's preface), so that the speech, gestures, and movements of the actors require little or no exaggeration or distortion. Scenic convention (environment) is particularized to show us a real kitchen in a nobleman's mansion in nineteenth century Sweden. The language is written in prose, and in dialogue that scrupulously avoids the artifices of soliloquies and asides. Clothing is characteristic of period, place, and character status, and there are no garments that attempt to generalize or abstract the human form. Characters are understood in terms of complex psychological configurations, stressing a modern scientific view of human behavior based upon heredity and environment.

Just as certain historical periods are characterized by distinctive environments, modes of speech and dress, and predominant philosophical beliefs, the theatres of these periods are characterized by consistent theatrical conventions that have been influenced by these ingredients. It would be unfeasible here to explore in detail all of the combinations of conventions that have emerged since the theatre was originated. Essentially, however, each theatrical period inevitably develops its conventions in terms of objective and/or subjective reality, and varies according to the degrees of representational or presentational perception that predominate.

Because the early part of this book made use of examples from a realistic play, *Miss Julie,* and the more realistic aspects of a somewhat more presentational play, *The Would-Be Invalid,* the emphasis at this point will be upon presentational conventions as exemplified by Greek classical tragedy and Shakespearean tragedy. A thorough examination of these styles, it is hoped, will familiarize the acting student with a methodology that he may apply to other theatrical styles.

CHAPTER 9

Fifth Century Greek Tragic Conventions

It is important, first, to state that many uncertainties exist regarding the conventions of the Greek physical theatre. Much of what is believed about those conventions is conjectural, and is derived from various sources including archeological remains, vase painting, minimal clues from Aristotle, allusions from the comedies of Aristophanes, the practical demands of the tragedies themselves, and the manner in which conclusions from each of these sources support one another. It is impossible to verify conclusions about a resulting acting style, except insofar as what seems to best support the style of the text. One of the benefits of this kind of examination, however, is the experience to be gained by the process of examination itself.

THE PHYSICAL THEATRE

The Greek theatre of the fifth century B.C. was an amphitheatre, located outdoors and formed by slicing into the side of a hill. The principal acting area was a circular space called the *orchestra*, which was approximately sixty feet in diameter. The audience sat on the slope of the hill above the orchestra and surrounded it on three sides (or two-thirds of its circumference). These area was called the *theatron*, and it is speculated that it accommodated at least 15,000 spectators, and in some theatres, up to 30,000.

At the edge of the *orchestra* opposite the center of the *theatron* was the *skene*, a structure with at least one entrance and a roof or *logeion*, which is

168

FIGURE 9-1. *View of the theatre at Epidaurus, Greece.*

believed to have provided an additional acting area. The *logeion* was used principally for the appearance of the gods, but no doubt also served as the watchtower for the sentinel at the opening of Aeschylus' *Agamemnon* and as the palace rooftop from which Medea flies off in her chariot at the conclusion of Euripides' *Medea.* The *skene* itself normally represented the abode of one of the principal characters. In *Medea*, it would have been the house in which Medea was forced to live.

The spaces between the sides of the *skene* and the audience were used as entrances for the chorus and for characters entering from locales other than the place represented by the *skene*. These entrances were termed *paradoi.*

The Impact of Size

Let us now consider the physical magnitude of this theatre and its demands upon the actor. First, it is a huge theatre. When the actor speaks from the front of the *skene*, he is approximately sixty feet from the first row of seats opposite him, and thirty feet from the first rows at each side. When he performs in the center of the *orchestra,* where it may be assumed most of his major scenes are enacted, he is approximately thirty feet from the entire front row. Add to this the consideration that he must also be heard and seen by audiences in the top row of the *theatron,* and the distance he must reach is doubled or tripled. It should be mentioned here that in the remains of Greek amphi-theatres, acoustics are perfect. In the last row of the theatre at Epidaurus, for example, a dropped coin or the crinkling of a piece of paper in the *orchestra* can be heard clearly. This does not mean, however, that a conversational level of projection will be acceptable. Such a level may be heard and understood, but its effect is incongruous to the vastness of the space. The sound of the voice must parallel the quality (in this case, the grandeur) of the space.

EXERCISES

From previous exercises (pp. 157-158) you have learned something about the demands of large spaces upon the voice and body. Now expand upon the previous exercise, using part or all of one of the Greek messenger speeches listed on page 200. Ideally the speech should be performed in an outdoor amphitheatre, but if the appropriate spot is unavailable, find an open space in which to perform that approximates the size of the acting area of the Greek theatre.

While working under such simulated conditions, you should discover the following:

1. Special demands upon voice and speech.
    a. You must use as much vocal strength at your command as possible without appearing to shout.
    b. Any of the messenger speeches will require speech variety. You must be able to project volumes ranging from strong to stronger. For example, in the messenger speech from *Medea,* the description of the Princess trying on the robe and crown should be light and delicate, but when the hideous effects of the gifts begin to manifest themselves, the messenger's volume should correspond to the mounting horror. There will be a similar build from the point at which the King appears to his tortured demise.
    c. There may be moments that require extreme softness, even a whispered or hushed quality, as might be the case in the following lines:

At last his life was quenched, and the unhappy man
Gave up the ghost, no longer could hold up his head.
There they lie close, the daughter and the old father,
Dead bodies, an event he prayed for in his tears.[1]

In such instances, the actor must speak very slowly, meticulously enunciating each word.

d. Vocal strength does not guarantee clarity. The larger the space, the slower the pace. In an intimate theatre, the actor can be understood if he slurs or runs words together (although there is an art to this also), but careless enunciation will not work in a space the size of a Greek theatre. The tendency of the young actor is to speak rapidly—too rapidly even for naturalistic drama. It makes him uncomfortable to deliberately measure each word, and he becomes self-conscious when asked to do so. Nevertheless, if he is to master all styles, he must work daily on slowing down so that eventually he can do so without labor when the text and the space demand it. An effective exercise is to take a poem, a newspaper article, or a few lines from a play, and read the material in what will appear to be an excruciatingly slow manner. One word should be read at a time, enunciated precisely, with pauses of two or three seconds between words.

e. Vocal clarity requires both crisp and precise consonant sounds and prolonged vowel sounds. It is the latter that gives inexperienced actors the most difficulty in poetic drama. In the Greek theatre, when vowel sounds are insufficiently extended, all the audience hears is a choppy series of meaningless consonant sounds. Exercises to correct this problem are often anguishing, too, but necessary if the actor is to develop clear vowel sounds as a matter of habit. The same exercise as that suggested in "d" above, but with a patient effort at extending the vowels, will prove beneficial. More comfortable and interesting, perhaps, would be the telling of a fairy tale to children, in which exaggerated vowel sounds make words more colorful and vivid—and more fun, too!

f. The greater the demands upon vocal energy, the greater the need for controlled breathing and phrasing. The following will demonstrate the problems that theatre size makes upon breathing:

Read lines 1204-1217 from the messenger speech in *Medea* as though you were performing in an intimate space, taking in breath (indicated by //) in the places specified below:

//But her wretched father, knowing nothing of the event//
Came suddenly to the house, and fell upon the corpse.//
And at once cried out and folded his arms about her,//
And kissed her and spoke to her, saying,// "O my poor child,
What heavenly power has so shamefully destroyed you?//
And who has sent me here like an ancient sepulcher,
Deprived of you?// O let me die with you my child!"//
And when he had made an end of his wailing and crying,//
Then the old man wished to raise himself to his feet.//
But as the ivy clings to the twigs of the laurel,

So he stuck to the fine dress,// and he struggled fearfully.
For he was trying to lift himself to his knees,
And she was pulling him down,// and when he tugged hard
He would be ripping his aged flesh from his bones.

Now read the lines again with the same phrasing, but in Greek theatre conditions.

Unless you are possessed of an extraordinary diaphragm and perfect breath control, you will run out of breath in several places before being able to complete a phrase. When this happens, you either are incapable of continuing the phrase without taking more breath, or your projection becomes considerably weaker at the end of the phrase. Besides developing a stronger diaphragm, the actor must become aware of additional methods of control when confronted with the challenge of a large theatre.

He must take in *more* breath before beginning each phrase and, without sacrificing meaning, find ways of shortening his phrasing. See what happens when you repeat the speech, breathing in more deeply before each phrase, and substituting the following phrasing:

//But her wretched father// knowing nothing of the event//
Came suddenly to the house, and fell upon the corpse.//
And at once cried out// and folded his arms about her,//
And kissed her and spoke to her, saying,// "O my poor child,//
What heavenly power// has so shamefully destroyed you?//
And who has sent me here// like an ancient sepulcher,

Deprived of you?// O let me die with you my child!"//
Then the old man wished to raise himself to his feet.//
But as the ivy clings to the twigs of the laurel,//
So he stuck to the fine dress,// and he struggled fearfully.//

For he was trying to lift himself to his knees,//
And she was pulling him down,// and when he tugged hard//
He would be ripping his aged flesh from his bones.

(*Note:* All breathing should be through the mouth. You cannot get as much breath inside your lungs as quickly through the nose, and you will find it awkward to have to close your mouth every time you breathe in.)

g. Work on your assigned messenger's speech for appropriate breath control.

2. Special physical demands

a. When you walk, the length of each step is determined by your physique, your emotional condition, and the reason for your action. But the size of your movement as viewed by an audience is relative to the size of the stage on which the actor walks. You will have learned from earlier exercises that a normal step in a very large space may

172

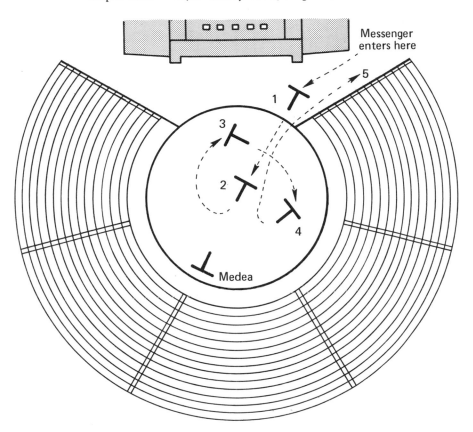

FIGURE 9-2. *Sketch of the* Medea *messenger speech and movements.*

appear to be mincing, or may make your crosses appear to be un-necessarily slow. The larger the space, then, the longer the stride (unless the character or action requires deliberate slowness or short steps). Using the *Medea* messenger speech again, follow the block-ing specified in the ground plan above and determine how long your strides must be in a large stage space.

1) Enter and stop before speaking.
2) Move toward Medea on line 1129 ("What! Are you right in the mind?")
3) Move to position indicated on Medea's cue, line 1135 (". . . they died in agony.") *before* speaking. Use this cross to relate to the area from which you came as you prepare yourself to recount the event to Medea and the chorus.
4) Move to Medea on line 1222 ("As for your interests . . .")
5) Exit *after* final speech.

3. Gestures and turns must be much broader. Small shrugs, vague or random gestures from the wrists or elbows come across as weak and incongruous in the large theatre space. It is important to realize that the size of a theatre does not dictate the *amount* of gestures (although arm gestures will, as a rule, be preferable to nods of the head) or turns to be made, but their execution and size. Justification for *all* movement is exactly the same as for any drama, and includes all internal and external stimuli discussed in Part I, although it is best to exercise even greater economy in Greek tragedy. The actor should begin with the above-stated principles for gesture. Rather than thinking of the physical theatre, he should concentrate on developing the expression of what the *character* thinks and feels, and to whom he relates and how, then go through the speech, allowing the body to respond freely to stimuli.

As a general example, let us find "appropriate" gestures for the *Medea* messenger:

The messenger enters agitated; he has been running, and his objective is to warn Medea. He kneels when he sees her.

Line 1122 ("run for your life"): *stretch out arms in appeal.*
Line 1125 ("she is dead"): *drop arms despairingly.*
Line 1129 ("What!"): *rise;* ("Are you right in the mind?"): *cross to Medea.*
Line 1130 ("The house of kings . . ."): *point to parados from which you entered.*
Line 1131 ("Do you enjoy it?"): *shift arm, palm up, to Medea*
Line 1136: *Before speaking, turn toward entrance and relate to offstage area of Princess and King. Then turn to Medea, and speak. Visualize the details you describe and locate the characters you describe in front of you.*
Line 1142 ("And I myself was so full of my joy."): *bring hands to chest.*
Line 1146 ("Was keeping her eye fixed eagerly on Jason"): *turn head only toward Jason.*
Line 1148 (". . . and she turned herself away from him."): *turn head away.*
Line 1151 ("You must not look unkindly on your friends."): *as Jason, reach arm out tenderly toward imagined Princess.*
Line 1154 (". . . And take these gifts . . ."): *gesture toward imaginary gifts.*

During the descriptive passages that follow, it is best not to illustrate all of the actions of the Princess, King, or servants. Visualize and respond to the imagined action, and *suggest* some of its details, such as stretching the arms to receive the gorgeous robe, raising the hands to the sides of the head to suggest putting on the crown, stretching out a foot and "looking along it," and taking one or two steps back on "staggered back." Gesture toward mouth on "the white foam. . . ." Reach for crown, to tear it off, on "The wreath of gold . . ."; clutch your body on ". . . was fastening on the unhappy girl's fine flesh"; shake head on "Shaking her hair. . . ."

Line 1195 (". . . she fell to the ground"): *relax, let arms drop. Look down to ground to describe the Princess.*

You will find that what will have been achieved, while honest and appropriate, probably will be too small to be apprehended or will be disproportionate to the magnitude of both the content of the speech and the physical theatre. Your next step is to enlarge the physical action you have discovered to be truthful. For example, when you point on line 1130, instead of merely bending your elbow and raising your lower arm while pointing your index finger, raise the entire arm away from the body and point firmly in the direction of the palace.

In the final suggestion for gesture in the example from *Medea,* the arms should be held away from the body as you point downward. The fingers also should be straight and pointing downward.

In those instances where you take notice of or allude to people, objects, or places, do not rely on merely focussing your eyes or nodding slightly in their direction; instead, move the entire head in a full, precise manner.

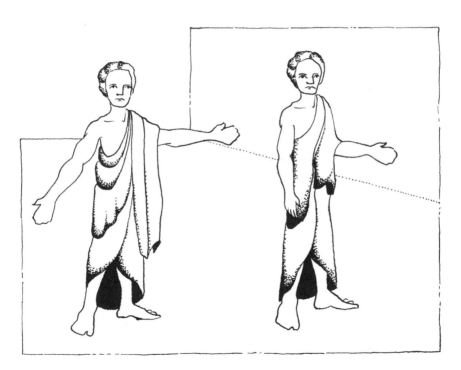

FIGURE 9-3. *Actor on left: right; actor on right: wrong.*

FIGURE 9-4.   *Actor on left: wrong; actor on right: right.*

(More will be said about the scope of movement and gesture when language is discussed.)

Work out appropriate gestures for your Greek messenger speech. Follow the procedure suggested above by first developing truthful expression, then enlarging it for the large open-air space.

The Impact of Space

Except for the possibility of painted panels attached to the front of the *skene,* or of *periaktoi* (three-sided panels that pivot to reveal a new design on each side), no stage scenery appears to have been utilized by the Greeks. Indeed, the extant texts do not stress the particulars of environment and make little or no issue of the relationship between environment and character. Locales were invariably set outdoors, and the *skene,* normally represent-

FIGURE 9-5. *Second Messenger in Euripides'* The Bacchae. *University of California at Santa Barbara production.*

ing the palace or domicile of one of the principal characters, was utilized principally for entrances and exits, or for the revelation of the bodies of characters who had met their demise offstage.

With the exception of an occasional chair for a weakened character such as Phaedre, or a litter for a wounded Hercules, the Greek theatre used virtually no furniture and a minimum of properties. The consequence of such austerity is that the possibilities for stage movement and personal business are severely limited. The actor cannot open or shut windows, relate to fireplaces, bookcases, chairs, tables, beds, or other accouterments of everyday life. The texts call for no cups or saucers, doorknobs, *objects d'art,* or whatever Greek habits or cravings paralleled our own use of cigars, pipes, or cigarettes. The actor is thrown upon his own resources: the expression of emotions and attitudes relies almost solely on the manipulation of his voice and body. The challenge to the actor in a naturalistic play is to make as much use as possible of environmental detail; in a Greek tragedy, he or she must try to be as interesting and affecting as possible with a minimum of environmental detail.

While the elimination of such detail certainly does result in limiting the amount of movement and personal business available to the actor and places greater emphasis on gesture and vocal variety, there still are a number of spatial factors that may justify physical action and demonstrate that Greek acting need not be completely static. Some of these factors are discussed here.

OTHER CHARACTERS. In Greek tragedy, unless you are a single prologue device, there will always be other characters on stage. Central characters come and go (there are never more than three speaking characters on stage at one time), but the chorus is always present. In the blocking plan proposed for the messenger in *Medea* (see p. 173), note the suggestions for the justification of movement that emerge from his relationship to Medea. Might he not similarly relate to the chorus? For example, before crossing on line 1129, he might, in his shocked reaction to Medea, turn to the chorus in order to share his amazement. When he begins to describe the Princess' action, he could be telling his story to the chorus as well as to Medea. He might direct line 1171, where he describes the transition from the fainting of the Princess to the entrance of the aged woman servant, to them. This might be further justified by audible reactions from the chorus to the horror of the fate of the Princess. Line 1202, "It was a fearful sight . . . ," also might be directed to the chorus—after all, Medea already is fully aware of the havoc she has wrought.

EXERCISE

Review your particular messenger speech, and determine if you are able to justify turns, crosses, or gestures on the basis of how certain lines relate to other characters on stage. What is your attitude toward those characters? What kinds of responses can you anticipate from them?

Because of the size of the acting area, characters cannot enact a scene for too long a period of time in close proximity to one another. Rarely does the text call for such intimacy, no doubt because the size of movement and sound demanded by the theatre would appear ludicrous when characters are too close to one another.

EXERCISE

Have two actors read through the first scene between Jason and Medea in a space the size of a Greek *orchestra*. Try to play the scene with the characters about one-and-a-half feet apart. What does this force the characters to do? How does this affect their relationship to the audience? Experiment with distance, and find one that does not destroy character relationship or the meaning of the scene, and yet is appropriate to the actor-audience configuration.

STAGE AREAS. We have seen that in addition to the *skene*, there are two *paradoi* through which offstage space may be associated with particular locales. It has already been suggested that in *Medea,* each *parados* may be associated with other places, and in the blocking example, it was proposed that the messenger gesture toward "The house of the King" (line 1130), and that he might turn and look sadly off in that same direction as he begins to recount what took place there (line 1136). It should be clear that even empty space can contain areas that have associative values. When a character leaves the stage, the remaining characters can allude to the area that he has occupied when referring to him. Not previously mentioned is the presence of a *thymele,* or altar, which occupied the center of the *orchestra.* In plays such as *Agamemnon* and *Oedipus,* this area is used for ritual offerings to the gods or as a place of prayer. Allusion to the gods or symbolic references to sacrifice and prayer may be made by relating to the *thymele.*

179

THE AUDIENCE. In the realistic theatre, the illusion of a "fourth wall" is always suggested. The fourth wall is an imaginary barrier between the audience and the actor which creates the illusion that the characters are unaware of being observed, and that the audience is viewing their actions through a wall. One of the consequences of such an actor-audience relationship is that the actor scrupulously avoids direct contact with the audience. He must never appear to see it or to speak to it. This means that he will usually avoid the "full-front" position, even preferring on occasion to act with his back to the audience. In addition to this, the proscenium stage, which fostered the realistic theatre, separates the audience from the stage completely. The seats and the stage face one another. In the Greek theatre, the audience surrounds the stage on three sides, and the text requires the actors and the chorus frequently to speak directly to the audience.

The result is that acting in Greek tragedy becomes more formal. In order for the entire audience to see and hear, actors must play more often in an open position, and when delivering a long speech, will more often than not have to occupy a position in the area between the *thymele* and the *skene*. They also will have to find justification to relate to all parts of the audience during a scene. Note how the blocking of the *Medea* messenger scene attempts to do this.

Another aspect of the audience-actor relationship is that the audience is *above* the stage. The stage is *not* a platform that, as in the proscenium theatre, requires the audience to look up at the action. When the audience stretches above the stage, then the actor must try to keep his chin up and avoid playing with his head down, except when it is absolutely necessary.

EXERCISE

In Greek theatre conditions, perform your Greek messenger speech with an awareness of your relationship to the audience. Be sure that your head is tilted upward when you address the other characters onstage.

The Impact of the Quality of the Environment

We cannot be certain of the architectural design, decor, or materials of the original theatres, so we do not know the kind of response it may have provoked in the actor. The quality of the *skene* actually is unimportant because actors do not perform *in* it, but in front of it, and because the same structure served all the plays, the actors would have had to *imagine* a gorgeous palace, or the run-down abode to which Medea was relegated, or Philoctetes' cave. What is of importance, however, is the natural environment of the Greek theatre. There is no roof but the heavens high above. Below the *orchestra,* in full view of the audience, stretch the orchards of Epidaurus, the natural topography of Athens, or the majestic mountains and valley at Delphi with their mysterious, moving cloud formations. The actor is performing in an unrestricted space, surrounded by nature's grandeur. There is more to its potential influence upon the actor than its size or space. The only way its impact can be described is to compare it to the exhilaration one experiences upon leaving the city and visiting an area that possesses natural grandeur. Places like Delphi, the Alps, Yosemite, or the Grand Canyon, although they dwarf us physically, have the capacity to free and enlarge the spirit and make us feel at one with the cosmos. That this experience is part of the nature of Greek tragedy is no doubt due to the quality of the environment for which it was written.

EXERCISE

Close your eyes, and try to recall your experience in the most beautiful natural environment you have ever visited. Recall specifically the smell and feel of the air, the colors, size, and scope of the terrain. It dwarfs you and may make you feel insignificant until you feel that you are part of it. Gesture, move, and make sounds that fully express your oneness with natural majesty.

LANGUAGE

Unlike the theatrical conventions of Greek tragedy that have been analyzed, in which so much is the result of conjecture, the language of Greek tragedy has been preserved in the extant plays. The dramatist's choice of words and his treatment of language are recorded for all to read, to speak, to hear. But while we have texts, we do not have any way of knowing how they were spoken. Indeed, many scholars believe that Greek tragedy was not spoken, but sung in recitative, probably to the accompaniment of musical instruments. We can be fairly certain that parts of, if not entire, choral odes (*stasima*) were sung, and that the chorus danced at the same time.

Another problem exists for the non-Greek actor who must rely upon translations that necessarily deviate from the original language to the extent of producing a different sound and meter than the original. Like the French alexandrine, the Greek metrical mode does not translate well into English, and the result is translation in prose or in blank verse. Essentially, however, the translator's problem is to capture the tone and spirit if not the rhythm of the original, and to provide the actor with speakable dramatic dialogue. Victorian translators tended toward a lyrical quality that was more literary than dramatic, while some contemporary writers have gone to the extreme of using a more conversational style, including contemporary idioms, which not only weakens the power of the play but creates contradictions between language and the other conventions—even themes—of Greek tragedy. Cosmic reverberations are difficult to reproduce in the language of the living room, the barracks, or the street corner.

The actor, then, is at the mercy of the translator for his acting style, since the actor's vocal and physical mode are determined to a great extent by the language to be used.

The requirements for an adequate translation of a Greek tragedy include the recreation of the poetic and formal qualities of the language and of a speech mode that characterizes the great archetypal characters of Homeric myth. It must resonate with the mystery of Fate and the sounds of universal anguish and joy. It is a language that magnifies and orchestrates, but at the same time does not lose touch with honest human emotion.

The speech of the characters in Greek tragedy is always formal in that it is dignified, carefully organized, precise, and devoid of the casual or colloquial qualities of everyday speech. At the same time, it varies in degree toward or away from common expression. Medea's first laments, for example, are ritual-like in their structure:

> *Ah, wretch! Ah, lost in my sufferings,*
> *I wish, I wish I might die.*
>
> (ll. 96-97)

Medea's behavior, described at the beginning of the play by the Nurse, also approaches the ritualistic:

> *And poor Medea is slighted, and cries aloud in the*
> *Vows they made to each other,* the right hand cloyed
> *In eternal promise.* She calls upon the gods to witness

What sort of return Jason has made to her love.
She lies without food and gives herself up to suffering,
Wasting every moment of the day in tears.
So it has gone since she knew herself slighted by him.
Not stirring an eye, not moving her face from the ground,
No more than either a rock or surging sea water
She listens when she is given friendly advice.
Except that sometimes she twists back her white neck and
Moans to herself, *calling out her father's name.*

(ll. 20-31)

When Medea herself appears, her language continues to be formalized, but even while she soliloquizes, it moves nearer to the quality of conversational speech as she directly addresses the women of Corinth. But still she is provided with poetic images such as "sea of woe."

Later, in scenes between Medea and Creon, Jason, or Aegeus, the language moves even closer to the quality of conversational exchange (*stichomythia*):

MEDEA
I beg you. By your knees, by your new-wedded girl.

CREON
Your words are wasted. You will never persuade me.

MEDEA
Will you drive me out, and give no heed to my prayers?

CREON
I will, for I love my family more than you. (ll. 324-327)

—ritualistic, conversational but poetic, and *stichomythia*—

These three levels of speech repeat themselves throughout the play and must be given readings appropriate to them. The modern actor, provided he is able to grasp the scope of the character, should have little difficulty with the more realistic speeches, but he may have trouble with the more formal, ritualized language.

We have become so accustomed to the speech and conventions of naturalistic drama, with its demand for "underplaying" and its reliance upon pauses to suggest underlying emotions, that we have become distrustful of broad and vigorous emotional expression. Somehow, we no longer believe that people can honestly express grief by keening, groaning, or wailing. Much of this is due, of course, to our own "stiff upper lip" life style and

FIGURE 9-6. *Size and gesture in Greek tragedy. Oedipus in Sophocles'*
Oedipus the King. *University of California at Santa Barbara production.*

the social constraints upon us to keep our emotions bottled up. Too many
aspiring young actors today rationalize their acting inhibitions by arguing
against "overplaying" and referring to enlarged behavior as "hamminess."
But "ham acting" only occurs when expression is out of proportion with
the demands of the text, and usually is the result of exhibitionism rather
than accurate interpretation.

The use of the *kommos* in Greek tragedy provides a clue as to the extent of emotional expression expected. The *kommos* is a lament (sung by the chorus or chanted by a character) for the fate of the protagonist and means "breast-beating," and suggests unsuppressed emotion. The language and the characters of Greek tragedy are momentous because their ideas and view of life are so, and in order to achieve the scope, dramatic excitement, and impact of these plays, actors must free themselves from a narrower vision and technique.

EXERCISES

1. *Release games.* The following improvisations should be developed and executed with a sense of fun. Do not be afraid to exaggerate or burlesque everything that you do:
   a. King Kong captures Fay Wray.
   b. Count Dracula tries to get Lucy's blood.
   c. The wicked witch consults her magic mirror, then makes her poisoned apples.
   d. Doctor Jekyll is transformed into Mr. Hyde.
   e. You are Nelson Eddy and Jeanette MacDonald singing a duet from an operetta.

2. *Archetypal expression*—working from the outside in:
   a. Spread your legs wide apart. Stretch your arms to the sky, with fingers outspread. Throw your head back and look upward. Expand your chest and breathe deeply. Smile. Say "AH," letting the sound come from deep within you, and extend it fully. Surrender yourself to what you are doing physically. What, if any, emotion is evoked?
   b. Cross your arms across your stomach and clutch your sides. Hunch your shoulders forward. Press your chin into your chest. Sink to your knees and begin to rock slowly. Let the sound of "OH" come from deep inside you, and extend it fully. Surrender yourself to your physical state. What, if any, emotion is evoked?
   c. Lie on your back, with legs and arms outstretched. Tense your entire body and arch your back severely, grunting as you do so. Collapse. Repeat this several times, then accelerate the repetitions faster and faster. Surrender yourself to your physical state. What, if any, emotion is evoked?

3. *Archetypal expression*—working from the inside out. Do not be concerned with exploring justifications for the following. Respond to the words intuitively and do the first physical thing that comes to mind. Follow the physical action with sound. Move and vocalize as broadly and as unrestrainedly as possible. These should be done as group exercises.

   a. Extreme ecstasy.
   b. Extreme despair.
   c. Extreme pain.
   d. Extreme rage.

4. Study Medea's scene with her children (II. 1021-1080). If you break it down, you will find that it consists of a pattern of constantly shifting emotions, such as the following:

1021 ff.	1.	Sorrowful lament over separation.
1028 ff.	2.	Bitterness over the futility of her suffering.
1036 ff.	3.	Anguish over the loss of her children.
1044 ff.	4.	Change of heart caused by innocence of children; tenderness and relief.
1049 ff.	5.	Recollection of hatred; defense of pride.
1053 ff.	6.	Determination to pursue goal; gathering of strength.
1056 ff.	7.	Change of heart again; pity.
1059 ff.	8.	Reversion to determination; hardness and cruelty.
1070 ff.	9.	Love, pity, sorrow in final farewell.
1078-1080	10.	Controlled fury.

   a. Perform the scene, expressing the emotional progression of the scene with *sound and movement only.*
   b. Perform the scene, using its language, but *incorporate* the sound and movement you had previously abstracted.

LANGUAGE AND CHARACTER

The types of characters created by the playwright are indicated to us by the meaning and form of the language and action with which he has endowed them. We have seen in dramatic analysis that most dramatic characters have a core, or spine, that contributes to their definition. In realistic drama writers such as Strindberg are interested in exploring the influences of heredity and environment as well as the many ramifications of their characters' cores as they relate to their daily lives. To make characters more "lifelike," they are provided with numerous particularized qualities including details of personal habits and idiosyncrasies, speech mannerisms, and the way in which they dress. Such details are foreign to Greek characterization, which prefers to distill rather than to complicate. All nonessential traits are stripped away, leaving the pure and simple essence of a human quality that is magnified and illuminated by a great crisis. This explains why it

186

is not difficult to determine the correct mask—the single expression that essentializes the character.

Medea develops in Euripides' tragedy only in terms of the extremes to which her personal pride as a princess and a woman will lead her. The major obstacle is her devotion to her children, and her decision to kill them demonstrates the strength of her self-esteem. She runs the gamut of emotion, but her mask, which should convey furious, burning pride, is a constant reminder that all her emotions and actions emanate from it.

EXERCISES

1. Determine the essences of Jason's and Creon's characters. Describe the masks that should be designed for them.
2. Select a protagonist from another Greek tragedy (see list at end of chapter), and determine the nature of the mask for that character. Justify your decision.

The use of archetypal expression of emotion in Greek tragedy was mentioned previously. Characters in these plays come closer to being archetypes than individualized, recognizable (social or psychological) types. Euripides is far more concerned with examining the human capacities for pride, jealousy, and barbarism than in presenting a "well-rounded" depiction of a woman scorned. Archetypal characters are less complex psychologically than particularized ones, and the writer will structure his character by simplifying, then amplifying them. This is why they come across as "larger than life." This is not because they are giants (though in many instances they are, spiritually and sometimes physically), but because such magnification clarifies and more powerfully dramatizes a vision of fundamental human potential.

With this kind of interest in characterization, the language of Greek tragedy is concerned less with individual idiosyncrasies than with the expression of a character's spiritual or philosophical essence manifesting itself in argumentation and in basic but powerful human emotion. Such language forces the actor to eliminate little "personal" touches and mannerisms. His movement and business must be as simple and uncluttered, as direct, and as powerful as the language.

EXERCISES

---

1. Read Medea's initial speech after her first appearance. What kind of personal business (gesture, use of hand properties, use of hands and body, etc.) does the speech justify? Repeat the speech, but add bits of individualized business such as handling parts of your costume, arranging your hair, playing with your rings or jewelry, pulling your ear-lobes, holding and relating to a glass of water in a distinctive personal manner.

     The results need not be ludicrous, and perhaps not totally incongruous, but notice how the meaning and impact of the scene change; how the emphasis shifts from an archetypal view of a wronged, suffering woman to the portrait of the small personal details of a wronged, suffering woman. Which type of emphasis is more appropriate to the play's language?

2. Do the same as the above with Miss Julie's speech that begins with, "You don't mean that. Anyway, everybody knows my secrets.—My mother's parents were very ordinary people, just commoners. . . ." What type of personal business is more suitable to Miss Julie?

Finally, we must recognize that the conflicts and confrontations in Greek tragedy are less physical than they are argumentative. The episodes in Greek tragedy are comprised chiefly of debates—usually over fundamental moral issues, with the result that a large portion of the language of Greek tragedy is rhetorical. The first confrontation between Medea and Jason is typical of this, and even includes references to good and bad methods of argumentation. The arguments are introduced, logically developed, and concluded, whereupon the responder, in a speech usually balanced in length, will not merely develop his own arguments, but will comment point by point on the quality or accuracy of his opponent's remarks.

The language of rhetoric is formal in terms of its careful organization and must be delivered rationally and clearly. Many people would argue that rhetorical speech is undramatic and theatrically dull. To many, the term mistakenly connotes affected oration, such as that which is characteristic of some politicians. Such critics must be reminded that courtroom drama, invariably rhetorical, is, when well-written, nearly foolproof theatre. Even nondramatic debates can be very "theatrical" and exciting. Of course, the debates in Greek tragedy will be dull if the characters are *solely* debaters. They are not. Their personal principles, their lives, and their destinies are wrapped up in their arguments. Jason must preserve his personal integrity and justify his decision to desert his wife. Medea must make him understand her position and the error of his ways. Both are concerned with their public images as they try to make their points with the chorus and the audience. Nor is there a dull, polite objectivity in the opponents. They organize their arguments rationally, but Jason is not above patronization and scorn, nor is Medea beyond vicious personal attacks upon her estranged husband. The actor has little justification for movement in these scenes, but there is sufficient intellectual and emotional provocation in the conflict of wills to challenge the vocal and physical skills of any actor.

EXERCISES

1. Analyze the mode of argumentation of the debate between Medea and Jason in their first scene together.
2. Analyze what the text and subtext reveal in terms of how each character relates to the principles of his argument, and how he relates to his opponent.

CLOTHING

In the modern realistic theatre, costume is selected primarily to reveal:

1. Character traits such as status, age, refinement or coarseness, eccentricity, occupation, etc.
2. Influences of locale, including climate, the particulars of national or regional garb, etc.
3. Accuracy of period dress.

The classical Greek tragic theatre, however, while it might have made certain modifications for status such as distinguishing between king and peasant, or occupation such as defining soldier or priest, required a fairly uniform, standardized costume for all tragedy. Vase painting indicates that selected garments of fifth century B.C. Athens were used, but to these were added formalized apparel such as the *onkos,* a high headdress, *kothurnai,* a thick-soled boot, and a mask.

Body Garments

The pieces that comprise body dress are so simple that they can be constructed and worn by the actor himself for rehearsals or exercise work by assembling a few rectangles of cloth and some pins. The basic body garment was the *chiton*, which was made of wool or linen, and which could be worn from the shoulder to just below the knee, or full length. It consisted of two rectangular strips of cloth pinned together at the shoulders and belted at the waist. Sometimes they also were pinned beneath the armpits, or else both pieces were folded at the top so that portions of the cloth could hang down from the shoulders to the waist. Long sleeves might be added, which may have been a permanent feature of the tragic costume.

The Greeks had a choice of two overgarments: the *chlamys* or the *himation*. The *chlamys* was a short rectangular piece that normally was pinned to the right shoulder and draped over the left arm, creating the effect of a short cape. It was a utilitarian garment that covered the torso for warmth. The *himation,* on the other hand, was a mark of status and was worn only by the nobility, the wealthy, or by statesmen. For this reason, it was utilized more than the *chlamys* in tragedy. It consisted of a lengthy rectangular strip of cloth that could be draped in several different ways. It might be gathered over the left shoulder and upper arm, from where it hung straight to the ground. Or it might hang to the ground in front of the left shoulder, while the rear section was wrapped loosely around the rear of the lower part of the body and drawn across the front of the body, where it might be pinned to the left waist or drawn over the left forearm.

EXERCISES

1. Put on a full-length *chiton.* Walk with long strides. Gesture broadly, first pointing the arms forward, then to the sides, and finally to the sky. You should find that the *chiton* is unrestrictive, and provides the entire body with complete freedom.

2. Gather a *himation* (about six feet wide) over your left shoulder (if you are left-handed, drape it over your right shoulder). It should be long enough to hang to the ground in front and back. The opposite arm will be quite free for gesturing, but what happens when you gesture broadly with the left arm? Do not be disturbed by the fact that the *himation* will slide down your upper arm. After all, Greek bodies were no different than ours and actors had to cope with the *himation* in the

FIGURE 9-7. *Medea's murder of one of her children is graphically depicted in this fourth century B.C. vase painting. Courtesy of the Louvre Museum, Paris.*

same way. You will find that you can still gesture with the *himation*-covered arm, and you are free to readjust it to your shoulder at any time. You may prefer to gesture *more* with your free arm, and use the covered arm only when gesturing with both arms. You must become accustomed to what at first seems to be a hindrance, and respond naturally and unselfconsciously to its presence.

Take long strides wearing the *himation*. What must you do to prevent it from constantly sliding down? The simplest method of control is to press against it with the *himation* hand. Might such a bent portion of the arm have become an accepted characteristic trait? Now gesture with your free arm. This might be another type of gesturing that was natural to the Greeks.

3. Experiment with the wraparound *himation*. Now you will find that you want to use your free arm for large, straight arm gestures, but that you may use the *himation*-covered arm for gestures that require the use of the forearm. Note that your body position is affected by this draping of the *himation;* the forearm over which the *himation* is draped must be bent.

4. Try a speech from *Medea* using the *chiton* and the *himation*. Medea's speech to her children (II. 1021-1077) is an effective one for women, while Jason's reaction to Medea's murder of the children (II. 1323-1350) is recommended for the men. In both speeches, gesture and movement should be geared to the size of the Greek theatre.

You will find that you cannot leave the adjustment of the *himation* to chance, but must anticipate and control its behavior.

The *himation* provides us with an example of a nonutilitarian garment. It is primarily decorative. If it can create the kinds of problems we have just discovered, why did the Greeks persist in wearing it? The answers can only be conjectural. First, the *himation* emphasizes verticality, thereby contributing to a sense of dignity and stature to the human form. Second, from all appearances the Greeks were fond of draping the body, and the *himation* adds to the total effect. Third, the *himation* tends to refine movement, allowing a subtlety of choice with which it may be manipulated, and providing a sense of physical control. Finally, we must assume that the posture, arm position, and other adjustments provoked by the *himation* resulted in a distinctive physical style that was pleasing to the Greeks.

Of course the actor will not always wear the *himation*. Considering its restrictive nature, he may want to discard it, let it fall, or use it like a prop in the more violent parts of the play. When he is wearing it, how-

Figure 9-8. *Greek tragic costume:* chiton *and* himation. *Oedipus in
Sophocles'* Oedipus the King. *University of California
at Santa Barbara production.*

ever, he should exploit the positive justifications for its use and attempt to
fully integrate the stylistic results.

ONKOS. We cannot be certain of the actual size or of the materials
used for the traditional high headdress of the tragic actor. It may have been
a wig, or a stylized headpiece to which was attached a crown or tiara. It
may have been attached to the mask. Its use surely was to provide added
stature.

193

EXERCISES

Using a rigid material such as cardboard or stiffened muslin, construct a circular headpiece about ten inches high to fit securely on your head.

1. Walk about.
2. Stand still and turn your head forty-five degrees to each side.
3. Tilt your head downward, then upward. How is your movement affected? How does the *onkos* make you feel?

When walking, you will discover that the tall headpiece makes your posture very straight, keeps your head upright, and prevents head bobbing. You must turn your head more slowly and in a more stately manner, and when you attempt to look down or up, you must move your head in a more deliberate and controlled way. On the whole, you should feel taller, more dignified, and more restrained.

KOTHURNAI. Again, the actual height and material of the footwear worn by the tragic actor are matters of conjecture. Some scholars believe that the sole of the shoe was as high as twelve inches, and made of wood or cork. The resultant restriction upon the actor's movement hardly seems practical. At this writing, platform shoes of excessive height are popular but clearly hazardous. Yet some kind of thickness would appear to be necessary in order to contribute to the heightening of the characters, and to maintain bodily proportions commensurate with the enlargement of the head created by the mask and *onkos*.

One solution to the problem would be to use a two-inch, thick-soled shoe made of leather, wood, or cork.

EXERCISES

Analyze the difference in length of stride and speed when walking in bare feet or sandals as compared to a thick-soled shoe.

1. Lie down, then rise in thick-soled shoes.
2. Make a 180-degree turn in thick-soled shoes.

You should discover that balance is the key factor in adjusting to thick-soled footwear. When you walk, you must do so with a bit more deliberateness and caution; the faster you walk, the shorter your strides. Your weight must come down firmly on the heel at first, or you might trip and stumble. Getting up from a prone position requires more caution in setting the feet.

You cannot pivot as easily when you turn 180 degrees; it is safer, first, to step back with one foot, then swing the other foot around when turning. The total effect of thick soles on footwork will be one of more deliberation, slowing down, and perhaps some rigidity or stiffness.

THE MASK. There are many good explanations for the use of the mask in Greek tragedy. The mask could distinguish the sex of the character (only male actors were allowed to perform); the mask enlarged the head and the features of the face so that they might more easily be seen in the huge Greek amphitheatre; since tradition demanded that only three actors play all roles (except for the chorus and "walk-ons"), the mask contributed to the actor's change of identity; the mask enlarged and emphasized the single most essential trait of the character (more will be said about this in the section dealing with Reality).

EXERCISES

If you do not have access to masks that have been constructed for Greek tragedy, you should use a novelty-shop type of full-face mask or a paper bag, with spaces cut out for the eyes, nose, and mouth, using rubber bands to hold the mask in place.

1. Using the mask, enact Medea's or Jason's soliloquy before an audience.

What was the effect of the mask? Did it make you perform differently than when you did not use it? In the opinion of the spectators, what did you do or should you have done differently?

2. Using masks, two actors should play any scene in the play requiring two characters.

How does the mask influence the manner in which each of you relate to the other character?

Do the following conclusions correspond to your answers?

1. A mask at first is frustrating because it completely prohibits facial expression.

2. The actor must channel all expression into his voice and his body. The voice and the body must become more expressive than usual.

3. Focussing upon other characters, stage areas, or objects cannot be done with the eyes alone. The head and sometimes the body must turn clearly toward the object in order to clarify the character's direction of attention. Glances are out of the question.

FIGURE 9-9. *Greek tragic costume and masks. Scene from Euripides'* The Bacchae. *University of California at Santa Barbara production.*

4. Peripheral vision is nearly impossible. The actor must face the object he wishes to see with his entire head. He cannot see the ground immediately in front of him, and consequently he must precisely set his movement in advance and move more cautiously.

The Complete Costume

The effect of the entire Greek tragic costume upon the actor is one that does not permit naturalness. A person cannot stand, move, or speak as he does in everyday life. His appearance, as well as the sensory impact of the costume, is one of solidity and weightiness. There are no airy, delicate, flighty, lightweight characters in Greek tragedy. The actor will also look and feel very tall, statuesque, dignified, and noble. The effect of costume on movement is to restrict speed and muscular flexibility; the actor must not be robotlike or appear to be mechanized, but he must move more slowly and with more deliberation and economy. Physical restrictions will force him to channel most of his expression into voice and gesture. There is no way he can compensate if his voice and speech lack the power and range to enthrall the audience, or if he is too inhibited to move and gesture with enormous size and strength.

THE "REALITY" OF GREEK TRAGEDY

It should be apparent at this point that the conventions of Greek tragedy are nonrealistic. The physical conventions of the theatre force the actor into a mode of speech and movement that cannot possibly mirror the normal speech and movement of everyday life. It is true that much of what has been concluded is conjectural, but we have seen in the texts of the plays how language and characterization confirm the acting style that the supposed theatrical conventions have been shown to produce. The structure and thematic concerns of the tragedies further support the nonrealistic "reality" in which they are conceived. The interruption of the action by *stasima* (choral songs and dances) serves to remind us that we are in a theatre watching a dramatic ritual rather than a "slice of life."

Greek tragedy developed out of ritualistic celebrations that honored the gods and celebrated fertility. The god of Theatre was Dionysus, and the *thymele* is presumed to have been his altar. Fifth century B.C. tragedy never deviated from these celebratory purposes in structure or theme. The use of song and dance, the mask, and retention of the circular threshing ground for the main acting area unquestionably originated in the religious rites that preceded, then evolved into, theatre and drama. The tragedies, with the exception of Aeschylus' *The Persians* (still one of the most ritualized of the extant plays), are set in legendary worlds and their characters are the gods or goddesses, heroes, heroines, and villains of mythology. Their concerns are with the relations between the gods and men, with the enormous responsibilities of great men, with the evanescence of good fortune, and with the mysterious workings of the universe. Even when *Medea* and some of Euripides' other works appear to descend into domesticity, they are heightened by the magnitude of the characters and their sufferings, the intervention of the gods, the poetic language, and the epitomization rather than the particularization of love, jealousy, and evil. The result is that even without the knowledge of the *onkos,* the mask, the *kothurnai,* or the exact size and shape of the Greek theatre, the text itself will require many of the same conventions of acting as those precipitated by the physical theatre.

One other important point must be made before completing our study of the stylistic demands of Greek tragedy. It is a curious fact that modern actors trained in the naturalistic school, and using methods (such as those investigated in the first part of this book) that stimulate honesty rather than clichés or facile tricks, forget all they have ever learned when attempting Greek and Elizabethan tragedy. They subconsciously assume that nonrealistic styles are forms of decoration to be embroidered upon, rather than integrated with characterization. In short, they try to play the *effect* of a particular style rather than its meaning. When Greek tragedy is performed today, many productions appear to be attempts to rebel against naturalism, and the results are often romanticized and self-indulgent approaches to the ritualistic and sensory—even orgiastic—nature of ancient Greek drama. This brings about stylized gesticulation, dancing, singing and chanting, creating "interesting" effects, all of which have little relevance to the language and meaning of the play. Actors magnify their movement, gestures, and speech, groan and keen uninhibitedly, but without an iota of honest thought or emotion. Often the language is thoroughly neglected in favor of visual spectacle, as though the writers of Greek tragedy were pre-Artaudian prophets. It is not difficult to understand the appeal to Artaud and his disciples of the ritualistic and theatrical qualities of Greek tragedy, but these are only a part of what Greek tragedy is all about. To stress these qualities, and neglect the equally strong emphasis that the Greeks placed upon the mind and upon verbal discourse, is to emasculate and reduce these great works to titillating exercises.

The purpose of any tragedy is to move us, put us in awe, make us cry, terrify us and, ultimately, purge us. None of these responses is possible to achieve in the theatre without the stimulus of recognizable and believable human emotion. Such terms as "formalized," "magnified," "controlled," and "austere" have been used to characterize the acting style of Greek tragedy. This does not mean that the characters in these plays are "living statues," devoid of basic human emotion, or that because expression is conventionalized, human qualities themselves are artificial. Nonrealistic modes of expression do not exclude the use of the methods previously advocated to make the ideas and emotions of dramatic characters meaningful and believable to the actor and, consequently, to the audience.

In whatever style the actor works, his first job is to discover what makes his character *human,* and to understand the nature of the character's emotions and attitudes. The actor must begin by analyzing his character's desires and characteristic behavior. He then sets out to find material from his own observation and experience that makes the character's actions personal, meaningful, and expressive. Once he has found the means of comfortably and appropriately giving shape to the character, he must adapt that shape to the environment and costume of the theatre, and to the language of the text. If he must use external methods and work from the outside-in (i.e., experimenting with archetypical techniques), these should result in actions in which the actor and audience will believe and be moved.

EXERCISES

1. Analyze Medea or Jason according to the methods described in Part II.
2. Using any of the major speeches of each character, do the following:
    a. Make a line-by-line subtextual analysis.
    b. Isolate the emotions and attitudes that the subtext reveals.
    c. Find parallels in your own experience, and try to recall what you did.
    d. Improvise a scene with given circumstances that parallel those of your speech.
    e. Play the speech in your own words.
    f. Play the actual scene and *adapt* to the language of the speech and to the environmental conditions of the theatre. (You may, but do not have to, use a mask.)
    g. If you or your observers feel that you have not found a magnitude appropriate to the language and the character, make use of the exercises suggested for archetypal movement.
3. If the above procedure is used as a collective exercise for a class, follow it with independent scenes from other plays, for which each performer will utilize the procedure outlined above.

Selected Messenger or Messenger-type Speeches from Greek Tragedy

Some of these selections may be interrupted by lines spoken by other characters. Most of them, however, include at least one long uninterrupted sequence on which the actor may concentrate, or he may prefer to put several interrupted speeches together to form one long delivery. The line indications are for the entire scene in which the messenger appears.

Euripides, *Andromache:* Messenger, ll. 1070-1165
——, *The Bacchae:* First Messenger, ll. 660-774
                              Second Messenger, ll. 1024-1152
——, *The Cyclops:* Odysseus, ll. 375-436
——, *The Heracleidae:* Second Attendant, ll. 784-891
——, *Heracles:* Messenger, ll. 910-1015
——, *Hippolytus:* Messenger, ll. 1154-1254
——, *Iphigenia in Tauris:* Herdsman, ll. 237-339
                              Soldier, ll. 1284-1419
——, *Rhesus:* Charioteer, ll. 733-807
Sophocles, *Ajax:* Tecmessa, ll. 201-330
——, *Antigone:* Messenger, ll. 1152-1243
——, *Oedipus at Colonus:* Messenger, ll. 1579-1665
——, *Oedipus the King:* Second Messenger, ll. 1223-1295
——, *The Women of Trachis:* Hyllus, ll. 749-812
                              Nurse, ll. 871-942

Selected Protagonists' Speeches from Greek Tragedy

WOMEN

Aeschylus, *Agamemnon:* Clytemnestra, ll. 855-913
                              Cassandra, ll. 1256-1294
                              Clytemnestra, ll. 1372-1398
Euripides, *Electra:* Clytemnestra, ll. 1011-1050
                              Electra, ll. 1060-1096, 1125-1170
——, *Iphigenia in Aulis: Clytemnestra,* ll. 1147-1207
                              Iphigenia, ll. 1466-1509
——, *Iphigenia in Tauris:* Iphigenia, ll. 1-62
——, *The Trojan Women:* Cassandra, ll. 353-405, 424-462
                              Hecuba, ll. 466-510
                              Andromache, ll. 634-683
                              Andromache, ll. 740-779
                              Hecuba, ll. 1156-1206
Sophocles, *Antigone: Antigone,* ll. 891-929

MEN

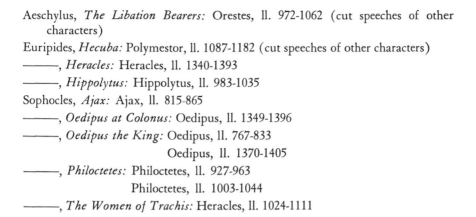

Aeschylus, *The Libation Bearers:* Orestes, ll. 972-1062 (cut speeches of other characters)

Euripides, *Hecuba:* Polymestor, ll. 1087-1182 (cut speeches of other characters)

———, *Heracles:* Heracles, ll. 1340-1393

———, *Hippolytus:* Hippolytus, ll. 983-1035

Sophocles, *Ajax:* Ajax, ll. 815-865

———, *Oedipus at Colonus:* Oedipus, ll. 1349-1396

———, *Oedipus the King:* Oedipus, ll. 767-833

Oedipus, ll. 1370-1405

———, *Philoctetes:* Philoctetes, ll. 927-963

Philoctetes, ll. 1003-1044

———, *The Women of Trachis:* Heracles, ll. 1024-1111

PART III

NOTE

1. All quotations from Euripides' *Medea* are from the translation by Rex Warner in *Euripides I*. David Grene and Richard Lattimore, eds. (Chicago: The University of Chicago Press, 1965).

SELECTED READINGS

Barton, Lucy. *Historic Costume for the Stage*. Boston: Walter H. Baker & Co., 1935.

Bieber, Margaret. *The History of the Greek and Roman Theatre*. Princeton: Princeton University Press, 1939.

Brockett, Oscar G. *History of the Theatre*. 2d ed. Boston: Allyn and Bacon, Inc., 1974.

Chekhov, Michael. *To the Actor*. New York: Harper and Bros., 1953.

Evans, Maria M., and Abrahams, Ethel B. *Ancient Greek Dress*. Chicago: Argonaut, 1964.

Glenn, Stanley L. *A Director Prepares*. Encino, Calif.: Dickenson & Co., 1973.

Gorelik, Mordecai. *New Theatres for Old*. New York: Samuel French, 1947.

Hope, Thomas. *Costumes of the Greeks and Romans*. New York: Dover Publications, 1962.

Kitto, H. D. F. *The Greeks*. Harmondsworth, Middlesex, Eng.: Penguin Books, 1951.

Laver, James. *Costumes in Antiquity*. New York: C. N. Potter, 1964.

Nicoll, Allardyce. *The Development of the Theatre*. 5th ed. New York: Harcourt, Brace & Co., 1967.

Penrod, James. *Movement for the Performing Artist*. Palo Alto, Calif.: National Press Books, 1974.

Rockwood, Jerome. *The Craftsmen of Dionysus*. Glenview, Ill.: Scott, Foresman & Co., 1966.

St. Denis, Michael. *Theatre: The Rediscovery of Style*. New York: Theatre Arts Books, 1960.

Selden, Samuel. *First Steps in Acting*. 2d ed. New York: Appleton-Century-Crofts, 1964.

Williams, Raymond. *Drama in Performance*. London: C. A. Watts & Co., 1968.

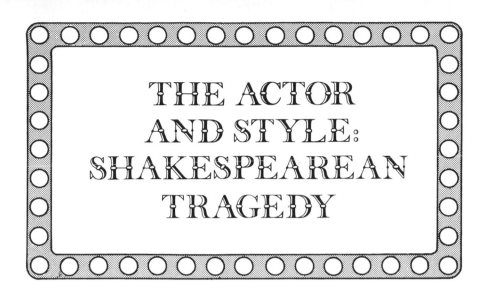

THE ACTOR
AND STYLE:
SHAKESPEAREAN
TRAGEDY

PART IV

Despite the numerous Shakespeare festival theatres that are in operation today, and that presumably are structured to emulate the Elizabethan public theatre, there is even less material evidence for the Elizabethan theatre than for the classic Greek theatre. Unlike the Greek amphitheatre, no archeological remains exist of the playhouses of Marlowe, Shakespeare, and Webster. Our suppositions about their theatres are based upon fragmentary evidence: the evolutionary trends of the medieval physical stages, the hypothesis of the innyard influence, a rough sketch of the Swan Theatre, recorded specifications for the Fortune Theatre, the Roxanne drawing, and the internal evidence provided by the plays.

Nevertheless, with the exception of such controversial details as the existence of an inner stage, we presently share certain accepted ideas about the conventions of the Elizabethan physical theatre. As was the case with the Greek theatre, one of the tests of the suitability of conjecture is the compatibility of the requirements of textual conventions with the stylistic requirements of the reconstructed Elizabethan stage.

CHAPTER 10

The Elizabethan Theatrical Environment

The chorus in Shakespeare's *Henry V* refers to his theatre as "this wooden O," and it is believed that it was indeed a building whose wooden sides formed a circle, probably an octagon. Although completely enclosed by its walls, exposure to the open air above resulted in a courtyard effect. The interior diameter formed by the octagon is believed to have been approximately fifty-eight feet. If true, it means that the entire theatre space would have fit into the *orchestra* of the Greek theatre. Three sides of the octagon's interior were utilized for the stage facade, masking the "tiring house" [retiring area?], from which entrances were made and which contained space for dressing and storage. Two doors are believed to have been used, one on each of the two outer sides of the three-sided facade; in addition, there may have been a curtained recess called "the study" or "inner chamber" in the center. We are fairly certain that the facade was at least two-storied, and that it contained windows or balconies above the doors and probably a second "study" over the one below. There may have been a third level for musicians, and we are reasonably sure that the "tiring house" was crowned with a small rooflike extension called "the heavens."

The "airing house" was the term used for the remaining interior space, one-half of which consisted of a platform (*platea*) that thrust out from the "tiring house." In the rest of the open space created by the octagon, a portion of the audience ("groundlings"), which may have numbered as many as 600 people, stood, surrounding the platform on three sides. Inside the theatre's remaining five sides, additional members of the audience were seated in two or three stories. Altogether, the theatre may have accom-

FIGURE 10-1.   *The Elizabethan playhouse. Model of John Crawford Adams's reconstruction. Reproduced with permission of The Folger Shakespeare Library, Washington, D.C.*

modated as many as 2,000 spectators. The *platea*, described in the prologue of *Henry V* as "this unworthy scaffold," was the principal acting area. It stood probably no higher than five feet and contained at least one trap door. Some favored members of the audience may have been permitted to sit on the stage.

The "heavens" that extended over the *platea* were probably supported by a pair of pillars, which might have been used for trees or as hiding places in some of the plays. In some reconstructions permanent benches have been attached to the front of each pillar, providing extra seats or another level for actors to utilize.

SIZE

By Greek theatre standards, Elizabethan public theatres such as Shakespeare's Globe were small in size. But if scholarly calculation is correct, they were much larger playhouses than the intimate theatres that were constructed for naturalistic drama in the twentieth century. Interestingly, these theatres appear to have combined intimacy and distance. The actor could be no further than sixty feet away from his audience, while at times he could be so close to the groundlings that they could reach out and touch him. We cannot be certain of the acoustical quality of the theatres, or of the influence of the open air upon sound. If we assume acoustical conditions to have been favorable, and draw our conclusions from the probable size of the theatres alone, then these theatres would have permitted quieter speech, more use of facial expression, and more subtle gesture than the Greek theatres.

Indeed, the language of the tragedies tends to support such conclusions, for many scenes and soliloquies suggest a quiet, often reflective or introspective quality. Hamlet's "To be or not to be . . . ," Macbeth's "Tomorrow and tomorrow and tomorrow . . . ," the farewell scene between Richard II and his queen, and Iago's confidences with the audience are more believable and effective when delivered quietly than bombastically.

EXERCISES

Study Richard's opening soliloquy in Act V, Scene 5 of *Richard II,* then do the following:
1. Speak it in an area the size of the Greek theatre.
2. Speak it in an area the purported size of the Elizabethan theatre.
Which delivery seems to you to be more advantageous for the speech? What is the opinion of the audience? Why?
3. Repeat the speech, justifying as much gesture as you can. Wear a mask and deliver the speech in Greek theatre conditions.

4. Using the same gestures and eliminating the mask, deliver the speech in Elizabethan theatre conditions.

What alterations have you found it necessary to make?   Why?

Though smaller than the Greek acting space, the Elizabethan stage is hardly confining. An area forty feet wide and twenty-nine feet deep allows plenty of room for free and vigorous movement, as well as for the pageantry and crowd scenes required by many of the tragedies and histories.

SPACE

As with the Greek theatre, the Elizabethan stage is relatively scenery-less. The same stage facade and open acting area serve productions of all plays presented. There is a similarity, too, in that the acting area is an open space in *front* of a building facade, and is surrounded on three sides by the audience. The Elizabethan stage structure is believed to have assumed a similar neutrality of decor. Just as the scene building may be any building and the *orchestra* any location, so may the "tiring house" represent any building, and the *platea* any location. In both theatres, efforts to visually particularize locales were minimal.

Yet there were some differences. In Greek tragedy, each play normally took place in one locale, whereas within a single Shakespearean tragedy the scene often shifted from house to house, or country to country any place in the world. *Richard II,* for example, is set in seventeen different locales. Where Greek tragedy is always set outdoors, Shakespearean tragedy may take us into many rooms of various kinds of dwellings, as well as to exterior locales.

Another difference provided by the Elizabethan theatre is in the more elaborate function of its scene building. In the Greek tragic theatre, one door was all that was needed for entrances into a building, and the roof of the building might also serve various functions. But Shakespeare's theatre was architecturally more varied and complex. Where only three entrance possibilities existed (four, if the roof, or *logeion,* was included) or were necessary in the Greek theatre, the Elizabethans may have had as many as seven: two doors, two windows, upper and lower studies, and the trap door(s). The result was a busier, less static use of space. More importantly, the actor would have had more justification for relating to spatial areas, and consequently more provocation for movement and focus of attention.

Because of the versatility of this type of stage, the Elizabethan playwright had greater freedom in terms of the limitless locales that he could utilize: the stage, in essence, was a cosmos, including its heaven and its hell. But while Shakespeare and his contemporaries exploited this freedom, little or no effort was made to represent *actual* locales. The result was a greater stress on imagination, as the chorus in *Henry V* suggests:

> *... Can this cockpit hold*
> *The vasty fields of France? Or may we cram*
> *Within this wooden O the very casques*
> *That did affright the air at Agincourt?*
> *O, pardon! Since a crooked figure may*
> *Attest in little place a million;*
> And let us, ciphers to this great accompt,
> On your imaginary forces work.
> *Suppose within the girdle of these walls*
> *Are now confined two mighty monarchies,*
> *Whose high upreared and abutting fronts*
> *The perilous narrow ocean parts asunder:*
> *Piece out our imperfections with your thoughts;*
> *Into a thousand parts divide one man,*
> *And make imaginary puissance;*
> *Think, when we talk of horses, that you see them*
> *Printing their proud hoofs i' the receiving earth;*
> For 'tis your thought that now must deck our kings,
> Carry them here and there; *jumping o'er times,*
> *Turning the accomplishment of many years*
> *Into an hour glass....*

> (Prologue,
> *Henry V*, ll. 11-31)

Shakespeare is not just asking the audience to use its imagination; he is suggesting, when his chorus says, "let us, ciphers to this great accompt,/ On your imaginary forces work," that the playwright and *the actor* must stimulate the audience's imagination.

The playwright does it, of course, with his language, which will be discussed later. The actor must make use of his sense memory in order to *himself* visualize the settings he describes; this, in turn, will stimulate expression and tone of voice, so that the audience *believes* in the character's relationship to an imagined environment. Rosalind says, "Well, this is the forest of Arden"; Viola, just washed onto the shore, asks, "What country, friends, is this?" and the Captain responds, "This is Illyria, lady." Rosalind must see and react to a forest, Viola and the Captain to the sandy shores of a strange new country. *The Tempest* opens on a ship in a violent storm, and *King Lear* encourages nature to "Blow, winds, and crack your cheeks! Rage! Blow!" In too many productions of both of these plays, realistic lighting and sound effects drown out the actors' words. These scenes were written for the *actors* to create the illusion; the reality is in the truth of their *response* to the imagined environment.

EXERCISES

Using the practice of sensory response (pp. 42-48), create imaginary environments for the following scenes from *Richard II*, and determine how you must respond to them. Determine, too, how you may relate to the structure of the Elizabethan stage.

1. Act II, Sc. 3. In addition to the textual clues regarding environment, imagine that a strong wind is blowing throughout the scene.
2. Act III, Sc. 2. (ll. 1-62)
3. Act III, Sc. 4.
4. Act V, Sc. 5.

Despite clear evidence that Shakespeare and his contemporaries used hand properties freely (unlike the setting, these were always materially accurate), the use of furniture was nearly minimal. Except for such important furnishings as Desdemona's bed, Juliet's bier, and thrones for kings, the texts rarely demand the illusion of completely furnished rooms. Constant furniture shifts would only make the plays cumbersome, whereas the scenes should move swiftly, fluidly, and uninterruptedly.

The result for the actor is similar to the demands of the Greek theatre, where the actor was forced to be more dependent upon posture, gesture, movement, and voice because for the most part he had little or no furniture to sit or lean upon, or to which he might relate.

As in the Greek theatre, Shakespeare's stage utilizes no "fourth wall"; the audience often is directly addressed in soliloquies and asides. The thrust stage convention demands more acting in the open position, since the actor's audience surrounds him on three sides.   When he is alone onstage, the actor's best position for soliloquy is upstage center, where the entire audience may have a good view of his face.   Or, if the soliloquy justifies it, the actor may move about the stage in such a way as not to favor any one section of his audience.   When two characters are on stage, they will of course relate to each other, but when either of them has a long speech to make, he will be forced to open up and face his audience.   For example, in *Richard II,* when Richard offers his crown to Bolingbroke (IV, 1) he will share the stage and address his adversary on "Here, Cousin, seize the crown . . . ," but when he describes the surrender of his kingly possessions (ll. 201 ff.), he will no doubt adjust to a full-front position.

Invariably there will be instances when the speaking character's back will be turned to a portion of the audience, in which case he will find that he must gesture so that the portion of the audience that does not see his face will be able to observe his movement.   When Richard II faces Bolingbroke

FIGURE 10-2.   *Soliloquy position on thrust stage.*

FIGURE 10-3. *Holding out the crown: a) wrong way;*

in the scene previously described, if he is at Bolingbroke's right, he must use his upstage hand to hold out the crown. The crown will be obscured from the audience sitting behind Richard. But the speech will require much gesturing with Richard's other arm:

> *The emptier ever dancing in the air,*
> *The other down, unseen and full of water.*

The actor should open up on these lines and gesture in the direction of the audience at his back.

The Elizabethan actor, unlike his Greek counterpart, performed on a *raised* stage. Instead of most of his audience being above him, a goodly portion was below him, while the rest were in galleries that extended above him. He could not hold his head so as to completely favor either the groundlings or the occupants of the upper gallery. For example, when Richard II sits and addresses the crown he holds in his hands in III, 2 ("For God's sake,

b) right way.

let us sit upon the ground/ And tell sad stories of the death of kings . . ."),
he must be careful that the audience in the upper gallery sees more than just
the top of his head.   In the earlier portions of the scene, when he speaks
proudly, asserting that God and the angels are on his side, he will want to
avoid sustaining a position too long that reveals only his jaw and nostrils to
the demonstrative "groundlings!"

EXERCISES

Using one of the soliloquies listed at the end of this chapter, perform it on a
platform of an imagined Elizabethan theatre (unless you are fortunate enough
to have access to one).   Your audience is on three sides below and above
you, and the "tiring house" with its various architectural openings is behind
you.
1.   Deliver the entire speech at the foot of the stage.
2.   Deliver the entire speech to the upper gallery.

3. Deliver the entire speech to the groundlings.
4. Deliver the entire speech to the audience on your right or left, but keep the opposite side interested.

Discuss the consequences of all four methods, then

5. Find the best stage positions for the entire speech.

The combination of the special demands of the thrust stage, the variety of playing areas, the numerous entrance and exit possibilities, and the frequent alternation of locales, most of which begin with entrances and conclude with exits, create a pattern of vigorous movement on the Elizabethan stage.

QUALITY OF THE ENVIRONMENT

Because the Elizabethan public playhouses were enclosed on all sides, they lacked the natural grandeur and open vista of the ancient Greek theatres. Neither were these theatres elaborately designed. They appear to have been simple wooden structures with thatched roofing over the galleries and "tiring house." Whether or not they owed part or all of their design to the innyards, there appears to have been a strong resemblance to them. Yet these theatres apparently conveyed something more significant in their physical design and associations than hastily erected gathering places for the presentation of plays.

The use of a platform for the principal acting area, the proximity of the actor to his audience, the absence of scenery, and the relative bareness of the *platea* combine to emphasize the physical presence of the actor. The actor is made to feel his dominance not simply because his stage is a pedestal, but because he can easily respond to and control the audience that surrounds him so closely.

Jacques' observation that "all the world's a stage," could easily be rephrased to state that, in the Elizabethan theatre at least, "the stage is all the world." We have observed already that Shakespeare can go where he chooses in his plays, and we have seen how his stage structure made this possible. But for the Elizabethan audience, its playhouse contained associative and symbolic values that transcended its rough appearance of wood and straw. Like the Greek theatre, the concept of the Elizabethan theatre originated in a religious environment. Centuries before Shakespeare's time, church interiors were the settings for the earliest medieval dramas. Although the church interior in no way resembled a Globe or a Swan structure, it made use of its space to create "stations": the illusion of multilocale settings, including heaven (the altar) and hell (door leading to basement), which formed the cosmos of the Biblical world.

The Elizabethan stage is a visual image of the universe, and its canopy and trap doors are a symbolic carry-over of the "stations" of heaven and hell. Unlike those of the Greeks, Elizabethan performances were not put on in connection with religious festivals, but the Elizabethan spectator consciously or subconsciously had to be aware when he was in the theatre of his confrontation with the Christian universe. Certainly such an impact is clear in the tragedies, all of which are concerned with Man's position in the Christian cosmos.

The actor, then, is operating in a symbolic, essentially religious environment, and his response to it must transcend material reality.

CHAPTER 11

Shakespearean Language Conventions

The language of Greek tragedy is completely poetic in form, and may have been intended to be sung. The language of Elizabethan tragedy is much more varied. *Richard II* is written entirely in blank verse, but includes rhymed couplets, often at the conclusion of a speech or scene:

> *There shall your swords and lances arbitrate*
> *The swelling difference of your settled hate.*
> *Since we cannot atone you, we shall see*
> *Justice design the victor's chivalry.*
> *Lord Marshal, command our officers-at-arms*
> *Be ready to direct these home alarms.*

(I, 1: ll. 200-205)

Frequently throughout the play, characters may shift to rhymed couplets, sometimes in the middle of a speech (i.e., IV, 1: ll. 214-221).

In other tragedies, Shakespeare will alternate blank verse with prose, sometimes to distinguish nobles from commoners, and sometimes for speeches with a more prosaic content. In all the plays, *stychomythia* is employed, sometimes in blank verse, and at other times in prose. Despite the tendency of the language of Shakespeare's tragedies occasionally to be more realistic than that of the Greeks, it should be stressed that in the former, blank verse is the predominant mode. When other ingredients of language such as choice of words, sounds, poetic contractions, formal use of "thee" and "thou," frequent use of metaphor, poetic images, and classical allusions are taken into consideration, the overall spoken effect of Shakespearean tragedy is by no means realistic.

The major problem in acting Shakespeare in the twentieth century has centered on the question of how to "handle" Shakespeare's diction. On the one hand, we have had the school that is overly conscious of the vocal range and utterance required for Shakespeare; and on the other, those who want to make his characters sound like "real" people by ignoring the poetic devices used by the playwright, suggesting that the words will take care of themselves. The first group is aware primarily of sound, while the second is concerned primarily with sense. What neither school seems to realize is that in the hands of a good dramatic poet, sound and sense are one, and the good actor will know how to relate them.

EXERCISES

1. Analyze the literal meaning of the following lines from *Richard II:*

    Richard: Down, down I come, like glistering Phaëton,
    Wanting the manage of unruly jades.
    In the base court? Base court, where kings grow base,
    To come at traitors' calls and do them grace.
    In the base court? Come down? Down court! Down King!
    For night owls shriek where mounting larks should sing.

    (III, 3: ll. 178-183)

    Literally, Richard is saying that he will descend from the ramparts. He compares himself to Phaëton, son of Apollo, who as he rode through the air, lost control of his horses (unruly jades) and plunged to his death. He plays on the term "base court," which means lower courtyard, and converts its physical connotation to a qualitative one. "Lower" becomes lowly, rank, despicable. He himself will become debased by descending and complying with the wishes of traitors. Finally, both court and king will be unnaturally debased, and, metaphorically speaking, the court will become a place where the cacophony of "night owls" (traitors) replaces the sweet and more appropriate music of the "mounting larks" (beings who maintain their exalted positions).

2. Read the speech neutrally for its literal connotation. Read it honestly and with the intensity it demands, but keep your reading "neutral," i.e., do not try to apply expressive sounds or to "color" the language. Does this reading satisfy you?

3. Now analyze how Shakespeare has "orchestrated" this speech by his selection of words and their sounds, and the images they suggest.

"Down, down I come,"

Note how both meaning and sound combine to suggest a descending quality in the voice. The vowel sound in "down" is a diphthong *(da-own),* which forces the voice to glide downward on "-own." It is repeated twice and completed with "come," which must be pitched as low or lower than the second "down." Note that Shakespeare repeats "down" consecutively. Try saying, "Down I come," just once. By itself it is somewhat literal. When you say it twice, with the second "down" lower pitched than the first, the full magnitude of the fall is conveyed; there is now a *sense* or *feeling* of falling, which is likened to Phaëton's fall from the heavens to the earth.

"Like glistering Phaëton, / Wanting the manage of unruly jades."

It is important here to imagine the beautiful son of Apollo, with whom Richard identifies, riding high in the heavens, close to the sun, whose dazzling light is reflected by Phaëton, a godlike youth, and his golden chariot. The sibilant sound of "glistering," plus the image it creates, is a contrast to the extended "O's" of "down" and "come." The combination of Richard's attitude, the sounds, and images of his language force the voice to soar back up.

"In the base court?"

Richard now recalls that he has been asked to come down to the base court.

"Base court, where kings grow base, / To come at traitors' calls

and do them grace."

He recognizes the ironic double entendre, and stresses the word "base" twice, emphasizing its derogatory meaning. "Traitors" is also derogatory, for it clearly is demeaning for kings to pay grace to traitors. The entire line must be pitched low.

"In the base court? Come down?"

These two questions may be subject to several interpretations. They might, with the remaining lines, confirm the judgment of Northumberland, who says, "Sorrow and grief of heart / Makes him speak fondly (foolishly) like a frantic man." Another possibility, however, is that of Richard repeating the request of his opponents for a second time, but now with an indignant sense of the humiliation of the descent. In his eyes, he has not simply been asked physically to come down, but to surrender his exalted position. Both remarks are interrogatory, requiring an upward inflection.

"Down court! Down King!"

As with the beginning of this speech, "down" is repeated twice and accompanied by the "o" of "court." The sense here is that if he comes down (falls), everything comes down. The sound of the extended "o's" makes for low ominous tones, becoming lower and lower with the literal descent suggested by the words.

"For night owls shriek where mounting larks should sing."

The traitors are the night owls, and in their triumph, their shrieks replace the harmony of an ordered world where the rightful king is ruler. The image of birds of the night (as opposed to "glistering Phaëton"), and the continued "o" sound in "owls" suggest a continuation of a lowered pitch, but "shriek" ("sh-ree-k") follows, then is contrasted, with its harsh consonant and rending vowel, with "mounting larks"—soaring birds—that sing rather than shriek. "Mount" reverses "down," and "sing" "shriek," in sound as well as sense.

The sounds of the words that Shakespeare has selected and ordered become aural reinforcements to the literal meaning of the speech. Sounds and images suggesting high and low, descending and ascending, expand the audience's response on imaginative and emotional levels. To speak such a speech "neutrally" is to limit such responses.

It is clear that the actor must be aware of the differences between poetic and prosaic speech, yet there may be pitfalls in such awareness. One is the tendency of some actors to become too conscious of speaking poetry, with the result that they begin to concentrate upon the sounds of their own voices. Words and sounds then are spoken with a sense of their effects only, and belief in the desires and conflicts within the characters is either minimized or generalized. But the poetic dramatist is not simply writing poetry; he is not concerned with creating pretty speeches for actors to recite in order to demonstrate their vocal virtuosity. He is, first of all, a creator of plot and character, and his use of language is based upon the most effective ways of expressing a character's needs, attitudes, feelings, and personal traits.

The speech from *Richard II* that has been analyzed has been well-orchestrated and contains some stunning images, but there is not a word or a sound that does not communicate the character and plight of a despairing king clinging to the notion of his divine right. The actor's responsibility in poetic drama is somehow to understand and make use of the devices of poetry, while at the same time realizing that they are the utterances of believable human beings. Let us now consider some of the common problems that confront the actor of Elizabethan poetic drama, along with some suggestions for coping with them.

MEANING

A prominent contemporary director once remarked that it wasn't terribly important for the actor to understand the more obscure words in Shakespeare because the audience wouldn't understand them anyway.   One can only hope that he was joking, for the actor must understand all the words he is to speak if he is to make clear to the audience the context in which those words are spoken.   Each word can only be uttered in terms of its meaning or of the image that it conveys.   An audience may not comprehend the exact meaning of "glistering Phaëton wanting the manage of unruly jades," but the actor who understands the mythological reference and its purpose, will say the line (and perhaps gesture) in such a way as to suggest the blinding fall of a golden god.   The actor's awareness that the character compares his fate to such an archetype will influence the way in which he utters the phrase, and this in itself will convey some sort of meaning to an audience.   His understanding of "base court" and the play on the word "base" is essential for the ironic and bitter tones with which they must be uttered if they are to have any effect on an audience.   The actor should study his speeches carefully, and not take anything for granted.   The meaning of words often may be determined by their context, but the actor would be wise to consult Shakespeare glossaries and dictionaries.   The Furness *Variorum* editions of Shakespeare provide detailed interpretations of obscure and ambiguous terms.

EXERCISES

1.   Study Richard's soliloquy in Pomfret castle (V, 5: ll. 1-66).   Read it aloud *before* investigating its obscure or ambiguous passages.   After you have done this, analyze the entire speech so that every word is intelligible to you.   Read the speech again, and note the many ways in which your expression and sense of security are affected.
2.   Learn one of the soliloquies listed at the end of Part IV so that you may independently apply the materials under investigation.   Start by interpreting the meaning of the entire speech.

IMAGES

The advantage of dramatic poetry over prose is that it can provide an additional stimulus for sensory and emotional expression.   In the first part of this book, it was demonstrated how the actor's recollection of his own sensory and emotional experiences might assist him in achieving honest and sometimes unique expression. This method depended on remembered images to touch off appropriate responses. The images provided in the language of a poetic dramatist such as Shakespeare can be, if properly visualized, just as effective a stimulus. Already we have observed the effect of comprehending, and consequently *visualizing,* "glistering Phaëton."

The poetic dramatist, as stated before, does not simply create sounds and images in order to prettify or embroider his language. Essentially, if he is a good dramatic poet, his concern is to aid us in comprehending his characters' imaginative, sensory, and emotional capacities. He is not satisfied merely to inform us what they think and feel, but to thoroughly explore *how* they think and feel. King Richard, in his "down, down I come . . ." speech, could merely have said very tragically, "I'm coming down and I debase myself in doing so." But the language that Shakespeare has chosen not only informs the actor and the audience of Richard's proclivity for self-dramatization, but communicates his sense of the awesome enormity of his fall. The actor must respond to the images by visualizing them in clear detail and responding to them with the despair or passion that they provoke.

EXERCISES

---

1. Following is a paraphrasing of Richard's famous "graves, worms, epitaphs" soliloquy (III, 2: II. 144-177). Read it aloud:

    Nothing matters any more. Don't anyone try to comfort me. Let's just talk about death. After all, everything which was ours belongs to Bolingbroke except our graves. Let's sit on the ground and talk about the way kings die—or are murdered. Death is always there, looking on, while we kings fool ourselves with our power, our vanity, our "invincibility." But when Death is ready, the king, like any other mortal, must go. Stop treating me like something special. I have the same needs as all men, so how do I deserve to be called "king"?

    This can be read with the same despair that motivates the character, and can convey the basic notion that is to be communicated, but lost are the sounds and images that stress the nature of death and decay; of the symbol of the crown as a place where death keeps court rather than its wearer; of the power of death, which can bore through a castle wall with a little pin and puncture the grand illusions of monarchs. But even these interpretive words fall short of the effect of the actor *imagining* the images and responding to them as he speaks them.

2. Read lines 160-170, and do the following:

    Take off your crown (imagined or otherwise) after ". . . all murdered," hold it in front of you, then speak the first line. On "Keeps Death his Court," see a black cloaked figure with a grinning skull perched upon the edge of the crown. On "Scoffing his state" to "vain conceit," imagine yourself as king, foolishly going through motions of pomp, power, and "vain conceit." On "this flesh which walls about our life," imagine a strong metal barrier. On "Comes at the last," see the image of death, still grinning, touch the wall with a little pin, crumbling it easily, spread his cloak and, on "Farewell! King!", cover the crown completely.

How do these images make you respond in terms of concentration? Vocal expression? Gesture? Facial expression?

3.   Using the soliloquy you have selected from another Shakespearean play, find the images and determine their effect on your delivery.

POETIC FORMS

Meter. For the most part, Shakespeare's verse is written in iambic pentameter. The actor must be aware of it and avoid violating it. But often there are metrical changes, and when this occurs, the actor must scrupulously observe them. In the following speech (III, 2: ll. 145-177) of thirty-two lines, nearly the entire first half is almost exclusively in iambics:

> Let's talk/of graves,/of worms/and ep/itaphs,
>
> Make dust/ our pa/per and/with rai/ny eyes
>
> Write sor/row on/the bos/om of t/he earth.

But line 163 begins with a trochee:

> Scoffing/ his state/ and gri/nning at/ his pomp

as do lines 169, 170, and 171. In each of these instances, the shift to a trochee cannot be argued because it corresponds to the sense of the line. But there are times when the metrical intention may be interpreted differently, resulting in a choice between several possible meanings, as occurs in the last line of the same speech:

> How _can_ / you say / to me / I am / a King?

or

> _How_ can / you say / to me / I am / a King?

or

> _How_ can / you say / to me / _I_ am / a King?

One of the problems encountered by the actor of Shakespearean roles occurs when he permits meter to become monotonously regular. This can occur when the actor insists on adhering to iambics even when the text suggests otherwise. More often it occurs when the actor's awareness of meter becomes more important than meaning, or when he subconsciously falls into a metrical pattern that sounds like doggerel. Concentration upon thoughts and images, however, will stimulate different stresses, pauses, changes of tempo, inflection, and volume, so that while the meter remains consistent, it does not dominate our response to the language. The speech with which we have been concerned is an interesting one because a large portion of it actually is dominated by the regularity of its meter. It is a mournful, despairing, deliberately monotonous dirge, with only subtle variations until Shakespeare introduces the trochee (l. 163)—where the image of Death as an antic watching the deluded king requires an ironic, mocking tone. The third trochee that begins a line ("Cover your heads . . .") is a complete shift from Richard's introspection to a command. It calls for an increase in volume, and perhaps in speed. The stressed syllables of "Cover," "mock," and "Throw away" are stronger than other stressed syllables in the speech. Yet, even with these variations in delivery, the iambic meter thoroughly dominates.

Another trap into which the actor frequently falls occurs when he gives the last word in each line the same stress:

Let's talk of graves, of worms and epitaphs,*

Make dust our paper and with rainy eyes

Write sorrow on the bosom of the earth.

Let's choose executors and talk of wills

And yet not so, for what can we bequeath

Save our deposed bodies to the ground?

Not only will such a pattern become inappropriately monotonous, but the last word in each line receives an additional emphasis that is not always correct.

* The double line (//) indicates a heavier stress.

EXERCISE

Scan your selected soliloquy and determine its meter. Is it always regular? If not, how do the metrical variations affect your reading? If it consists of fairly uninterrupted iambics, what justifications are there for variety?

Rhymed couplets. Much of what has been said about meter can be applied to the reading of rhymed couplets. They have been worked into the language for a reason, and the actor must recognize their existence and accept the formalism they impose. In Act IV, Scene 1 (the so-called "deposition" scene) in *Richard II,* Richard often shifts from blank verse to rhymed couplets. For example, in his soliloquy beginning on line 200 and ending on line 221 (he has a half line more, which is completed by Bolingbroke, but it is a transition line following a complete body of thought), Richard begins with a rhymed couplet, follows with eleven lines of unrhymed verse, and returns to rhymed couplets for the next eight lines. The speech is almost equally divided between blank verse and rhymed couplets. Actually the entire speech is ritualistic as the king emphasizes the procedural quality of his abdication ("Now mark me how I will undo myself."). Its meter is regular and there is a strong use of repetition. Lines 204-206 end with "head," "hand," "heart"; lines 207-210 begin with "With mine own . . . ," and each of these lines also contains references to parts of Richards body: "tears," "hands," "tongue," "breath." Lines 211-214 end with similes: "forswear," "forgo," and "deny."

Then Richard moves into the use of couplets, as though to intensify and bring the ritual to a climax. The speech might almost be sung or chanted. The actor recognizing this intent will then exploit the character's conscious and deliberate efforts to ritualize. Too often the modern actor, steeped in realism, tries to obscure the formalistic qualities of poetry by underplaying or "throwing away" the words that form the couplets, sometimes mumbling them or rapidly moving on to the first word in the next line.

At the opposite extreme are those who chant without sense or subtext, and those who unconsciously utter the rhymed words with exactly the same double emphasis and downward inflection, as is the case with the monotonous delivery of poetic meter.

The solution, in both cases, is the same. The actor must concentrate upon his subtext, upon his justifications for saying what the character says, and upon the emotions and attitudes that underlie his utterances and allusions. In *Richard II,* the protagonist seems to relish self-dramatization, and prefers to reflect, philosophize, and even poetize the events rather than to take action. The abdication speech is a conscious effort at language formalization by the character. At the same time, beneath his outward show, his heart is breaking; during the scene he constantly refers to his grief and his tears. Even while ritualizing his offer of crown and scepter, he cannot bear to part with them. As he moves into the artifice of couplets, he is ironically reproachful toward his enemies when he declares, "God pardon all oaths that are broke to me!/ God keep all vows unbroke that swear to thee!" And at the end, in bidding Henry long life, he sinks into his preoccupation with death and nothingness.

These are the things on which the actor must concentrate in performance, and if he does nothing to obscure poetic artifices such as rhyming couplets, the poetry will take care of itself.

EXERCISES

One actor and one actress should read ll. 81-102 from the farewell scene in *Richard II* (V, 1):
1. Placing strong emphasis on the last word of each line.
2. Trying to avoid *any* emphasis on the last word of each line.
3. Placing emphasis wherever meaning and character attitudes dictate.

    The rhymed couplets provide a formalism—a kind of ceremonial farewell —that cannot be ignored, but the scene is one in which the characters are deeply affected by their parting.

PUNCTUATION

PROLOGUE: If we offend, it is with our goodwill.
    That you should think, we come not to offend,
But with goodwill. To show our simple skill,
    That is the true beginning of our end.
Consider, then, we come but in despite.
    We do not come, as minding to content you,
Our true intent is. All for your delight,

We are not here. That you should here repent you,
The actors are at hand, and, by their show,
You shall know all, that you are like to know.

THESEUS: This fellow doth not stand upon points.

LYSANDER: He hath rid his prologue like a rough colt, he knows
not the stop. A good moral, my lord. It is not enough to speak,
but to speak true.

HIPPOLYTA: Indeed he hath played on his prologue like a child on a
recorder—a sound, but not in government.

THESEUS: His speech was like a tangled chain—nothing impaired, but
all disordered. Who is next?

(*Midsummer Night's Dream*, V, 1: ll. 108-126)

There is controversy over much of the punctuation in Shakespeare's texts.
This is due to suspected inaccuracies and ambiguities in the quarto and folio
editions. Later editors attempted to correct the punctuation according to
their interpretations, but some of these corrections are also disputable. For
example, if you were to use the text of *Richard II* edited by G.B. Harrison,
you would find in Richard's soliloquy in Act V, Scene 1, a comma used in
the middle of line 5:

I cannot do it, yet I'll hammer it out.

The first folio edition, however, uses a colon:

I cannot do it: yet I'll hammer it out.

Each punctuation mark suggests a different reading. The comma suggests
the briefest of pauses, if any, and excludes the possibility of a transition.
This would indicate that from his first sentence Richard has already decided
that, despite the discrepancies in his analogy of his prison and the world,
he'll work out a solution anyway. This would appear to contradict the
finality of "I cannot do it . . . ," and the suggestion of a spontaneous deter-
mination to do so with the word "yet." A colon or a period, then, seems
more suitable, because it dictates a pause for reflection after deciding the
analogy would be fallacious.

Another aspect of punctuation that seems to trouble some actors of poetic drama is the run-on line. The end of a line written in iambic pentameter does not always end with a period or a comma. Actors who memorize
lines by recalling the way they are printed, or who mistakenly believe that

the end of a line completes a sentence, inflect downward and/or stress
the final word in a line, then follow it with a pause. On occasion, even when
there is no period at the end of a line, this tendency may be suitable, as in
the following:

> *And nothing can we call our own but* death//
> *And that small model of the barren earth.*
>
> (Richard II, III, 2: ll. 152-153)

> *...and humored thus//*
> *Comes at the last ...*
>
> (ll. 168-169)

But in the same speech, there are several occasions when the line should run
on to the words that begin the following line:

> *Cover your heads and mock not flesh and blood*
> *With solemn reverence. ...*
>
> (ll. 171-172)

Punctuation is a guide to meaning, but the actor must use common sense
for oral punctuation by ascertaining for himself the meaning of every speech
and the mental processes that justify their utterance. We have already seen
that sometimes textual punctuation may be misleading; more often, the
spoken speech requires more that the text provides. The following extract
from *Richard II* begins and ends with a comma, but there is no punctuation
indicated in between:

> *..., and humored thus*
> *Comes at the last and with a little pin*
> *Bores through his castle wall, ...*
>
> (ll. 168-170)

The actor, however, can justify the addition of the following oral punctuation:

> *..., and humored thus/*
> *Comes at the last/ and with a little pin/*
> *Bores through his castle wall, ...*

227

EXERCISES

Apply the following things to your selected or assigned soliloquy:

1. If your speech contains rhymed couplets, determine where the stresses should be, and which word or words in each line have the strongest stress.
2. Analyze the punctuation of your speech as it appears in your copy of the play. Do you agree with the punctuation that is printed?
3. Are there lines in your selection that end with no punctuation?   Which of these should be run-on lines?
4. Phrase your lines according to the printed punctuation only. Now add any phrasing that you feel will make the lines clearer and make you more comfortable. Make comparisons; do not be reluctant to admit it if your innovations prove to be ineffective.

SPEED

The fearful passage of their death-marked love,
And the continuance of their parents' rage,
Which, but their children's end, naught could remove,
Is now the two hours traffic of our stage.

This innocuous reference by the chorus in the prologue to *Romeo and Juliet* to "the two hours traffic of our stage" has led to unfortunate excesses by those who have used it to justify the acting of Shakespeare at breakneck speed. There was apparently good cause for the movement to increase the tempo of Shakespearean production in the modern theatre. Sir Harley Granville-Barker, in his *Prefaces to Shakespeare,* informs us that English speech in the eighteenth and nineteenth centuries had slowed down, "and, in the nineteenth, as far as Shakespeare was concerned, it grew slower and slower, till on occasions one thought—even hoped—that shortly the actor would stop altogether."[1] He places the blame for the slowdown on actors' efforts to make antiquated phrases understood, and on the increasing size of the physical theatre. In addition, there was the effort of the actor to enable the audience to appreciate the "eloquence" and "poetry" of the Divine Bard, not to mention the beauty and virtuosity of his own voice and diction.

Unfortunately, as is often the case, one excess simply replaced another, and acceleration replaced deceleration; the actor was now directed to race rather than plod. Whereas the audience had been lulled to sleep by the actor's efforts to enable it to understand and appreciate Shakespeare's language, it now was left confused (and ultimately as bored) by his efforts to "energize" Shakespeare. The fact is that simplistic generalizations about tempo are anathema to the acting of drama in any period or in any style, because they force the actor to concentrate upon effect rather than upon principles of adaptation and communion. Language is the handmaiden of character; when it stops expressing one's thoughts, attitudes, desires, and emotions it ceases to be dramatic. When the actor uses language purely for its own sake, he ceases to be dramatic.

It is true that plays have their own tempos and will vary in overall patterns of speed. A melodrama such as *The Front Page* demands the effect of a rapid typewriter, while *The Three Sisters* will be much more leisurely, but the pace of each play is determined by the justification of the characters, their environments, their life styles, and the circumstances in which they find themselves—*not* because someone has pronounced that melodrama should be fast and Chekhovian drama should be slow. Shakespearean tragedy as a rule is vigorous and contains much action that is swift, but it is also contemplative and subject to moods best expressed by more measured tempos.

A good example of the wide range and variety of speed possible in Shakespearean tragedy occurs in Act III, Scene 2 of *Richard II,* during which the king's virtually manic alternation of exhilaration and despair requires strongly contrasting tempos. In his first long speech, "Needs must I like it well . . ." (ll. 4-26), Richard sentimentally greets the land from which he has been long absent, then calls upon it to rid him of his foes. The speech is measured and moderately paced, starting slowly but quickening in intensity as he refers to his enemies. When the Bishop of Carlisle and Aumerle tactfully suggest that Richard replace fancy with action, he reassures them with confident rhetoric filled with images of glowing strength, using verbs such as "fires" and "darts," which suggest quickness. He slows down to moralize that "Not all the water in the rough rude sea/ Can wash the balm off from an anointed King," then quickens his pace on "For every man that Bolingbroke hath pressed . . . ," building to the climactic image of glorious angels fighting for his right.

As soon as Salisbury brings the bad news about the deserting Welshmen, Richard immediately is plunged into despair: "Have I not reason to look pale and dead?," suggesting a much slower pace. Almost immediately, reacting to Aumerle's few words of comfort, Richard snaps out of it and berates himself being so forgetful: "Awake, thou coward majesty! Thou sleepest." His rediscovered self-assurance will encourage a more rapid tempo. As worse news follows, Richard's confidence ebbs, but his immediate responses now are bitter attacks upon his former allies, and require rapidity—especially in his "Oh, villains, vipers, damned without redemption!" speech, after which he appears to have become drained of his will, settling into the somber mournfulness of "Let's talk of graves, of worms and epitaphs . . ."

It is true that the contemporary ear is unaccustomed to the syntax and idiom of the Elizabethans, perhaps making it often necessary for the actor to phrase a bit more deliberately in striving for clarity. On such occasions, the actor must never make his audience suspect that this is his purpose. He should never sacrifice clarity for speed, but at the same time he must never allow his clarity to become patronizing.

EXERCISES

1. Study John of Gaunt's speech about England in Act II, Sc. 1 of *Richard II* (ll. 31-68). After you have analyzed it for meaning and for Gaunt's objective in speaking it, determine with what speed it should be spoken. Take into consideration the following factors:
   a. Gaunt's age
   b. Gaunt's physical condition
   c. The nature of the images that are evoked
   d. Gaunt's attitudes toward the subjects of his speech
   e. Justifications for acceleration and/or deceleration during the speech.

2. Experiment with tempo in your selected or assigned soliloquy:
   a. Try speaking it as rapidly as possible, but with clarity of enunciation and phrasing.
   b. Try speaking it slowly and deliberately, making all of it ponderously clear.
   c. Concentrate upon meaning and character and allow your interpretation to motivate speed.

While the truly interpretative method (c) should provide the best reading, (a) and (b) should be taken seriously. They provide good exercises in control, and may be effective in dealing with the actor's personal tendency to speak too rapidly or too slowly.

THE SOLILOQUY

The realistic proscenium theatre discouraged the use of soliloquies and asides, and attempted in the performance of older plays to keep those conventions behind the "fourth wall," suggesting that the characters were merely thinking aloud to themselves. The result was often even less realistic than talking to the audience, and sometimes absurdly ineffectual. While we cannot be certain about the Elizabethan actor's delivery of soliloquies, many of these passages strongly suggest that they be directed to the audience. When Iago, alone, asks with mock innocence, "And what's he then that says I play the villain?" (*Othello,* II, 3: l. 342), it makes little sense to suppose that he is talking to himself. He takes an enormous pleasure in *sharing* his wickedness with the only ones who can't do *anything* about it: the audience. The same might be said for Edmund and Richard III, and for most of Shakespeare's villains.

But there are soliloquies that might well be interpreted as introspective, in which the character actually is contemplating aloud to himself. Hamlet might address the audience on "Oh what a rogue and peasant slave am I!" (II, 2: l. 576), but his "To be or not to be" (III, 1: l. 56) could easily be internalized. Richard II has only one soliloquy alone onstage, when he opens the scene in his prison at Pomfret Castle (V, 5). A sense of his isolation, and of his efforts to keep his mind occupied, might appear to be better served as internal rather than including the audience. Essentially, it seems wiser to avoid a dogmatic approach to this aspect of the soliloquy, and to allow the actor and director to determine how each passage is better served in terms of the nature of the speech itself and the need of the character who is speaking.

EXERCISE

Using your chosen soliloquy, try delivering it two ways. First, enact it as though it is purely contemplative, and avoid a breakthrough of the "fourth wall." Then present it directly to an audience. Which way works better?

Once the decision is made that certain speeches are to be addressed to the audience, the actor must be able to manage his relationship to the audience. He is better off and more comfortable if he treats the audience as another character in the play; in other words, he uses the same principles of relating, adapting to, and communing with it. He should, as a character, desire to share his thoughts and plans with his viewers. Invariably, the speaker of a soliloquy in Shakespeare is totally honest with the audience. Iago has nothing to lose by letting us in on his deviltry; what he gains is the satisfaction of knowing that someone in this world can appreciate, if not approve of, his magnificent guile. The actor must adopt an attitude toward his listeners. If Richard II is to address his final soliloquy to the audience, the decision must be justified by his desire to inform it of how he has been spending his time, and to share his new-formed view of himself and the world.

When the actor engages his audience in this way, he should avoid both of two extremes: he should not appear to be making a speech over the heads of his viewers, nor should he discomfort the audience by deliberate and sustained eye contact.

Another common problem in the performance of Shakespearean tragedy is the delivery of a well-known speech. Often the first thought of the actor who must deliver "All the world's a stage," "Romeo, Romeo, wherefore art thou Romeo?," "To be or not to be," "Friends, Romans, Countrymen," etc., is: "How can I do this differently?" This is only natural, but it is a mistake. There is only one way to interpret any speech, and that is on the basis of the character's justification in uttering it. When the actor begins such a speech, it is difficult to ignore the fact that the audience knows it as well as he, is anticipating its every word, and usually has its own conceptions of precisely how that speech is supposed to be enacted. Instead of saying to himself, "I'm going to surprise them," the actor had best decide what the speech is all about, what stimulus has necessitated it, what the character's objective is in speaking it, and what emotional or attitudinal factors it entails.

Finally, the actor must determine how much movement and gesture are justified during his soliloquies. Once again, contemporary actors tend toward one of two extremes. Some, venerating the language, believe that movement or gesture will be distracting, and deliver their soliloquies like operatic arias; others, in order to avoid such stilted delivery, fill the speeches with "business," and in essence obscure their language, and consequently, their meaning. Once again the best course of action is to move and gesture on the basis of what the character, the circumstances, and the language make you *want* to do. There are no set rules or restrictions regarding the relation between Shakespeare's language and the actor's physicalization because the characters and moods of his plays are so variable. The quietly introspective and simple nature of Hamlet's "To be or not to be . . ." is probably best played with a minimum of movement or gesture, while Mercutio's flamboyant Queen Mab speech in *Romeo and Juliet* (V, iv) may justify considerable choreography and illustrative invention.

The following is an example of a possible movement and "business" pattern for Richard's prison soliloquy in Act V, Sc. 5 of *Richard II*. It should be stressed that this example is but one of many methods that may be employed by the actor to project honestly the imprisoned monarch's thoughts and emotions.

Richard begins his speech by stating that he has been trying to make an analogy between his prison and the world. The scene might begin with Richard silently contemplating such a comparison. He could be standing to one side of the stage, looking at the space of his cell. After a few moments, he shakes his head and speaks:

> *I have been studying how I may compare*
> *This prison* (gesture toward cell space) *where I*
>   *live unto the world* (look up and spread arms),
> *And for because the world is populous,*
> *And here* (arms drop straight down, indicating his
>   prison world) *is not a creature but myself,*
> *I cannot do it.* (Shrug, pause, then decide to work
>   it out anyway. Determined.) *Yet I'll*
>   *hammer it out* (sit at stool center. Pause and
>   begin to think it through)
> *My brain I'll prove the female to my soul,*
> *My soul the father, and these two beget*
> *A generation of still breeding thoughts,*
> *And these same thoughts people this little world*
>   (gesture toward cell space around him)
> *In humors like the people of this world,*
> *For no thought is contented.* (Lean back, trying
>   to find first thought. Pantomime, "aha! I have it!")
>   *The better sort,*
> *As thoughts of things divine, are intermixed*
> *With scruples, and do set the word itself* (extend
>   lower arm palm upward as though weighing
>   *"the word itself"*)

Against the word (extend other arm, palm upward, to
   indicate other word of equal weight).
As thus, "Come (stretch out arm invitingly) *little
   ones," and then again,* (raise same arm, palm
   outward, as though creating a barrier)
"It is as hard to come (shaking head negatively) *as
   for a camel
To thread the postern of a small needle's eye."*
   (Drop arm.   New thought comes.)
*Thoughts tending to ambition; they do plot
Unlikely wonders—how* (extend both lower arms forward,
   palms down, looking at fingernails) *these vain
   weak nails
May tear a passage* (bend fingers like claws)
   *through the flinty ribs
Of this hard world, my ragged prison walls*
   (visualize walls straight ahead)
And, for they cannot, die (drop hands between legs)
   in their own pride. (New pause.   Thought.)
*Thoughts tending to content flatter themselves
That they are not the first of fortune's slaves,
Nor shall not be the last, like silly beggars
Who, sitting in the stocks* (hold arms outward making
   fists, *and* stretch legs forward as though wrists
   and legs are locked in stocks)
   *refuge their shame,
That many have and others must sit there.
And in this thought they find a kind of ease* (open
   fists, relaxing hands),
*Bearing their own misfortunes on the back
Of such as have before endured the like.*
   (Put hands in lap and bring legs back to normal
   position on following line)
*Thus played in one person many people,
And none contented.* (erect posture, head high on:)
      *Sometimes am I King,
Then treasons make me wish myself a beggar,* (slump)
*And so I am.   Then crushing penury
Persuades me I was better when a king.
Then I am kinged again* (head erect as though being
   crowned) *And by and by*

Think that I am unkinged by Bolingbroke,
And straight am nothing. (Pause. Images of death,
    nothingness) *But whate'er I be,*
Nor I nor any man but what man is
With nothing shall be pleased till he be eased
With being nothing. (Pause. Music sounds. Richard
    listens.) *Music do I hear?* (Rise, move toward
    door—or direction of music. Listens, perhaps
    beats time with hand, then notices missed
    timing)
Ha! ha! Keep time. How sour sweet music is
When time is broke and no proportion kept! (Thinks
    sorrowfully of his own wasted and discordant
    time as he leans back against door)
So it is in the music of men's lives.
And here have I the daintiness of ear
To check time broke in a disordered string,
But for the concord of my state and time
Had not an ear to hear my true time broke. (With agony)
I wasted time, and now doth time waste me.
For now hath Time made me his numbering clock. (See
    image of clock, and visualize self as clock,
    with hands stretched sideways)
My thoughts are minutes and with sighs they jar
Their watches on unto mine eyes (point hands inward,
    fingers touching eyes), *the outward watch,*
Whereto my finger, like a dial's point,
Is pointing still (shut eyes in pain), *in cleansing*
    them from tears. (Pull self together to complete analogy)
Now sir, the sound that tells what hour it is
Are clamorous groans, which strike (hit heart with
    fist) *upon my heart,*
Which is the bell. (Pause) *So sighs and tears and groans*
Show minutes, times, and hours. (Bitterly:) *But my time*
Runs posting on in Bolingbroke's proud joy
While I stand (reveal self mockingly) *fooling here,*
    his Jack-o'-the-clock. (Hands on ears, move
    forward, away from door:)
This music mads me, let it sound no more,
For though it have help madmen to their wits,
    (Sit on stool, still clutching ears.)

In me it seems it will make wise men mad.
  (Long pause; Richard drops hands slowly, looks
  up with a kind of amazement.)
Yet blessing on his heart that gives it me!
For 'tis a sign of love, and love to Richard
Is a strange brooch in this all-hating world.

EXERCISES

1. Work out movement and business for your assigned soliloquy. See if the following procedure is helpful:
    a. Determine what the scene represents, and visualize the quality of your space.
    b. Can you justify the use of properties? If so, determine the logical place for them.
    c. Do not work out your movement and business mechanically. When you feel that you understand all the ramifications of your speech, begin to relate yourself to your space. Where should you be at the start of the speech? What stimulus has provoked your decision?
    d. Begin the soliloquy, and without premeditated action, allow yourself to respond to your thoughts and feelings as the character. Use sense and emotion memory when you can in order to stimulate honest physical responses.
    e. Eliminate anything that feels awkward or untruthful. Select and sharpen what appears to work for you.
2. After working out a scheme, enact the soliloquy again with as much honesty and intensity as you can, but make it purely internal: eliminate all movement and gesture. How does this feel? Do you find that you are too restricted? Do some things actually work better now with less movement?

MANNER OF DELIVERY

We have talked about how Shakespeare's language may justify movement and business, but not about the manner of delivery and its relationship to movement and business. Shakespearean character and costume will have

236

FIGURE 11-1. *Richard Pasco in the Royal Shakespeare Company*
production of Richard II. *Photo by Cock's Studio, Stratford-Upon-Avon.*

FIGURE 11-2. *Ian Richardson in the Royal Shakespeare Company production of* Richard II. *Photo by Cock's Studio, Stratford-Upon-Avon.*

a bearing on manner, and these will be discussed shortly. For now, the question of the influence of Shakespeare's dramatic poetry is the issue.

Shakespeare's language is generally straightforward and direct. Words rather than pauses (although pauses are essential for logic, mood, and dramatic impact) convey what is necessary to know about character. This means that the words cannot be mumbled or slurred. *Everything* must be clearly enunciated. It would be inconsistent, then, for movement and gesture to be sloppy and slurred. Little, careless half-gestures from the wrists or elbows, shuffling feet, and random nods with the head are generally out-of-place with Shakespeare's diction.

His language is not the language of commonplace conversation or expression. Its phrasing, word usage, and metrical form collectively do not permit casualness in speech delivery, posture, movement, and gesture. The actor must be relaxed, yes, but only in the sense of avoiding tension. Speech and movement are sharp, energetic, precise, and always controlled. Interjections of "uh's," naturalistic tendencies to run sentences together, and nasality will almost invariably contradict the nature of the language and its formal structure. Jokes have been made about a popular movie star in period films in which his Bronx speech proved to be embarrassingly incongruous. But Americans from other regions also have difficulties, such as contracting words, running them together, and failing to enunciate consonants sharply enough. The following is a typical, unexaggerated example of the kind of speech one can sometimes expect in American productions of *Hamlet:*

> *T'be or not t'be—thadis the queschin.*
> *Whether 'tis nobler in the mine t'suffer*
> *The slings an darrows of outrageous forchin,*
> *Or ta take arms against a sea a troubles*
> *An by opposing endem. T'die, t'sleep—*
> *No more, n'by a sleep t'say we end*
> *The heartache n' the thousan nacheral shocks*
> *That flesh is heir ta.*
>
> (III,1)

We have seen that Shakespeare's language makes regular use of metaphor, imagery, fanciful allusions, and phraseology. None of his passages can be spoken in the casual manner of everyday speech. The actor must make such language his own, but must speak it with the size and dimension that it demands, and with a corresponding mode of movement and gesture. Shakespeare himself provided very good advice in Hamlet's speech to the players, in which his admonishment against vocal and bodily excesses might be applicable to any period (III, 2). But when he speaks of holding the mirror up to Nature, he is not necessarily advocating naturalism. As we shall observe later, the medieval concept of "mirror" has a special meaning, and the "nature" of which Hamlet speaks is based on sixteenth century conceptions of the human personality. The actor shows "the very age and body of his time, his form and pressure" (ll. 26-27), and the standard for his time is the *ideal* "accent" and "gait" of the sixteenth century Christian gentleman. Anyone who would interpret Hamlet's coaching as advocating naturalism is forgetting that most of Shakespeare's characters speak in blank verse.

EXERCISE

Speak your assigned soliloquy naturalistically; try to make it sound as much like your everyday speech as possible. Stand and move accordingly. It is important not to mock this procedure; perform honestly, but pretend you are in a play by Tennessee Williams or William Inge. Do you sense any incongruity? Do your viewers?

CHAPTER 12

Other Shakespearean Conventions

LANGUAGE AND CHARACTER

The language of Shakespeare's tragic protagonists reveals characters of breeding, intelligence, imagination, and in several instances, wit. From the quality of their speech alone it is clear that they are not ordinary men and women, but persons of stature and nobility who are fully aware of their responsibilities (as rulers, statesmen, officers, etc.) to their community and to the metaphysical order, of which the community is but a part. Richard II is a shallow, irresponsible king, but he, perhaps more than any of Shakespeare's other rulers, is aware of the external forms of his position. When he loses his crown, his awakening to his mortality endows him with a deeper and, ironically, a more divine dignity. Like the rest of Shakespeare's tragic heroes, crisis and suffering inspire closer inspection of man's condition in both the material and spiritual world. The loftiness of characters' positions and their metaphysical concerns justify the poetic and formalistic quality of their speech, which must inspire a corresponding physicality.

Unlike the Greeks, actors in Shakespearean tragedy do not wear masks. Nevertheless, the characters are structured on essences rather than on intricate psychological explorations. This is due in great part to conventions of the medieval dramatic forms from which the tragedies of Marlowe, Shakespeare, Webster, and Ford evolved. In the morality plays, characters were personifications of abstracted human qualities of the various forces of virtue and vice. Protagonists represent Mortal Man beset by externalized virtues

241

and vices as he journeys through life toward a hoped-for salvation. Shakespeare, of course, replaces abstractions with recognizable human beings, but more often than not he retains and emphasizes the struggle between good and evil forces (both within and without the protagonist) for a man's soul. Richard II, in the first half of the play, is seen subjected to the advice of both good (York, Gaunt) and evil (Bushby, Bagot, Green) counsel, as well as to his personal temptations of tyranny and excessive luxury. His character essence is arrogance, and is based upon the fallacious belief that since he is "the deputy anointed by the Lord," he can do no wrong.

Here another medieval influence upon character can be seen at work. "Histories" of kings and princes were a popular form of literature, but their purpose was less to report and objectify historical fact than to provide moral examples for the nobility to learn by. *The Mirror for Magistrates* was such a history, and the word "mirror" was understood as a moral lesson rather than a mere reflection. The characters that emerged were based principally upon the sin or error of the prince that contributed to his inevitable downfall. Unlike the mask in Greek tragedy, the "mask" in *Richard II* (and this is the case in most of his tragedies) begins to be replaced by a new one as the protagonist's downfall progresses. Richard submits without a struggle, though he chastizes and complains, and what emerges is a kind of philosopher-artist (actor-poet) who chooses to do no more than reflect ironically and fancifully on his newly discovered views.

While this kind of character delineation may be more complex than that of Greek tragedy, it remains far removed from naturalistic characterization. First, the concerns of Shakespeare's characters are more with the spiritual than the mundane. Except for deformities such as Richard III's twisted body, there is very little emphasis upon surface details of character, and little emphasis upon environmental influences on character. Second, we must take these characters as they are and not expect behavioristic explanations for their motives. We do not know what made Richard II selfish, vain, and arrogant, nor are we aware of what lies behind his failure to act or to choose the course he follows. He is defined by actions and choices themselves rather than by explanations of how they were motivated.

EXERCISE

Analyze your Shakespearean character in the usual way, but add the following questions:
1.   What is the social status of your character?
2.   What social qualities are revealed by his language?

3. What is his essence, and can you propose a "mask" that symbolizes it?
4. Does the "mask" change during the course of the play?   Explain.
5. What are the concerns of the character as he progresses throughout the play that relate to his justification for action and his response to his fate?

CLOTHING

The evidence provided by sketches and by allusions to dress in the plays reveals that the Elizabethan actor was clothed primarily in the fashion of his own time.   Unlike the theatre of the Greeks, there was no standardized theatrical costume.   The actors wore clothes appropriate to the status of their characters, and on occasion, as in the Roman plays, an item or two of Roman garb was mixed with Elizabethan clothing.

This is not the place to argue about the problems of costuming Shakespearean plays in today's theatre, which chiefly involve decisions concerning the use of historically and geographically accurate costumes versus Elizabethan costumes or the use of a time and place that touches neither place, but costuming implies some kind of special relevance by its use.   Our concern, as was the case with Greek tragedy, is with the relationship between the nature of the costumes for which the plays were written, their possible influence upon the plays' language and characters, and what effect all of this might have upon the actor's movement and speech.   Our emphasis upon Elizabethan dress is not meant to suggest that it is the only or the best costume solution, nor should it be assumed that all male and female characters in any of the plays wore precisely the combinations to be discussed.   For example, all characters probably did not wear a ruff; older nobles probably wore gowns rather than doublets and hose, ceremonial costumes were undoubtedly utilized, and the use of military garb was varied.   Nevertheless, as we shall see, certain qualities and effects are shared by all costumes worn by principal tragic characters.

Female Dress

As with the Greeks, men played women's roles in the Elizabethan theatre.   But the latter, with its more realistic costume conventions, offered clear-cut distinctions between the clothing of the sexes in everyday life.

243

FIGURE 12-1. *Elizabethan female costume. Painting by Elizabeth I by Marcus Gheeraerta, the younger, c. 1592. Reproduced by courtesy of the Trustees, The National Gallery, London.*

The basic female garment is the *farthingale,* which clothes the lower half of the body. It is a floor-length garment whose understructure of a bolster, or hoop, plus several skirts and petticoats, extended the hips and outer skirt far beyond the normal shape of the body. The Spanish far-thingale used a hoop and created a bell-shape, while the French farthingale created a square shape by using a bolster tied to the waist.

The torso was bound from the chest to below the abdomen by tight metal corsets; breasts were bound and pushed up, creating a flat-chested appearance, but permitting some cleavage to appear. A *stomacher,* which further flattened the front of the torso, might also be worn. It consisted of a triangular piece of cloth-covered wood that was tied to the torso from chest to abdomen.

Over the bodice and farthingale, a gown was worn. It was open at the front of the farthingale, revealing part of a fancy petticoat. The gown had sleeves that puffed out considerably to the wrist and often were slashed, revealing the sleeves of the chemise, or lining, beneath. Fancy collars gen-erally were worn at the neck. Sometimes a ruff was formed by the top of the chemise, or a separate thick ruff was worn in either an open or closed fashion. One of the extreme pieces worn was the *de Medici collar,* a wing-like structure stiffened by wire and worn from the shoulders to above the ears, and fancifully decorated.

Accessories included lots of jewelry: rings, sometimes one on each finger; beads, jewels in the hair and sewn into the gown. Women some-times held stiff, decorative fans, carried more for decorative than utilitarian purposes. Shoes were comparable to walking oxfords, with a two-inch heel. Head coverings included wigs that were shaped to permit high foreheads (shaved to emulate Queen Elizabeth's), and small decorative hats that often were perched on the side of the head.

INFLUENCE ON POSTURE AND MOVEMENT. The rigidity of the bodice, created by the corset and/or stomacher, forced the wearer to stand stiff and erect. The ruff set off the head (as ruler of the body), and forced it to be held erect with the chin up. The de Medici collar prevented the head from turning sideways; the body and head had to be turned at the same time whenever the wearer wished to look sideways. The wide skirt did not allow the elbows to be next to the bodice, and prevented the arms from being held loosely at the sides. When the French farthingale was worn, the elbows could rest on the bolsters, with the lower arms dropping below and bent inward. With the Spanish farthingale, elbows were bent, and a graceful curve was found for the arms while the hands rested away from the body on the hoops. Because of the tightness at the shoulders, gestures had to be made with the lower arms, and had to originate from the center of the body in order to appear graceful. The thickness and detail of the sleeves often stiffened the elbow, preventing up and down motion of the lower arms. Hands and fingers compensated for the restrictive use of the upper arms, and more expressive use was made of them.

The stiffened torso had to be maintained when the wearer was moving —bending from the waist was prohibited by the stomacher or corset. The high-heeled shoes forced the weight of the body to be supported by the toes and balls of the feet. The walk had to be smooth and even, preventing the extended skirts from swaying. When moving past other persons and objects, the woman was forced into a curve wide enough to avoid brushing against anything with her farthingale. It may even have been necessary to enter sideways through doors or arches.

The costume required that women be seated on the edge of a chair in order to prevent skirts from popping up. Since the waist could not be bent, women virtually had to kneel, stiff-spined, onto the chair.

When the woman curtsied, it had to be done with an upright torso and with a good sense of balance. One leg had to curve in back of the other, with the arms spread out to the sides, the wrists turned with thumbs up, the index fingers out and the others turned in, as the lady bent her knees and curtsied.

Male Dress

The male torso was covered by a *doublet,* a form-fitting garment that reached from the neck to a few inches below the waist, where it may have been skirted. It was either buttoned up the front or laced at the back. The shoulders were padded, as was the front (peascod belly). There was a standing neckband and, as with the women, a ruff or large collar was normally attached. A shirt was worn beneath the doublet, and its cuffs were pulled out to edge the arms of the doublet. Trousers were short, and varied in length from above to just below the knees. "Pumpkin breeches" were short and balloonlike, ending high on the thigh; "venetians" were tight on the thigh, ending just below the knee; "canions" were skintight and worn just above the knee, and "slops" were very full and extended below the knee. Legs were covered with hose and were sometimes cross-gartered. Shoes were generally flat, but some had half-inch heels. The "romeos" worn today resemble male Elizabethan shoes. Boots might be worn. A short cape ("mandillion") could be worn over one shoulder.

FIGURE 12-2. *Elizabethan male costume. Painting of Sir Walter Raleigh and son, artist unknown, 1602. Reproduced by courtesy of the Trustees, The National Gallery, London.*

247

Hats varied in size, and were often decorated with feathers and worn at rakish angles.

Accessories included rings, heavy neck chains with medallions, earrings, and swords that hung at the side opposite the sword hand. Moustaches and small goatees were popular.

INFLUENCE ON POSTURE AND MOVEMENT. While men were not as rigidly bound as women, the padded front and ruff, and probably custom, provoked a stiff, arched spine and erect head. The exposed legs led to deliberate leg positions in order to prevent awkward stances and to exhibit full calves. Paintings show the male keeping one leg straight while bending the other slightly at the knee and turning slightly outward. The walk was long-strided and masculine. When the sword was worn, the hand on the sword side was often clasped on the hilt in order to prevent the sword from jiggling.

While there was nothing in his costume to prevent the male from sitting comfortably back in a chair, he looked more poised, dignified, and handsome if he sat at the front edge, spine straight and head erect, with one foot forward and pointed slightly outward and the other bent at the knee and perched on the toes. One hand might have been placed upon the extended knee, while the other tilted the bottom of the sword backward.

The male bowed by stepping back with one foot and "dipping" as his arms extended outward and slightly behind the back. The back had to be kept straight. If he was bowing to royalty, he would bow his head too. On occasion, instead of extending both arms, one hand might be kept on the sword hilt. If he wore a hat, he might either hold it to his chest or in one of his outstretched hands. If he knelt, he had to make sure not to bend his torso, and he had to tilt the sword so that it would not touch the ground.

The Complete Costume

For both male and female, clothing was designed to beautify and decorate the body and to exhibit wealth and power. Fabrics were rich and heavy, often with elaborate patterns and ornamented with jewelry. The Elizabethan concept of the ideal form was neither natural nor comfortable. The stiffened torso, the arched back, the head set off from the body by the ruff—all contributed to a posture of pride and dignity. It was a very formal kind of dress and required a certain formality of standing, sitting,

FIGURE 12-3. *Scene from Shakespeare's* The Two Gentlemen of Verona, *showing the costumes worn.* University of California at Santa Barbara *production.*

and moving. Its formality and ornateness corresponded to the language of the plays, which accounts for the discrepancy that occurs when Shakespeare is performed in modern dress—or, as was the case in a recent production of *Hamlet,* in "rehearsal" clothes.

It is important that the same principles of interpretation of dramatic poetry should apply to the use of costume: while the formality of both must be taken into account, physical action, like speech, must be honest and unself-conscious. The actor must convince his audience that the clothes he wears, like the words he speaks, are natural and comfortable to him. Unless his character calls for it, he must not self-consciously pose and strut as though he were modeling. His goal is to avoid bringing undue attention to costume. On the other hand, if he ignores costume completely and moves in Elizabethan garb just as he would in jeans and a t-shirt, he will create as much distraction by incongruity as by flagrant exhibitionism.

EXERCISES

1. If you do not have access to Elizabethan costumes, women should find a corset, a ruff, a bolster for the hips, a long skirt, and shoes with cuban heels. Men should find a corset, a ruff, a pair of tights, and a sword with a scabbard to hold it. Let your external image reflect the actual finery of Elizabethan clothing. Walk about the stage, sit, bow, and gesture until you feel at ease with the discomforts you encounter. Learn to enjoy the costume; let yourself believe that the clothing and what it makes you do actually elevate and beautify your form and action.

2. Rehearse your soliloquy in costume. How does the costume affect your delivery? How can costumes or accessories be made to relate to dramatic elements?

THE "REALITY" OF
SHAKESPEAREAN
TRAGEDY

Much of what has been concluded about the "reality" of Greek tragedy is also applicable to the "reality" of Shakespeare's serious plays. The conventions of the Elizabethan theatre appear to have been, for the most part, theatrically functional rather than realistic. The architectural stage symbolizes the universe rather than particular locales, and its openness, its thrust into the audience, and its relative emptiness plus the formality of the costumes force the actor into patterns of speech and movement that must deviate from those of everyday life. Textual conventions corroborate this style with poetic language and conventions of asides, soliloquies, and the occasional use of a chorus. The protagonists are royal, enlarged in stature by the scope of their responsibilities and suffering and by the grandeur of their language. The emphasis is upon the archetypal nature of their virtues and vices rather than upon particularized personal traits or idiosyncrasies. The tragedies all are concerned with the relation of man to his cosmos, and his position in the great chain of being. God, his angels, and the devil, though never seen, are invariably present not only thematically but in the very nature of the composition of all men. The conventions of Elizabethan tragedy, like those of the ancient Greeks, evolved from religious ritual; the stage, along with the language and thought of the plays, continued to reflect the theatre's medieval ecclesiastical heritage.

Unlike Greek tragedy, however, Shakespearean tragedy is also more secular and earthy. More real props are utilized: tables, stools, letters, rings, handkerchiefs, etc.; prose alternates with poetry, costumes resemble the clothes worn by the populace, and become an important aspect of action and plot, especially disguise. Much more personal business is suggested: physical intimacy and stage violence are more prevalent and suggest far more physical interplay among characters. Except for use in realistic business (as in the ball scene in *Romeo and Juliet*), the mask is not a convention; and there is ample evidence that realistic makeup (including blood) was utilized. Granville-Barker sums up this hybrid reality nicely when he states:

> However high, then, with Shakespeare, the thought or emotion may soar, we shall always find the transcendental set in the familiar.[2]

Ultimately, the same suggestions that were made for the stylistic interpretation of Greek tragedy are applicable to that of Shakespeare in terms of accepting and integrating its nonrealistic conventions without any loss of belief and honesty. Understanding character in terms meaningful to yourself and your experience, and willingness to shape that understanding in terms of poetic convention and textual integrity, are the basis of the actor's approach to style.

EXERCISES

1. Apply the exercises at the conclusion of the section on Greek tragedy to your soliloquy from a Shakespearean tragedy.
2. Choose one of the scenes listed for two characters, and with your partner, analyze the characters and their relationship to each other. Then:
   a. Improvise a scene in which you play the objectives and given circumstances of the scene in your own words.
   b. Perform the scene as written in costume, paying particular attention to what it does to your physical relationships.

Selected Soliloquies from Shakespeare's Serious Plays

WOMEN

Coriolanus: Volumnia, V, 3: ll. 132-182
Henry VI, pt. 3: Margaret, I, 4: ll. 66-108
Henry VIII: Katherine, II, 4: ll. 13-64
Macbeth: Lady Macbeth, I, 5: ll. 1-31, 39-54
Richard III: Margaret, I, 3: ll. 188-214, 216-234
Romeo and Juliet: Juliet, III, 2: ll. 1-36
                      Juliet, IV, 3: ll. 14-58
The Winter's Tale: Hermione, III, 2: ll. 23-54, 93-117
                      Paulina, III, 2: ll. 178-204

MEN

Coriolanus: Coriolanus, IV, 5: ll. 71-107
Hamlet: Hamlet, I, 2: ll. 129-158
            II, 2: ll. 576-634
            III, 1: ll. 56-88
            IV, 4: ll. 32-66
Henry IV: 1, Hotspur, I, 3: ll. 29-68
Henry V: Henry, III, I: ll. 1-34
            IV, 3: ll. 18-67
Henry VI, pt. 3: York, I, 4: ll. 111-168
                    Gloucester, III, 2: ll. 124-195

Julius Caesar: Antony, III, 2: ll. 78-201 (cut citizens)
King Lear: Lear, II, 4: ll. 267-289
Macbeth: Macbeth, I, 7: ll. 1-28
                 II, 1: ll. 33-64
Othello: Othello, I, 3: ll. 126-170
          Iago, II, 3: ll. 342-368
Richard III: Richard, I, 1: ll. 1-41
Romeo and Juliet: Romeo, V, 3: ll. 74-120

Selected Two-Character (Male-Female) Scenes from Shakespeare's Serious Plays

Coriolanus: Coriolanus and Volumnia, III, 2: ll. 1-138 (cut other characters in scene)
Cymbeline: Imogen and Iachimo, I, 6: ll. 12-210 (cut other characters in scene)
Hamlet: Hamlet and Gertrude, III, 4: ll. 7-217 (have someone speak Ghost's lines and have Hamlet react)
Macbeth: Macbeth and Lady Macbeth, I, 7: ll. 28-82
                                  II, 2: entire scene
Measure for Measure: Angelo and Isabella, II, 4: ll. 54-152
                              Claudio and Isabella, III, 1: entire scene
Richard III: Richard and Anne, I, 2: entire scene
Romeo and Juliet: Romeo and Juliet, III, 5: ll. 1-64
Troilus and Cressida: Troilus and Cressida, III, 2: ll. 64-203 (cut Pandarus)
A Winter's Tale: Leontes and Hermione, II, 1: ll. 36-125 (cut other characters in scene)
                      Leontes and Paulina, II, 3: ll. 39-142 (pantomime Antigonus' presence)
                      Leontes and Paulina, III, 2: ll. 155-244 (cut other characters in scene)

PART IV

NOTES

1. Harley Granville-Barker, *Prefaces to Shakespeare,* vol. 1 (Princeton, N. J.: Princeton University Press, 1946), p. 13.
2. *Ibid.,* p. 20.

SELECTED READINGS

Adams, John C. *The Globe Playhouse.* New York: Barnes & Noble, 1961.

Barton, Lucy. *Historic Costume for the Stage.* Boston: Walter H. Barker & Co., 1935.

Beckerman, Bernard. *Shakespeare at the Globe.* New York: The Macmillan Co., 1962.

Bentley, Gerald E., ed. *The Seventeenth Century Stage.* Chicago: The University of Chicago Press, 1968.

Brockett, Oscar G. *History of the Theatre.* 2d ed. Boston: Allyn and Bacon, Inc., 1974.

Brown, John Russell. *Shakespeare's Plays in Performance.* Baltimore: Penguin Books, 1969.

Flatter, Richard. *Shakespeare's Producing Hand.* London: Wm. Heinemann, Ltd., 1948.

Fluchère, Henri. *Shakespeare and the Elizabethans.* New York: Hill and Wang, 1956.

Glenn, Stanley L. *A Director Prepares.* Encino, Calif.: Dickenson and Co., 1973.

Gorelik, Mordecai. *New Theatres for Old.* New York: Samuel French, 1947.

Granville-Barker, Harley. *Prefaces to Shakespeare,* vol. 1. Princeton, N. J.: Princeton University Press, 1946.

Hodges, C. Walter. *Shakespeare's Theatre.* London: Oxford University Press, 1964.

Joseph, Bertram L. *Acting Shakespeare.* London: Routledge and Kegan Paul, 1960.

———. *Elizabethan Acting.* 2d ed. Oxford: Clarendon Press, 1964.

Knight, G. Wilson. *Principles of Shakespearean Production.* Harmondsworth, Middlesex, Eng.: Penguin Books, 1949.

Marowitz, Charles. *The Method As Means*. London: Herbert Jenkins, 1961.

Morse, H. K. *Elizabethan Pageantry*. New York: The Studio Publications, Inc., 1934.

Nicoll, Allardyce. *The Development of the Theatre*. New York: Harcourt, Brace & Co., n.d.

Reynolds, G. *Elizabethan and Jacobean, 1558-1625*. London: Harrap & Co., 1951.

Rockwood, Jerome. *The Craftsmen of Dionysus*. Glenview, Ill.: Scott, Foresman & Co., 1966.

St. Denis, Michael. *Theatre: The Rediscovery of Style*. New York: Theatre Arts Books, 1960.

Speaight, Robert. *Shakespeare on the Stage*. London: Collins, n.d.

Sprague, Arthur. *Shakespeare and the Actors*. Cambridge, Mass.: Harvard University Press, 1945.

Styan, J. L. *Shakespeare's Stagecraft*. Cambridge, Eng.: University Press, 1967.

Watkins, Ronald. *On Producing Shakespeare*. 2d ed. New York: The Citadel Press, 1964.

Williams, Raymond. *Drama in Performance*. London: C. A. Watts and Co., 1968.

THE ACTOR AND COMEDY

PART V

THE NATURE OF COMEDY

The neoclassicists, with their obsessiveness for order, created stringent rules for anything that could be controlled by man—including the arts. In dealing with dramatic genres, they decided that among the differences which distinguished the serious from the comic, two of the most important were the choices of proper subjects and the selection of suitable characters for each. Serious subjects dealt with elevated matters involving the nobility, while comedy was expected to be concerned with domestic matters involving the middle and lower classes. Democracy has changed all that, of course, and there are few, if any, subjects and social classes that are locked into a particular genre.

If there is an all-encompassing principle regarding dramatic genre, it is in the *treatment* of subjects and characters. Aristotle observed that the ends of drama were aesthetic and were directed toward the evocation of certain responses in the audience. Tragedy inspired, then purged pity and terror; comedy evoked ridicule, which in turn was purged by laughter. The playwright's task is not merely to create stories, themes, and charac-

ters, but to find ways of treating them in order to make the audience laugh
or cry, be joyous or sorrowful. The actor's task is not merely to create a
character, but to find the means whereby that character will evoke sympathy or hatred, admiration or ridicule.

In *Richard II,* an essentially serious play, Shakespeare manipulates our
response to his king with drastic extremes. In the early part of the play,
Richard's selfishness, arrogance, and cruelty make us dislike him. But beginning with his return from the Irish wars, Shakespeare forces us to pity,
love, and ultimately admire Richard. The king's first speech on his return
(III, 2) begins with a warm, tender greeting to his native land, which he
personifies; he then pleads that it destroy his enemies. The entire tone of
this speech is serious. Without changing any of the words, how may this
speech be made comic? Here are some suggestions:

1. Make Richard bowlegged.
2. Give him a lisp.
3. Let him wear sunglasses with his Elizabethan costume.
4. Allow his tights to be wrinkled and baggy.
5. His entrance is preceded by fanfare and by his followers, who line up
   on two sides of center stage. Let him trip and fall as he marches downstage between them.
6. After "I weep for joy/ To stand upon my kingdom once again," Richard
   blows his nose noisily.
7. Richard should then go down on his knees to greet the land. After
   "Dear Earth, I do salute thee with my hand," let him touch the ground
   then realize he should take off his gloves. He should have enormous
   difficulty trying to remove the gloves, which are skintight.
8. Somewhere later in this speech, his knees should begin to hurt.

Note that it was not necessary to alter the situation or the words in this
part of the scene. But the hypothetical treatment of the character emphasized a technique essential to comedy—*the use of incongruity*. Incongruity
occurs when a character's physical and behavioral patterns deviate from
established norms, or when there is a contradiction between expectation
and actuality. In the example from *Richard II,* our comic king's bowed
legs, lisp, and wrinkled tights are ludicrous because they deviate from
normative physical characteristics and because they are unsuitable to one
holding the high office of king. The sunglasses are ridiculously anachro-
nistic and do not belong with Elizabethan finery. His fall after the preparation of a grand entrance punctures expectation. Blowing his nose is
undignified, as is the difficulty Richard has in removing his gloves, an

act that should not effectively interfere with the ritual he is trying to perform. His aching knees also are out of place in the ritual, where there is no place for trivial physical discomfort.

Incongruity or deviations from physical or behavioral normalcy may not always be ludicrous. The deformity of Richard III is not comic, nor is Gloucester's blindness in *King Lear,* and Medea's extreme stubbornness must be taken seriously. It is when incongruity approaches the absurd that the actor receives his cue to apply his comic imagination. He then finds absurd and disharmonious things to do, and utilizes a certain degree of exaggeration. When the actor who portrays Richard II blows his nose, for example, he can either do it with serious restraint or exaggerate both sound and movement, which would stress the ridiculous.

EXERCISES

1. Repeat your Shakespeare soliloquy, but now attempt to evoke laughter with it.
2. Create a serious improvisation using the following circumstances:
   Your wife (or husband) has just left you. You have just returned home on a very cold day. Everywhere in the room you are reminded of your mate, but especially strong are the potted plants that he or she tended so lovingly. You fill a watering can and water the plants. The telephone rings. It is your spouse, offering reconciliation.
3. Using the same circumstances, make this a comic scene by utilizing incongruity.

Besides incongruity and exaggeration, there is another important device that comedy requires, but it is one more difficult to define. You may have noticed, when you performed the exercises above, that your feelings or frame of mind differed from your experience in performing serious scenes. The subjective condition of the actor in performing comedy might be termed "the comic spirit"; actress-author Athene Seyler refers to it as "good nature."[1] Comedy has a festive quality that probably is related to its origins in Greek ritual. It is believed that comedy developed from the *komus,* the "joyful return" that concluded the ritual worship of Dionysus. The *komus* was characterized by the spirit of fun and playfulness, during which the participants, clothed in colorful masks and costumes (probably of animals), felt free to ridicule public officials and to joke about sex and marriage. The Mardi gras, costume balls, New Year's Eve celebrations, and bachelor parties are some of the contemporary parallels to those ancient fertility events. Playing comedy requires much of the same kind of freedom and release; it requires a kind of infectious joy.

EXERCISES

1. Improvise a simple action from your daily life such as preparing and eating breakfast, preparing to shave or make up, making a telephone call, etc. (In the classroom, three persons might be asked to go onstage and perform simultaneously.) Do *not* try to make your actions comic; perform them straightforwardly.

2. Repeat the action to a piece of serious music such as the second movement of Beethoven's Seventh Symphony. Listen to the music for a few moments. Let the music's mood fill you and genuinely influence the way you perform your action.

3. Repeat the action to a very light piece of music such as Strauss's *Im Krapfenwald'l* or an overture to a Gilbert and Sullivan operetta. First, listen to the music, let it absorb you, then perform your action in the spirit of the music.

4. Pair off with another member of the class, and take turns playing the mirror to the other's action, which must concentrate upon the ridiculous. Make faces, assume absurd poses and movement, make foolish sounds. Let yourself go! Enjoy it!

5. Partner "A" silently wills "B" to perform a simple action. When "B" responds, "A" should, automatically and without thought, respond with an action, to which "B" responds with an action to which "A" will react, and so on.

6. Repeat number 5 (with a new set of responses) to serious music, reversing the roles of "A" and "B."

7. Change partners and repeat the exercise to comic music.

8. Partner "A" manipulates "B" into a ridiculous pose. "B" then walks, runs, and sits according to the dictates of his pose. Repeat with "B" manipulating "A."

9. Each partner assumes the character suggested in number 8 and improvises a dance to a Strauss waltz.

Not all comedy is alike: plays will emphasize ludicrous characterization or incongruous situations, or wit, or combinations of these. There are two extremes into which comedy may be categorized: "high" comedy, which is so-called because it appeals primarily to the mind and requires a worldly, knowledgeable audience; and "low" comedy, which is essentially physical and whose humor can be appreciated by the unsophisticated. It would be erroneous to assume that, in terms of sheer pleasure, one is superior to the other. Molière's farce *The Would-Be Invalid* will appeal more to an unsophisticated audience than Congreve's *The Way of the World,* but it is the sophisticate's loss if he regards *The Would-Be Invalid* to be beneath him.

For the actor there is as much challenge and ultimate pleasure in participating in either high or low comedy, but each involves its own special demands and techniques. The rest of our exploration of comic acting will concentrate upon the differences between farce, representing low comedy, and the comedy of manners, which represents high comedy.

CHAPTER 13

Farce

Farce has been defined as ". . . an extreme form of comedy in which laughter is raised at the expense of probability, *particularly by horseplay and bodily assault.*"[2] Because farce is often so physical and so frenetic, it requires superb physical conditioning and control. Running and rapid-fire speech and stage business have been farce characteristics since Aristophanes' time. The actor cannot be short-winded or physically inflexible for the blows, falls, and, in many instances, acrobatics required by farce. The ideal actor of farce should also be a good tumbler.

PHYSICALITY

Most often farce is realistic. Beatings should look like actual beatings, and "pratfalls" like genuine "pratfalls." Clearly, however, much of the physical "suffering" that farce demands must be faked. Oliver Hardy's career would have ended prematurely if the violence he underwent in his films had been real. In Molière's *Scapin,* a character hides in a bag in order to conceal himself from pursuers whom he mistakenly believes are after him. Scapin, who promises to prevent his discovery, pretends to be one pursuer after another who rush onstage and beat the bag mercilessly to demonstrate what they would do if they caught their victim. The actor playing Scapin must be able to run on and offstage many times, deliver a series of angry diatribes, and relentlessly and vigorously swing his stick against the body in the bag. To be successful, this scene requires two things of the actor: first, he must get through it effortlessly; second, he must control his blows or seriously injure the actor in the bag. No other form of drama consistently requires such risks or is so potentially dangerous.

The concern of the farce actor is not simply to find funny actions, but to carefully work out his comic business with absolute precision. Unstructured and uncontrolled chaos is not only dangerous, but also very *un*funny. During rehearsals, actors must first plan how they are going to "fake" physical violence, then they must carefully rehearse what they have worked out until it is mechanically perfect. Not even the smallest change or variation should ever be introduced by one actor without consultation and adequate rehearsal with the other actors involved.

Safety, of course, is a major concern, but the effectiveness of physical comedy relies upon skillful execution, which in turn depends upon the actor's sense of security. Mutual trust is important for any type of interaction, but it is especially necessary for scenes of violence. It is difficult to execute any type of scene well when you are unsure of the reliability of your co-workers.

EXERCISES

1. Pair off. Actor "A" turns his back to actor "B." Actor "A" is to fall back into the arms of "B." Determine first, however, the exact distance necessary between the two in order to avoid a miss. Plan how the catch is to be made: will "B" catch "A" under the armpits of "A," or clasp his torso around the arms? Both parties should be relaxed. Try several falls and catches. Reverse roles.

2. In a stage performance, action must appear to be spontaneous. In the first exercise, "A" should not have to look around to see if "B" is in the correct position. "B" should not appear to anticipate "A's" fall. It is important, then, for "A" to be in a precisely prearranged stage area, and for "B" to be alerted by a special cue for "A's" fall. Perform the exercise again, but this time "B" should face the opposite direction and be further away from "A." On a cue such as a gasp or an exclamation such as, "Good heavens!," "B" should move to the correct position to catch the falling "A." Timing is important: "A" cannot fall *on* the sound that cues "B." Instead, "A" makes his sound, "B" turns and steps in, then "A" falls. Work on the mechanics of this routine, then reverse roles.

3. Actor "A" runs across the stage and leaps into "B's" arms. There are two ways in which this may be done. The safer method is for "A" to

throw his arms around "B's" neck, then jump up into his arms. Try this first. The second method requires more trust. "A" runs to "B" and leaps into his arms without clutching or holding. (With actors of unequal size and strength, "B" should be the bigger and stronger.)

4. There are several ways of faking stage slaps, but all of them require expert timing for effectiveness. Especially important is reaction time. Without trust, the recipient usually flinches too soon; or the aggressor, not trusting himself, swings unconvincingly. Try the following technique of slapping, and rehearse it carefully until equal confidence is developed by both actors. The recipient of the slap ("B") should have his back to the audience, and place his right hand, palm open, under his right jaw, with fingertips touching the jaw. "A" stands upstage of "B," and with his right hand slaps "B" by hitting "B's" palm with his closed fingers and following through. A good, sharp sound is important. Practice this several times for accuracy, and also in order to get "B" used to receiving the slap without flinching. When both actors are confident, "B" should begin to practice his reaction by moving his head as though it actually has been struck. The movement must occur upon contact—as soon as "A's" hand strikes that of "B." If "B" anticipates and moves too soon, or moves too late, he will have destroyed credibility. Reverse roles.

5. Rehearse slapping each other alternately, and see how rapidly you can develop a sequence of slaps.

6. Practice backhand slaps using the same techniques described above.

Scenes of physical struggle and violence are not limited to farce, and the principles of safety and trust are as applicable to melodrama as they are to comedy. But there is a difference between the playing of melodramatic violence and farcical violence. Melodrama's intention is to make us anxious about the fate of the protagonist. We fear for his safety and suffer with him in his struggle, which we take seriously. We must believe in the possibility of harm (not to the actor, but to the character). Farce's intention is simply to make us laugh at physical mishap, therefore true harm or danger is minimized. When someone slips clumsily on a banana peel we want to laugh at the physical incongruity, but only when we are certain that the accident has not resulted in an injury. When a brick bounces off Oliver Hardy's head or a door slams in his face, why do we laugh? There are actually several reasons, but one of the most important is that his reaction will either be exaggerated or incongruous. If the actor wishes to provoke a serious reaction to a brick falling on his head, he will react with the reality of shock, then pain. The reaction will be restrained and will endure for some time. The actor tries to convince us that his character

FIGURE 13-1.   *Clowns: Oliver Hardy and Stan Laurel.*

truly is hurting. The comic actor will overdo his response, so that his facial expression is comically contorted; he may vocalize with "ooh, ooh, ooh!" then gingerly touch the lump on his head with his fingertips, react again, then forgetting the pain, decide that he is furious. The comic spirit or sense of fun of which we spoke earlier is useful in guiding an actor's intuitive response to catastrophe.

It is important to recognize that credibility on the part of the actor is still important. In both the serious situation and the comic one, the actor still must rely upon sense memory and observation in order to come up with truthful and imaginative rather than stock responses. The comic actor distorts and exaggerates his discoveries, but still retains a sense of truth. Recall the example used in sensory study in Part I, of Argan's footbath in *The Would-Be Invalid*. The same set of responses can be used to effect in serious or comic drama, depending upon the degree with which they are expressed. Remember that the audience must believe, but not take seriously, what you believe and *appear* to be taking very seriously.

266

EXERCISES

1. Practice stage falls. Trip and fall forward to the floor. Slip and fall backward. (It might be wise to start with a mattress on the floor until you have learned how to "break" a fall.)
2. Try each fall with the intention of "worrying" the audience about the character's safety. Use appropriate vocal responses.
3. Try each fall with the intention of evoking laughter. Use your voice.
4. Discuss what you did differently in number 2 and number 3. Discuss how you felt (in terms of mood or state of mind).
5. Choose a partner and prepare a farce struggle scene of your own invention. Create a simple situation that will force your characters into immediate conflict.
6. There are two excellent scenes that include comic violence in *The Would-Be Invalid:* the first act chase between Argan and Toinette, and the third act scene where Toinette is disguised as a doctor. Work on these scenes with an emphasis on the credibility and discipline of the slapstick suggested by the text.

COMIC INVENTION

The word "farce" is derived from the Latin verb *farcire,* which means "to stuff." Possibly the verb was applied to ancient comedy because of its use of the exaggerated phallus. But its use also might be attributed to the fact that it is characteristic of farce to be packed full with stage business. Of all dramatic forms, farce is probably the least satisfying in literary form because it is more dependent upon the performer's invention than are other genres. Farce texts are closer to scenarios in that they provide plots and situations that invite much physical embellishment. Serious drama tends to be more internal in its concerns with character delineation and issues from the spectrum of human values. The ludicrous is also concerned with values and judgments, but character traits are exposed with broad, physical strokes; revelation is made by external rather than by internal or reflective means. The challenge to the actor in farce, then, is not in exploring the subtleties and complexities of character, but in finding the funniest ways of revealing basic foibles or developing and amplifying the nucleus of comic situations provided by the playwright.

267

FIGURE 13-2. *Fleurant in* The Would-Be Invalid. *Humboldt State College production.*

The stage business used by the *Comédie Française* for *The Would-Be Invalid* no doubt includes a great deal of traditional comic stage business, some of it created by Molière's company itself. A good example of the kind of invention that is kindled rather than specified by the text is the *Comédie's* business for Thomas Diafoirus in the second act of the play. Thomas is wearing the traditional doctor's garb, but with a blonde wig and large horn-rimmed glasses. He is carrying a huge tome, which is supposed to be his thesis. His father must cue him for every social amenity, so when his father removes his hat in greeting his valued patient, Thomas quickly does the same, but drops his thesis in so doing. Later, discovering the thesis to be missing, he searches desperately for the huge volume, but his near-sightedness interferes. Molière's dialogue makes it clear that Thomas is a boob: he performs his social obligations by rote, and mistakes the maid for the mistress. When he *is* told to make his compliments to Angelique, he bumps into Argan, who is between Angelique and the elder Diafoirus. He begins his memorized speech once again (the actor uses a monotone and fails to orally punctuate his speech), but at several points he "dries up," whereupon he must cross back to his father to be prompted. Each time he bumps into Argan, until finally Argan tries to prevent a collision by sidestepping, but so does Thomas.

Finally Toinette is asked to arrange chairs for everyone, and Thomas is seated on a stool about six inches high. As Diafoirus begins his lengthy speech describing his son, Thomas is disturbed because he can see nothing but feet. As he strains to see better, he falls off the stool. Everything is delayed while Toinette goes off for a new chair, and she brings out a child's high chair. Thomas, with some difficulty, climbs up, finds the chair too tight, and sits on top of the backrest. As soon as he is settled, he looks around and becomes terrified because he can see no one. When he makes frightened noises, everyone below turns to Thomas, but can't see him. Thomas finally slides down into the seat, sitting on one of his legs. As Diafoirus drones on, Thomas begins to swing his free leg for a few moments, then looks down and is horrified because one of his legs is missing! None of this business is in the text.

At this point a word of caution is necessary. An all-too-common mistake in performing farce is that, as with food preparation, too much stuffing can spoil the dish. When actors become carried away and create too much comic stage business, the plot is delayed too long and the purpose of the scene or situation becomes obscured. Restraint is necessary even in farce. Besides knowing how much invention is correct, the actor must use discretion in his choice of stage business. Too many aspiring comedians are interested only in getting laughs, and invent themselves *away* from the play with no regard for relevance. Such exhibitionism is ultimately destructive, because irrelevant invention, besides confusing the text, is usually not very funny. You can amuse babies for a while by making funny faces and noises, but clowning without a context is an embarrassment for most of us past infancy.

There is very little visual comedy that is new in the world, but this does not mean that none of it can be effective. The most tired "gags," when performed with apparent spontaneity in the right place at the right time, continue to be hilarious. The *Comédie Française* treatment of Thomas Diafoirus works not just because it is skillfully executed, but because it emerges from character and situation. All the "stuffing" in the scene is utilized to stress, and at the same time to take advantage of, Thomas's stupidity and lack of common sense. Thematically, it makes more comically appalling the fact that Thomas is certain to be a successful doctor!

An awareness of the necessity that comic invention be organic provides us with the appropriate stimulus for the comic imagination. Instead of striving for effect—trying to "be funny"—the actor in comedy should resort to the same justification for action that he would use in other genres: his understanding of a character and its amplification by relating to other characters, setting, hand properties, and costume. But in comedy, such amplification is characterized by incongruity and exaggeration.

COMIC CHARACTERIZATION

A starting place for the invention of comic characteristics would be to find a way of stating the character's objective so that it stimulates comic rather than serious action. In *An Actor Prepares,* Stanislavski found, when he was rehearsing the role of Argan, that his first objective, "I am sick," induced actions that were pitiable rather than ludicrous. When he altered the objective to "I wish to be thought sick," he not only came nearer to the crux of Argan's comic excess, but now possessed a justification for more inventive comic action. He had to find ways of persuading other characters that he was sick, despite the fact that he was perfectly healthy. But this too can be done with serious results. If Argan is played craftily like Ben Jonson's *Volpone,* and if the role of the invalid is enacted successfully, then it is his victims who become ludicrous.

The key to playing "I wish to be thought sick" is to overdo his manu-factured symptoms, and wherever possible, to unconsciously betray himself. For example, the actor could have exaggerated coughing fits that conclude with gasping and self-pity. He could constantly (before others, of course) pop pills into his mouth, feel his pulse, check his temperature, and ache with pain every time he gets up or sits down. All of this should be done in an obvious manner for the effect it would have on others, rather than out of any actual affliction. Molière provides a clue in several scenes in which Argan wants to be thought frail and helpless, but as soon as he is contradicted, he explodes into a vigorous temper tantrum. Such revealing contradictions should be exploited as often as possible; when he walks "lame," for example, he could forget which leg is supposed to be arthritic.

FIGURE 13-3.   *Scene from* The Would-Be Invalid.
Comédie Française.

271

In Part I, it was suggested that Argan's major objective might be "I want to be indulged," and that wishing to be thought sick is one of his methods to receive attention. Such behavior is incongruously characteristic of the spoiled brat; it is truly infantile. Knowing this, the actor might actually assume the characteristics of a child by whimpering, pointing, talking baby talk, and purring with ecstasy when Béline accommodates him. His facial expressions might be similar to those of children when they cry, become irritable, and pucker up self-pityingly.

The way in which Argan copes with obstacles provides us with cues for comic invention. He becomes tyrannical when obstructed by his family and servant and intimidated by the threats of his doctors. It has already been mentioned that when he becomes angry, especially with Toinette, he becomes irrational and forgets to be sick. At such moments, his actions might reflect a child's tantrum: arms and legs flailing, turning purple by holding his breath, or forgetting to inhale when he berates others. He could become comically ineffectual with his threats of physical violence. His clumsiness in chasing Toinette is contrasted to her agility. He swings his walking stick awkwardly, perhaps stumbling or falling in the follow-

Figure 13-4.   *Scene from* The Would-Be Invalid. *Humboldt State College production.*

through, and becomes more and more frustrated by his failure to punish his maid.

When he is intimidated by Dr. Purgon, he reveals a lack of proportion by behaving as though the world were coming to an end. He can sob (exaggeratedly), plead by getting on his knees, then moving on his knees (always a ludicrous sight) to the doctor, perhaps tripping on his robe as he does so.

Farce characters often are eccentric. We have dealt with Argan's behavioral eccentricities and ways in which they may be physicalized. Often the playwright suggests certain physical eccentricities such as Falstaff's bulk, Sir Andrew Aguechek's spindly legs and stringy, flaxen hair, Chandebise's cleft palate in Feydeau's *A Flea in Her Ear,* Epihodov's perpetual clumsiness in *The Cherry Orchard,* or the implied metaphorical characteristics of the characters in *Volpone.* But physical deviation may, in many instances, be applied to characters whose playwrights have not specified any. De Bonnefoi, the notary, and Fleurant, the apothecary, are two such characters. De Bonnefoi is an oily, sneaky hypocrite, who can shrewdly twist the law to accommodate his clients, and consequently his purse. He may easily be compared to an eel, a snake, or a rat, and the actor may use their characteristics in order to create physical eccentricity. The actor can wear an oily black wig. By keeping his shoulders and elbows in, clutching his damp hands together, assuming a narrow base, peering up from bushy eyebrows, and moving with short, quiet steps as his body undulates, he can physically suggest the kind of despicable character Molière had in mind.

Fleurant is going to be amusing simply because he is holding an enema. But he will be even more amusing if he considers his job to be a holy one. A man offering an enema is going to appear more ridiculous if he holds it pompously, as though it were the Holy Grail or the golden fleece. We also might take a cue from his name, Fleurant, which contains the French word for flower (*fleur*). Imagine the incongruity of a delicate, perhaps foppish, snob, decked in ribbons and bows, whose occupation is giving enemas.

We are informed quite specifically that Thomas Diafoirus is a good-natured boob, totally lacking a mind of his own and most desirous of pleasing his humorless father. With what physical traits would you endow him?

Note that in each of the aforementioned examples, the source and justification for the invention of action and physical characterization have come from our conclusions about the playwright's character. It would be a mistake to arbitrarily apply comic qualities, no matter how amusing, which are irrelevant, or which obscure and contradict the essential quality of the char-

FIGURE 13-5. *The clown: Charlie Chaplin.*

acter in the play. Giving Argan a lisp might be funny for a while, but eventually it will become apparent that such a trait contributes nothing to the revelation of Argan's real foibles and deserves to be branded as "gimmickry."

Many actors have achieved fame for having created such distinct comic personalities that playwrights have written roles especially for them. This was true of Shakespeare, Molière, and possibly Aristophanes. In motion pictures, scenarios have been written for the characters created by Charlie Chaplin, Buster Keaton, Harold Lloyd, Laurel and Hardy, and others. In the contemporary theatre, such actors are often cast in famous comic roles and are permitted to develop those roles in terms of their own comic identity. The late Bobby Clark, for example, enjoyed success in the title role of Molière's *The Would-Be Gentleman,* and Bert Lahr applied his trademarks to *Volpone.* These actors are often referred to as "clowns," and their appeal has been in their simplicity and their uniqueness. Simple, because their creations are uncomplicated and immediately comprehended, and unique because of their remarkable fusion of physical and behavioral eccentricities. Chaplin's tramp is recognizable by his mustache and his costume, consisting of a worn derby, a tattered and ill-fitting suit (the coat is too small, the pants too baggy), and oversized shoes. His bow tie and cane create a jaunty attempt at elegance that is incongruous with the actual poverty of the costume. He has a distinctively jerky gait, with toes pointed outward. Behaviorally, he is society's "little man," downtrodden by the rich and powerful, by the police, and by occupational superiors such as bosses or sergeants. He gets into all kinds of difficulty usually by accident rather than design, and must use his agility and wits in order to extricate himself. He is—and perhaps this partly explains his wide appeal—naive and accident-prone, but he possesses extraordinary resiliency and endurance.

For some reason there are not many such clowns in the theatre today. They are more prevalent in nightclubs as stand-up comedians, and the emphasis is upon the verbal rather than the physical. Actors need to be encouraged, if they have a comic talent, to try to develop new clown characterizations, not only because of the affection and delight with which they are viewed, but because they stimulate and challenge the comic imagination of playwrights.

EXERCISES

1. Improvise a scene with two characters, one of whose objectives is "I am sick," while the other's objective is "I must make this sick person happy."

Afterward, the same actors should improvise a scene in which one character's objective is "I wish to be thought sick," and the other character's objective is "I must ignore his tricks."

2.   Create an eccentric character. Concentrate on a few physical deviations (features, movement, clothing) and one major behavioral trait.

3.   Place the character into a situation that is very simple, but one that will get him into absurd difficulties. Give him a particular objective, and use his behavioral trait to determine how he will attempt to achieve his goals and how he will respond to obstacles.

4.   After you have performed your scene and have had an opportunity to refine the character, prepare another scene in which your eccentric is paired off with another actor. You can work as a team (on the order of Laurel and Hardy) or as antagonists in a new situation.

SETTING

The actor, of course, does not design the set, but his awareness of the details of the physical environment will provide further nourishment for comic invention. There are occasions, too, when an actor may make suggestions about set additions or alterations that emerge from ideas in rehearsal. It might be suggested, for example, that a door open onstage instead of offstage in order to facilitate an accident, or in order to create comic suspense by concealing a character behind the opened door with the constant threat of discovery.

The comic actor should consider every possible action that could result from relating to the set. Windows that become stuck, roller shades that are uncontrollable, rugs over which to trip, appliances that do not function, treacherous staircases, and flimsy, breakable furniture are a few of the potential hazards that make farce possible. In working out Argan's pursuit of Toinette in the first act chase of *The Would-Be Invalid,* the translator has provided stage directions of the sort that actors and directors would develop in rehearsal. Note how chairs, tables, and finally the bed are used to provide as much variety to the chase as possible. Note too the comic effect of Argan standing on his bed shouting angrily. The actor might climax the chase with one more action not included in this version of the play. Argan, in furious frustration, could jump up and down on his bed as he screams, "If you don't stop her, I will put my parental curse on you!" Then, with Toinette's saucy reply, his jumping could get perilously close

FIGURE 13-6. *A more classic clown: Launce in Shakespeare's*
The Two Gentlemen of Verona. *University of California at*
Santa Barbara production.

to the edge of the bed, where he could slide thumpingly to the floor (rather than first collapsing on the bed), justifying his line, "Oh, oh, oh, I'm done for! This will kill me . . . Oh, oh, come here darling."

The same bed might be used for the disguised Toinette's "examination" of her patient in Act III. As she pokes and threatens, Argan could back toward his bed for security—perhaps on his line, "Yes, but I need my arm." He might bump into the bed into a sitting position at the end of the line. Toinette notices his eye and forces him backward on the bed as she examines it. When she suggests its removal, Argan, terrified, could slide on his back toward the head of the bed. Toinette, on hands and knees, could follow until he is trapped by the headboard.

(Exercises using sets as a stimulus for comedy are incorporated into the exercises for hand properties that follow.)

HAND PROPERTIES

Farce is a property manager's nightmare. Hand properties are consistently more abundant in farce than in any other genre, except perhaps in melodrama. Physical objects are necessary for physical comedy. If comic violence were restricted to wrestling, pushing, and shoving, audiences would soon tire of it. Actors require objects to express comically their characters' attitudes, feelings, and idiosyncrasies. Comic properties often are specified by the texts themselves. In *The Would-Be Invalid,* Fleurant's enema, Thomas Diafoirus's thesis, Argan's medications and footbath, and the pillows in Act One are a few of the props called for by the text. But it is the actor who must exploit them for comic purposes. Note that in the pillow scene, the dialogue clearly indicates that pillows are to be used and it actually suggests some of their comic usage, but the translator, in his stage directions, has expanded their use as might the actor or director. No reference is made to the pillows after the line, "Oh, you rapscallion, you want to smother me to death!" Morris Bishop adds three more items of comic business that are perfectly justified, though not explicitly required by the dialogue:

1. Argan, in his fury, throws two more pillows at the departing Toinette. This helps to justify Béline's line, "There, there, there!"
2. Argan, unassuaged, throws another pillow as Béline is trying to clear up the room and hits her accidentally in the rear. This gives more justification to her line, "What's the matter with you anyway?"

3. Argan gives up, but as he collapses into his chair, he sits on a remaining pillow, and enraged, throws it into the wings. Béline's next remark, "Why do you get so angry?" is again further justified by the action.

Compare this with another translation, which makes less effort to provide the actor's invention for the reader:

ARGAN: (*Rising up in a passion, and throwing all pillows after Toinette as she runs away.*) Ah! jade, thou wouldst stifle me.

BÉLINE: Oh so, oh so! What's the matter then?

ARGAN: (*Throwing himself into his chair.*) Oh! oh! oh! I can hold it no longer.

BÉLINE: Why do you fly into such passions?[3]

But even with texts that include more details than others, it is the actor who must execute the stage business. The "whats" of stage business may be described, but not the "hows." We know, in the scene just discussed, that Argan is angry and that this will influence the way he throws the pillows, but there are many ways of throwing things angrily. There are also numerous ways of varying repetitious action. What is Argan's reaction to hitting Béline by mistake? Can he do a double take after sitting on the last pillow? His execution of trying to convince Béline that he is all worn-out, and his contradictory action when he discovers the last pillow, will determine whether or not the stage directions will be successful.

In the same play we have already indicated how Fleurant's *relation* to his enema can make the use of a funny prop even funnier. Decorating the enema with ribbons to match a foppish Fleurant may add yet another comic element. Thomas Diafoirus's attitude toward his impressive looking manuscript adds to its comic potentialities. He loves it; it is proof of his right to practice medicine. Personifying the manuscript and treating it with human affection, followed later by Thomas's hysteria at its loss—as though his own child had disappeared—will magnify Thomas's disproportionate perspectives and further add to the comedy.

It is generally true that by the time a performance of a farce is ready, the number of hand properties will have doubled since its first rehearsal. This is because inventive actors and directors will find comic uses for objects that, although not indicated by the text, will enrich it. Although medicines are referred to in *The Would-Be Invalid*, there is little indication of the kind of medicines Argan might use. Pills the size of golf balls, throat sprays that can misfire, and foul-tasting fluids are some types that might be utilized. When Toinette enters in Act III disguised as a doctor, she might carry a medical bag. As she begins her long speech, beginning with "I am a roving doctor," she may begin to remove instruments of torture from the bag. This will add to Argan's discomfort as well as to the absurdity of Toinette's disguise. As the scene progresses, Toinette can make use of some of the exaggerated instruments. For instance, as she approaches Argan on "And I shall be delighted, sir, if you had all the diseases I have just named . . .," she might point at him with a large hand drill. A bit later, when she examines him to determine his "illness," she might take out a few other instruments: a stethoscope whose cold surface would be applied to Argan's bare skin, and a tongue depressor that is one foot long and two inches thick. When Toinette discovers his "parasitic" left arm, she could reach for a carpenter's saw, and she might threaten his useless left eye with a screw driver.

EXERCISES

1. For a single actor. Use the props suggested in Part I (pp. 66-67) for comic purposes. You may add three or four more objects if you wish.
2. For two actors. Create a pantomimic scene that emphasizes the use of properties for comic effect in the following circumstances:
   a. A customer and a waiter in a restaurant.
   b. A lazy husband who wants to watch television and an irate wife who wants attention.
   c. Two thieves who attempt to break into a house.
   d. Two strangers sitting next to each other at a movie.

COSTUME

Normally the actor will not have a great deal to say about his basic costume. In the professional theatre, where stars often have the privilege of making certain costume choices, and where there is more time, money, and assistance, costumes for comic purposes may be allowed to evolve in rehearsal. In amateur theatre, however, the director and costumer often have to make decisions before the play is cast, in which case the actor will have little to contribute in terms of costume design. But the actor still may have opportunities to apply his comic imagination to costumes. When he knows what his costume is to be like, he can allow its features to stimulate ideas about its use. If Argan knows that he will be wearing a long nightgown, he can raise it to his knees and reveal his bare legs when chasing Toinette, or he can forget its length and trip on it. He can use his hat, if one has been designed for him, to pound or strike with when angry; he may then put it on backward, or Toinette may pull it over his eyes during one of her arguments with him.

Thomas Diafoirus can make a perfectly normal costume look ridiculous by buttoning it wrong, wearing both shoes on the wrong feet, or letting his shoelaces remain untied, wearing a hat in the wrong way, and nervously twisting whatever loose garment he is wearing when he tries to recite his memorized speeches. Toinette's disguise, of course, must be planned in advance, and the actress must know what comic device it will incorporate so that she may develop appropriate comic stage business in the

FIGURE 13-7. *Comic costume: Petruchio's servants in Shakespeare's* The Taming of the Shrew. *University of California at Santa Barbara production.*

disguise scene. The costume may be far too large for her: she may plan on the hat constantly falling over her eyes, having to gather up yards of material in order to walk, and having to pull back an extra foot or two of sleeves in order to manipulate hand props.

Even when actors have little to say about the basic costume design small adjustments and additions may be made at their suggestion. Such items as suspenders, hats, and gloves, and accessories such as jewelry, fans, lorgnettes, and handkerchiefs may be added with minimal difficulty. Toinette may wish to have half a dozen pockets sewn into her doctor's robe for medical instruments; Thomas may request loose-waisted trousers, so that they can drop to his ankles at the appointed moment, and De Bonnefoi can ask that his clothes be made to look a bit seedy with worn elbows, a hole in one of the fingers of his gloves, a dirty collar, and scuffed shoes. He might want a filthy handkerchief to repeatedly wipe his clammy hands (if he takes off his gloves) and his freely perspiring brow and neck.

EXERCISES

1. If costume played a major role in your creation of an eccentric in a previous exercise, do you now believe that you made effective use of it? Review that scene and determine if you could have made richer use of costume.
2. If costume played a minimal role in your "eccentric" improvisation, invent another character for whom costume incongruity will be dominant.
3. If you have access to a costume collection, choose a few items of clothing and create a comic character from them. If not, go to the Salvation Army or a comparable used clothing agency and find items of clothing that you believe are ludicrous, or that may be made to appear ludicrous. Create a three-minute scene in which your costume is the major source of comedy.

MECHANICS

Control, timing, and clarity already have been treated as vital disciplines in the preparation of farce. *Pace* is another important factor. One of the characteristics of most farces is that they involve much that is improbable, with the result that a popular rule for farce is to play it as fast as possible so that the audience has no time to recognize its improbabilities. This is an acceptable principle as long as it is not taken too literally: if there is no change of pace, the speed will become monotonous and the performance will seem too labored. Farce, like any other genre, has its built-in rhythms and tempos, and pace should depend upon its appropriateness to each scene. Nevertheless, most farces generally do demand more speed and vitality than other genres. Speed in language must never be so rapid that it becomes slurred or misunderstood, nor should the speaker appear to be frenetic unless, of course, the part calls for this characteristic. The most effective way in which to suggest a rapid spoken tempo is to pick up cues in a series of exchanges without pause or hesitation. One of the textual cues for a rapid-fire exchange is when *stichomythia* (short, abrupt sentences) is used.

There are many such instances in *The Would-Be Invalid*. The first occurs early in the play, when Toinette finally answers Argan's desperate calls. From the moment she enters until Argan says, "All right, all right; let it go," twenty-three speeches later, no pause—not even the briefest— should be permitted between the last word of each character's speech and the first word of the response. The essential problem actors generally encounter in such situations is caused by their desire to take a breath before speaking. Of course this is necessary, but the pause can be avoided if the actors will inhale before the preceding speech has been completed.

EXERCISES

1. Read the first scene between Toinette and Argan up to the break indicated above. When you are familiar with it, act it out in a leisurely manner without markedly picking up cues.

2. Repeat the scene, but pick up all cues instantly. Do not feel obliged to speed up the words—just work on cues.

3. Do the same with another scene between the same characters, starting with Toinette's, "What, sir! You have actually done this silly thing?" Up to Toinette's, "Careful, sir. You're forgetting you're sick." Analyze this scene for tempo. Which sequences demand a rapid-fire exchange? Where are changes of pace and pauses necessary?

4. During your rehearsal of a farce scene (either from *The Would-Be Invalid* or an assigned segment of another play) and after learning your lines, march back and forth across the stage—crisscrossing with your partner— and speak your lines energetically with instantaneous cue pickups. Do not perform any stage business—simply concentrate upon energy and pace. This is also an effective way to warm up for a farce performance.

Another problem for the novice comedian is adjusting to audience laughter. This is a practice that must become intuitive, for in performance there is no time to think about what you must do when the laughs come thick and fast. After several performances, actors will have a good idea when to expect laughs and will anticipate the quantity of laughter each time. Knowing this, they can wait for laughter on a comic line or action, and will know how long to wait before proceeding. But in the first few performances of a comedy, no one can be sure of what will work or of the kind of response each comic moment will incite.

During early performances, and even later when there may be inconsistencies in the responses of different audiences, the actor must take cues from the audience and handle them in certain ways. First, the audience must be sure to hear certain lines because they may be the preparation for a comic line or action. If the preparatory line is not clear, the later line or action will fall flat. In the following extract from the scene in which Toinette dupes Argan as she pretends to be a doctor, lines that might be lost if the actors failed to stop for laughs are bracketed. Determine what the results might be for the other lines in the scene:

TOINETTE: Give me your pulse. (*He extends his arm apprehensively. A pause; she shakes his arm.*) Come on beat properly. Oh, I'll make you behave. (*Shakes his arm violently.*) [Oho! This pulse is trying to cut up; I see it doesn't know me yet.] (*Flings Argan's arm from her; it hits the arm chair; he grimaces. In a scornful tone*) [Who is your doctor?]

ARGAN: Dr. Purgon.

TOINETTE: Purgon? That name is not on my list of the great doctors. [What does he say is your illness?]

ARGAN: He says it is the liver. (*Toinette indicates amazement.*) But others say it is the spleen.

TOINETTE: (*Rolls up her sleeves, taps Argan's chest smartly; goes behind his chair, bends his head back, inspects his eyes, opens his mouth. Argan sticks out his tongue; she feels it with her finger. She closes his mouth by clapping him under the chin; Argan bites his tongue. She returns to face him.*) [They are all blockheads. It's the lungs that are causing the trouble.

ARGAN: The lungs?

TOINETTE: (*Facing audience, with air of knowing all the answers, and seeking only supporting evidence.*) Yes. How do you feel?

ARGAN: Sometimes I feel pains in my head.]

TOINETTE: Exactly. The lungs.

FIGURE 13-8. *Scene from* The Would-Be Invalid. *Comédie Française.*

The actor, when laughter begins, must hold the next line until the laughter subsides. If he fails to do this, not only will he lose subsequent understanding and laughter from the audience, but soon the audience will refuse to laugh because it will be reluctant to lose lines. If the actor has begun a line and a delayed laugh interrupts, he should stop, wait for the laughter to begin to subside, then repeat the line.

An actor can signal the audience to stop laughing (although he should never do this too soon, but allow the audience to fully enjoy whatever it is that has amused it) by some kind of pantomimic action related to his next line. While the audience is laughing its loudest, however, he must avoid unnecessary or distracting action. Sometimes just holding a position in character (not a freeze), or relating to another character or object with a

285

glance, will be all that is necessary. As long as the actor does not panto-mime too much and remains in character, he will have no problem in waiting out a laugh.

The actor must learn to be discriminating about the proper occasions to wait out laughter. Light titters do not justify waiting, but hearty, noisy laughter does. The actor must learn to react appropriately to varying de-grees of laughter.

EXERCISES

1. Perform a farce scene for the class. Select a leader to cue the audience. He signals when it should laugh, how hearty its laughter should be, and how long it should endure. The actors onstage must cope with the audience's responses.

2. Perform one of the scenes listed below. Apply to it all of the principles of farce with which we have been concerned. Analyze your character and determine his incongruities. Devise a setting, hand properties, and a costume for the scene that are germane to the text but that reflect your imaginative response to it. In rehearsal work on timing, clarity, and control. Eliminate clutter. Work on pace. Be prepared for handling laughter.

Selected Farce Scenes in Costume

(Some of these scenes may require a few lines from an additional character.)

SCENES FOR ONE MALE AND ONE FEMALE

Aristophanes, *Lysistrata:* Kinesias and Myrrhine
Chekhov, *The Boor:* Mrs. Popov, Smirnov
Feydeau, *A Flea in Her Ear,* II: Raymonde and Tournel
     Wooed and Viewed: Emma and Hector[4]
Molière, *The Miser,* II: Frosine and Harpagon
     The Physician in Spite of Himself, I: Martine and Sganarelle
Shakespeare, *The Taming of the Shrew,* II, 1: Katharine and Petruchio

SCENES FOR ONE MALE AND TWO FEMALES

Feydeau, *Keep an Eye on Amélie!,* II: Amélie, Irene, and Marcel[5]
Molière, *The Would-Be Gentleman,* III: Jourdain, Mdm. Jourdain, and Nicole
Prévert, *A United Family:* Gaspard-Adolphe, Gertrude, and Jacqueline[5]

SCENES FOR TWO MALES AND ONE FEMALE

Anon., *The Farce of the Worthy Pierre Pathelin,* Scene 3: The Draper, Pathelin, and Guillamette
Chekhov, *A Marriage Proposal:* Chubukov, Lomov, and Natalia
Labiche, *An Italian Straw Hat,* I: Anais, Emile, and Fadinard[6]
Molière, *Tartuffe,* IV: Elmire, Orgon, and Tartuffe

SCENE FOR TWO FEMALES

'Mr. S.', *Gammar Gurton's Needle,* III: Chat and Gammar

SCENE FOR TWO MALES

Molière, *Scapin,* III: Geronte and Scapin

CHAPTER 14

The Comedy of Manners

The comedy of manners is concerned primarily with idealizing the conventions and behavior of an elite social class, and with ridiculing those who fail to conform to its standards. The protagonists usually are brilliant wits such as Millamant and Mirabell in *The Way of the World,* who are to the manner born. The deviants fall into two classes: those who are ignorant of social decorum such as Sir Wilfull Witwould, and those, such as the fops in Restoration comedy, who abuse it because of a lack of moderation, or because of some excess such as Lady Wishfort's refusal to accept old age gracefully. The deviants, more often than not, belong in the realm of farce because their comic incongruities are exaggerated: the socially inferior are coarse and accident-prone; the fops overdress and labor futilely to be witty, and those who struggle against the inevitabilities of nature become grotesque.

Because farce already has been analyzed, there is no need to deal with the deviational characters of high comedy. Instead, our concern will be with the challenge of another, and quite different, comic level. It has been stated that the protagonists of the comedy of manners generally represent ideals of social behavior, although some of them are depicted with certain flaws: Loveless, in *Love's Last Shift,* is in need of sexual reform; Charles Surface, in *The School for Scandal,* has been too prodigal; Jack Worthing, in *The Importance of Being Earnest,* has been deceitful; and Jack Tanner, in *Man and Superman,* is smug and loquacious. But all of them are likeable characters, and each one is admirable for his intelligence and his social grace.

The essential difference between farce and high comedy is that the former is physical, earthy, and frenetic while the latter is intellectual, urbane, and restrained, with an emphasis on verbalism. This is one of the reasons why the appeal of high comedy is more limited than that of farce; physical action is more readily understood by nearly everyone (farce scenes from *The Would-Be Invalid* may be enjoyed even if the play is performed in a foreign language), but language that is ironic, subtle, and cleverly phrased offers delights that only the sophisticated may appreciate.

EXERCISES

1. Perform the Toinette-Argan chase scene, or the disguised doctor scene, without the words. Convert it into a scene of pure pantomime.
2. Perform the "proposal" scene between Millamant and Mirabell in Act IV of *The Way of the World* without words.

You will find that while the essential comic ideas of Molière's farce may be successfully communicated by pantomime alone, there is no way, no matter how skillful the pantomime, to convey the essentially comic elements of the scene from the Congreve play. You may convey the idea of a mock proposal, but there is no way outside of language to communicate the discrepancy between the surface appearance of a rather negative and unsentimental marriage bargain with its subtext of mutual affection. Nor is it possible to effectively mime the intellectual brilliance of the characters and their satirical reflections on marriage.

EXERCISES

1. Without undue concern for style, prepare the same scene including the dialogue from *The Way of the World* with as much comic stage business as you can invent. Your objective is to stimulate laughter by means of visual effects.
2. Perform the scene again with all of your concentration upon language. Make the scene a verbal fencing match.

The result once again should be obvious. High comedy requires less "stuffing" than farce; too much visual invention can only make the scene cumbersome and interfere with the effectiveness of the language.

LANGUAGE

We shall observe that, as is the case with any play, the comedy of manners requires physical action, and that there is much more for the actor to do than merely speak the words. But, as the previous exercises have demonstrated, the major source of laughter in high comedy is its language. Typical of Restoration comedy are lengthy scenes in which little is accomplished in terms of plot or character. Instead we are presented with exchanges of wit often in the form of a game in which the participants attempt to outdo one another in attacking the foibles of other persons or institutions. Because of its emphasis on language, a major portion of the success or failure of the comedy of manners in performance will depend on the actor's ability effectively to verbalize the distinctive qualities of the language.

One of the most serious errors in contemporary interpretation of the comedies of the Restoration and of the eighteenth century is that because they deal with an idle, leisured class, whose dress, speech, and manners are artificial, their characters move and speak with languorous affectation, with the result that the normative characters in the plays become comic deviants. We are prone to judge the social behavior of other times and places by our own standards of "naturalness." More will be said about this problem later, but our present concern is with language, and it is essential to realize that the society for which *The Way of the World* was written aspired to speak as brilliantly and artfully as possible, with the lightness and quickness of mind of Millamant and Mirabell. These are characters who do not have to strain to come up with exactly the correct phrase or witticism. Their wit flows as freely, as easily, and as sparklingly as champagne at a millionaire's wedding reception. Millamant is able to remark, "Let us be as strange as if we had been married a great while; and as well bred as if we were not married at all," without labor or hesitation.

The airiness of the language is a result of the apparent detachment with which the characters speak. Emotion is mistrusted and sentimentality is scorned; the former leads to loss of control—and self-control is *de rigueur* to a society that considers itself rational above everything else—and the latter to the exposure of blighted perception. The proper perspective for man is to view human behavior, including his own, coolly and objectively. The quality that removes this attitude from the realm of scientific observation is that one also views things humorously. In *The Way of the World,* Mirabell and Millamant are *deeply* in love. They are attracted to one another intellectually and sexually. But rarely will they display emotion, not even when they discuss their marriage in Act IV. Instead, each appears to insist upon certain concessions, which are critical of what is, apparently, typical marriage behavior. Instead of speaking idyllically of the joys of conceiving and raising a family, Mirabell uses such unendearing expressions as, "When you shall be breeding," referring to it as a result of their "endeavors." Millamant responds to the first with, "Ah. Name it not," and to the second with, "Odious endeavors!" Yet they know and we know that when they bed it will be fantastic, and that both will take pride in her gestation period, though they will take great pains to conceal or restrain overt expressions of joy.

Quickness of mind, lightness, and detachment are important for speech delivery, but these cannot be achieved if the actor seems to be laboring. This defect usually occurs when actors are not in complete control of the language, when they feel uncomfortable with it, and when they try too hard to appear witty. While Restoration comedy emphasizes intelligence, wit, and *savoir-faire* as standards for ideal behavior, none of these are acceptable if one must struggle to display them. Social effortlessness is the ultimate sign of the well-bred person. Witwould, as his name indicates, *would* be a wit, but Mirabell *is* one. Mirabell does not seem even to be *trying* to be witty or elegant. He emanates casualness, a kind of negligence, a nothing-to-it-ness, while delivering the most perfectly worded, perfectly phrased, perfectly polished commentary. Shakespeare exquisitely expresses this quality in *Henry IV, Part 1,* when Vernon describes Prince Hal:

> *I saw young Harry, with his beaver on,*
> *His cuisses on his thighs, gallantly armed,*
> *Rise from the ground like feathered Mercury,*
> *And vaulted with such ease into his seat*
> *As if an angel dropped down from the clouds*
> *To turn and wind a fiery Pegasus,*
> *And witch the world with noble horsemanship.*

> (IV, 1: ll. 104-110)

Hal's genius is in making a difficult action appear to be absurdly easy. Characters like Mirabell do the same with conversational art. Nor does Mirabell have to "punch" his points, for that would destroy their subtlety. Besides, his words are meant for the intelligent listener, not for those whose inferior wits require assistance in keeping up with him.

If the actor is to convey this important facet of characterization successfully, he himself must convey the same elegant ease and nonchalance in line delivery as was expected of the true Restoration wit.

EXERCISES

1. It would be advisable to work with a tape recorder in preparing the following exercises:
   a. Learn one of Millamant or Mirabell's speeches from the proposal scene in Act IV. Lines should be word-perfect, and as usual, you should understand the meaning of every word. Paraphrasing will be useful.
   b. Work very carefully on phrasing, so that complete clarity is achieved via verbal punctuation rather than by "punching" or by lengthy pauses.
   c. Strive for perfect enunciation, but do not appear to be working at it. In fact, with experience, language precision should become second nature.
   d. Deliver the lines with speed, but without allowing your tongue to out-race your mind. Quickness of thought is the justification for quickness of speech. You must never appear to be racing. Never allow yourself to gasp or to run out of breath. Plan your phrasing so that you can speak with rapidity.
   e. The lines must appear to be your very own. They should be spoken unaffectedly and confidently. Although as observers we admire Congreve's brilliant dialogue, as characters we must appear to take it for granted.
   f. Listen to the recording of your work and evaluate it in terms of the above criteria. Work on eliminating your defects.
2. Listen to professional recordings of comedies of manners. A splendid example is the recorded production of *The School for Scandal* with John Gielgud. Using the criteria suggested in the preceding exercise, evaluate scenes or speeches from the recording.

MANNERS

When we deal with manners we are concerned with external behavior. A consciousness of manner, such as is only possible in an organized society, leads to the establishment of customs and standards for external behavior. Leisured classes are inclined to place greater stress upon the refinements of external behavior because they are possessed of greater freedom, time, wealth, and educational opportunities. Characteristic of such classes are preoccupation with their life styles and with making an art out of day-to-day living.

Because manners are based less upon necessity for survival than upon artificial rules and customs, acceptable modes of behavior vary from society to society. What is considered tasteful by one group may be regarded as vulgar by another, and what is considered important by one group may be regarded as trivial by another. In order to appreciate works of art whose main concern is with the manners of a particular social group, it behooves the observer to familiarize himself with its rules for external behavior. Our attempts to find appropriate modes of expression for tragedy were based less upon the need to learn about superficial modes of behavior than to find ways of aesthetically supporting deeper human concerns. Tragedy focuses upon the inner person and his moral and spiritual conflicts. This is why poetic accuracy outweighs the accuracy of material time, place, or custom for those plays. The comedy of manners, because it attempts to mirror the external behavior of a particular society, requires that its actors accurately represent that behavior.

The plays themselves will provide us with much that we need to know because they are *about* manners. But when those plays are as remote in time as Restoration comedy, it becomes necessary to go beyond the text and to familiarize ourselves with whatever written and graphic data are available. The following material, which will concentrate upon Restoration comedy, is intended less as a comprehensive investigation into its manners than as a useful guide for such a study.

PHILOSOPHY OF LIFE STYLE

Any code of manners is based on interpretations of the nature of man. Comedies of manners are not unduly concerned with exploring the nature of man, but the outer behavior that they attempt to represent is the result of a society's assumptions about itself. When the importance of verbal expression in Restoration comedy was discussed, it was observed that the high regard for artful conversation was based on a capacity to exercise a witty and precise intellect, while revealing a detached and unemotional response to the world. Reason, clarity, order, and restraint were the foundations for speech decorum.

The society that produced Restoration comedy consisted primarily of the court of England's Charles II. Its members were all too familiar with death and violence: most of them survived a civil war from which many had narrowly escaped execution, and which had forced many into exile for nearly two decades; they were exposed constantly to the ravages of the plague; London was filled with poverty, and its streets were unsafe. Religious doubt had been increasing and its new substitute, science, could not provide consolation and solace for the nastiness of life. Cynicism was the inevitable result: the world is bleak; men essentially are corrupt and bestial, and not to be readily trusted. Survival requires one to be suspicious and constantly on guard. Emotion weakens the judgment; excessive emotion produces chaos. The best safeguards against exploitation and danger are a knowledge of "the way of the world," and firm control of emotion. The more positive view of man is that he is endowed with reason and will, which enable him to control his baser nature, to steel him against adversity, and to protect him from the machinations of others. It is also possible to create a life of beauty and harmony by the implementation of rules for any aspect of life that can be controlled, such as language, dress, and personal behavior (manners).

Beauty, of course, is relative, but the criteria for the seventeenth century aristocrat, besides order and harmony, included elegance, grace, and decorative embellishment. We have observed these qualities in Congreve's dialogue, where the witty manipulation of language proved to be more important than functional communication. Mirabell and Millamant will not simply say, "Let's get married!" Instead, they play delightful games with elegantly embroidered word patterns that ultimately lead not merely to a marriage agreement, but to the realization of a completely compatible life style that will make their marriage work.

The generalizations that follow are intended to describe some of the customs of Restoration high society and the correlation with their philosophical sources. It is not feasible to include descriptions of the daily routines of court society; such routines are accurately reflected in the plays. Nor is it possible to describe all of the detailed rules for various social functions. For those who are interested in further exploration, references to materials dealing with such matters are included in the bibliography. Our major concern is with the investigation of materials that can provide the actor with foundations upon which he may base his choices.

CLOTHING

As was the case in Elizabethan drama, the costumes worn in Restoration comedy duplicated the clothing of the time. An essential difference, however, was that unlike most of the plays performed earlier in the century, the time and place of the action in Restoration comedy was contemporary London, with an emphasis upon fashion itself. Costume then becomes important in and for itself, and becomes symbolic of not simply how the upper class dressed, but of the purpose and value of its apparel. For Restoration society, the naked human body represented the bestial aspect of man. Just as manners were imposed upon behavior in order to control and refine it, the purpose of clothing was to "civilize" the body, not by merely covering it up but by transposing it into an ideal shape—an external form that would be rich, elegant, graceful, beautiful, and which would encourage similar qualities in posture and movement. It is important to realize that the dress of this society is not intended to appear natural; its purpose is to conceal rather than reveal natural shapes. To these ends fabrics such as velvets, lace, satin, and fur were combined, and garments were lavishly decorated with bright dyes, jewelry, ribbons, brocade, feathers, and floral patterns.

Female Dress

As with Elizabethan female dress, the Restoration lady adopted the stiffened torso. Corsets or modified stomachers were worn and the bodice was attached tightly to a tapered waist. A short peplum (skirt) frequently was attached to the bodice and extended over the top of the outer skirt. Now that women were permitted to perform on the stage, the female costume could more effectively emulate whatever sexual emphases were in vogue. Shoulders were bare and there was ample décolletage. Sleeves were three-quarter length, revealing more of the lower arm, and varied in fullness

FIGURE 14-1. *Seventeenth century costume: female. Victoria and Albert Museum, Crown Copyright.*

and styling. Skirts continued to be full, but were no longer extended at the hips by a farthingale or widened by hoops (which did, however, make a return early in the following century). Instead, numerous petticoats were used to fill out the lower part of the body. The outer skirt was left open in front and pinned back, revealing a richly decorated skirt beneath.

Sleeved jackets and short capes could be worn over the bodice. Shoes were high-heeled, squared-off at the toes, and decorated with ribbons. Elbow length gloves were fashionable.

INFLUENCE ON POSTURE AND MOVEMENT. With the disappearance of the ruff and the extended stomacher, women's postures now were less rigid than earlier in the century. But the stiffened bodice kept the torso straight and rigid for both standing and sitting postures. The shoulders continued to be tight so that gestures were made with the lower arms. The arm could be held more naturally than before because of the disappearance of the farthingale. The high heels forced the weight of the body to be supported by the balls of the feet, which the lady placed down before the heel when walking. All in all, the posture and movement of the Restoration lady were more relaxed and natural than those of her Elizabethan counterpart.

Male Dress

Even more significant changes were made in the masculine costume. Now the male was to be more decorated than the female. In the comedies, very little ado is made over women's fashions, but comments about men's wear appear with regularity. One of the stock characters of Restoration comedy was the male fop, whose clothing excesses were ridiculed. Fops must have gone pretty far because the acceptable mode already was quite elaborate.

Breeches continued to be worn, but with a narrower look. Some were loose and tubular, ending just above the knee. Petticoat breeches were longer and fuller, and almost skirtlike in appearance. The doublet was lengthened, sometimes to the knee, and flared. Fancy vests and waistcoats were worn beneath the doublet, which was left partially unbuttoned so that the rich undergarments might be seen. Instead of a ruff, falling bands of lace circled the throat, or the *steinkirk* (a loose cravat) was worn. Stockings were worn and covered all of the leg not covered by the breeches. Sometimes they were gartered over the breeches. They were dyed and often had patterns embroidered on their sides. The doublet sleeves

Dessiné par I.D. De St Iean 1694.   auec priuilege du Roy.

FIGURE 14-2. *Seventeenth century costume: male. Victoria and Albert Museum, Crown Copyright.*

were full length, and lace cuffs protruded from beneath them, covering a good portion of the hands. Lace was often added below the breeches, sometimes falling to the shins.

A very important development was the wearing of periwigs, which were curled and worn shoulder length. Hats were more often carried than worn, and were wide brimmed, stiff crowned, and decorated with feathers and ribbons.

Shoes had high cuban-type heels, which were often painted a different color than the rest of the shoe. They were square-toed and decorated with ribbons. Unlike that of the female, the male body was almost completely covered, with the face and fingertips often providing the only visible skin.

INFLUENCE ON POSTURE AND MOVEMENT. Generally speaking, the overall elegance of masculine dress requires a certain pride of bearing. Posture should be upright; slumping positions would be incongruous. The doublet is tight across the back and constricted in the upper sleeves, creating a certain arm stiffness. Elbows cannot be fully bent, and gestures are restricted to the lower arms, wrists, and hands. The male, however, has plenty of freedom of movement in walking and turning. The full wig, of course, makes it necessary for him to turn his entire head toward the object of his attention. As with the Elizabethan male, his calves are exposed and he must stand and sit so that they present the most handsome and graceful appearance. The suggestions made for leg positions for Elizabethan men may be applied to those of the Restoration. The higher heels of the shoes will require more careful strides, and will thrust the weight to the balls of the feet. The heels will bring attention to a well-turned ankle.

The lace cuffs must be controlled when the character handles objects. Turning them back, or raising the lower arm and flicking them with the wrists, are some of the techniques used to free the hands. This should be done naturally, and only when necessary.

Arms may hang loosely at the side, but a favorite position is resting the back of the knuckles of one hand against the hip and bending the elbow slightly. Usually the male will sit with torso erect, but unlike the corseted female, he may lean back into his chair casually, but with casual elegance.

When he is carrying his hat, he should permit it to rest on his lower arm, which will be held horizontally across his stomach. There is nothing wrong with dropping the arm holding the hat if such action is justified. Gesturing when carrying a hat should be executed with the free arm.

FIGURE 14-3. *Seventeenth century costumes: male and female. Victoria and Albert Museum, Crown Copyright.*

Removing the hat is never done in a careless manner, but as with the handling of other objects, it should be performed as a kind of ritual. The wearer must first extend his arm out to his side, then allow it to sweep toward the front brim of the hat, which he grasps in his fingers. The hat is then raised off the head and swung in an arc as the arm stretches sideways and down, where it should be held away from the body.

FIGURE 14-4. *Influence of Restoration costume upon physical stance. From the National Theatre production of Congreve's* The Way of the World. *Photo by Dominic Photography, London.*

EXERCISES

---

1. Locate and study the portrait paintings of Jonès, Knellar, Lely, and Van Dyke, and the engravings of Bosse for their depiction of dress.   Concentrate on posture and stance.
2. Assume similar poses, and with an external image provided by a portrait, move as you feel the model might have done.
3. If costumes of the period are available to you, put some of them on and practice moving, standing, and sitting in them.   Use a full length mirror to observe yourself.   If you do not have access to period costumes, use items of clothing and materials that might provide you with similar body influences.

ACCESSORIES

Accessories were like toys to Restoration high society, and were subject to similar rules and rituals as the removal of a man's hat previously described. Most accessories were nonutilitarian and were used either to further decorate the body or to provide objects whose handling might contribute to overall appearance or provide something to occupy the hands.   Whatever their purpose, rules were created to govern *how* accessories were to be used. A familiarity with accessories and their use provides the actor with the kind of details that may best demonstrate a society's obsession with order and control, even for the most trivial external behavior.   Ignorance was the cardinal sin and one's command of the most trivial details demonstrated that he or she was "in the know."   It behooved every member of this society not only to know the abstract principles of the way of the world, but every detail of social behavior which that world dictated.

Following are descriptions of the major accessories used by men and women, with some examples of their usage.

Women's Accessories

Jewelry was worn abundantly, and included earrings, necklaces, bracelets, and rings, which sometimes were worn on all the fingers.   A woman might toy with an earring or turn her rings; she might touch them in various ways to indicate coyness, shock, or flirtatiousness. A walking stick was sometimes carried when going for a stroll or a visit. It was decorated, sometimes with valuable gold or silver knobs, and ribbons. It would not be used to support the body. Instead, it would be held lightly with the fingertips over the head of the stick or just beneath it. It would be held a comfortable distance away from the body when walking. When standing still, the lady might ignore it (but not the correctness of its position), gesture subtly with it, and use it to complete telling poses. For example, an indignant reaction could be displayed by raising the chin and bosom while extending the arm and hand holding the walking stick, so that it would be angled away from the body. Parasols were carried outdoors, ostensibly to protect the skin from the sun. But even with a functional purpose, parasols were used decoratively and, as with the walking stick, to aid body language. When open, parasols were permitted to rest against the shoulder, where they might be twirled easily by the fingertips. They could be closed and used as walking sticks.

Handkerchiefs of lace or silk were carried and were held either in a ring, bracelet, or sleeve. They were never used to blow the nose, but to add further adornment and to aid gesture. In a tearful or mock-tearful scene, the actress might use it to touch the area beneath the eye or the nostrils, but she would never actually wipe with it.

Perhaps a woman's most important single prop was her fan, which she carried everywhere. It was the folding type and was usually made of fine materials that were, of course, hand painted. One did not use a fan because of the heat. It was a pretty object to hold and with which to occupy one's hand. When open, it was held in front of the bosom, about eight to twelve inches away, and was fluttered, but not constantly. When closed, the fan was an unconscious extension of the hand, and was used to point and gesture. There was an art to opening it with a flick of the wrist, followed by a quick fluttering. The fan was probably used more than any other object for visual communication. There was even a special vocabulary of the fan to convey specific signals to the observer. For the actress this is less important than mastering a more universal visual language with the fan. Discovering ways of expressing outrage, fear, flirtatiousness, innocence, indifference, or other emotional reactions with facility is her vital concern.

The following scene from Etherege's *The Man of Mode* (1676) provides us with an excellent example of the use of the fan to communicate deliberate impressions. In the scene, Young Bellair and Harriet, whose parents want them to marry but whose hearts belong to others, attempt by looks and gestures to convince their elders that they are passionately in love.

YOUNG BELLAIR: Now for a look and gestures that may persuade 'em saying all the passionate things imaginable.

HARRIET: Your head a little more on one side. Ease yourself on your left leg and play with your right hand.

YOUNG BELLAIR: Thus, is it not?

HARRIET: Now set your right leg firm on the ground, adjust your belt, then look about you.

YOUNG BELLAIR: A little exercising will make me perfect.

HARRIET: Smile, and turn to me again very sparkish.

YOUNG BELLAIR: Will you take your turn and be instructed?

HARRIET: With all my heart!

YOUNG BELLAIR: At one motion play your fan, roll your eyes, and then settle a kind look upon me.

HARRIET: So!

YOUNG BELLAIR: Now spread your fan, look down upon it, and tell the sticks with a finger.

HARRIET: Very modish!

YOUNG BELLAIR: Clap your hand up to your bosom, hold down your gown. Shrug a little, draw up your breasts, and let 'em fall again gently, with a sigh or two, etc.

HARRIET: By the good instructions you give, I suspect you for one of those malicious observers who watch people's eyes, and from innocent looks make scandalous conclusions.

YOUNG BELLAIR: I know some, indeed, who out of mere love to mischief are as vigilant as jealousy itself, and will give you an account of every glance that passes at a play and i'th' Circle.

HARRIET: 'Twill not be amiss now to seem a little pleasant.

YOUNG BELLAIR: Clap your fan, then, in both your hands; snatch it to your mouth, smile, and with a lively motion fling your body a little forwards. So! Now spread it, fall back on the sudden, cover your face with it and break out into a loud laughter— take up, look grave, and fall a-fanning of yourself.—Admirably well acted!

HARRIET: I think I am pretty apt at these matters.

Another accessory, though used more limitedly, was the *vizard*, or mask, which was worn in places such as the theatre, where it was fashionable to be unrecognized, or at fancy balls. They usually were half-masks covering the upper part of the face, and were either held to the head by ribbons or held with the hand by an attached stick. In the comedies the detached mask could be used to greater advantage, for it might be handled playfully so as to reveal and conceal, and it could be used like previously mentioned objects, for expressive purposes.

Although not accessories in the true sense of the word, knitting, sewing, and embroidering are useful and accurate activities for the female, and may be expressively utilized by changing speeds, arrested movements, and other motions.

Men's Accessories

Men also carried decorated walking sticks and used them similarly, though they were longer and might be used less formally. For example, the cane might be tucked diagonally under the arm with the knob held forward, or a casual stance might be achieved by placing both hands in front on the head of the cane, as though leaning on it. If a greeting was required while a cane was in use, it was moved to the left hand, which was then extended full-armed to the left, while the other hand removed the hat or took the lady's hand to kiss it.

Handkerchiefs also were carried by men, but were much larger than those of the women and were more frequently exhibited. Like those of the ladies, men's handkerchiefs might be attached to rings or placed in the sleeve, but they might also be tucked into a pocket placed low on the doublet. China silk was a most effective material for the ceremonious use of the handkerchief because it billowed so gracefully. As with the women, the handkerchief was used more for decoration and expression than for functional reasons. A gentleman might fan himself with it after exerting himself, use it to wave at a lady, or touch his brow or upper lip with just the edge of the handkerchief to suggest or mock the removal of perspiration. It could be used effectively to clear the air of bad odors or of the aura left behind by an odious character.

Men actually carried more objects on their persons than women; purses, mirrors, snuffboxes, combs, swords, and small vials of perfume were accommodated in one way or another on a man's person, for these were "necessities" at home and abroad.

While handling snuff is often overdone by actors in Restoration comedy, there are no better examples (outside of the fan) of decorum in the management of objects than the rules concerning the taking of snuff. Schools were even created to teach a "snuff curriculum!"[7] An advertisement in the *Spectator* (August 8, 1711) announced, "The exercise of the Snuff

Box, according to the most fashionable Airs and Notions in opposition to the exercise of the Fan will be taught with the best plain or perfumed Snuff, at Charles Lille's & C."[8]   The snuff ritual went something like this:

1. A small snuffbox was kept in a pocket of the doublet, and was drawn out by the left hand.
2. With the fingers of the right hand, three taps were applied to the top of the box in order to settle the dispersed grains of snuff.
3. The box was opened and a pinch of snuff withdrawn with the thumb and index finger of the right hand. The lid of the box was then closed with the left thumb. The right hand was shaken once or twice to get rid of excess grains. At this point, one of several alternatives could be chosen for the next step.
    a. The pinch of snuff might be placed on the back of the left hand.
    b. The snuff might be placed on the left thumbnail, assisted by the index finger.
    c. The snuff might be kept in the fingers and thumb of the right hand.
4. The snuff was raised to each nostril and sniffed in.
5. The snuffbox was replaced in the pocket.
6. The handkerchief was drawn sharply forward and ceremoniously waved back and forth across the chest, to clear away loose grains which may have fallen on the doublet.
7. The imbiber might, if he wished, delicately touch each nostril with the handkerchief—but he must not sneeze or blow his nose.

As with other accessories, while the rules of application are fairly rigid, the manner of performance may communicate status or attitudes, such as "pinch military . . . pinch malicious . . . pinch dictatorial . . . pinch sublimely contemptuous . . . pinch polite,"[9] etc.

Men also smoked long, slender, curved clay pipes, which were smoked at home and in taverns or coffeehouses. The pipes were held at the stem behind the bowl, which rested on the lower joint of the thumb and was held by the index finger curved over the stem, or by the fingertips held under the stem near the bowl.

EXERCISES

WOMEN

1. Practice the removal and replacement of handkerchiefs from rings, bracelets, and sleeves.

2. Work with a fan. Practice opening and closing it with precision and facility.
3. Stroll with a closed parasol. Open it and stroll some more. Close it and continue strolling.

MEN

1. Stand, walk, and sit with a walking stick about four feet tall.
2. Practice removing your hat while in the possession of a walking stick.
3. Learn the snuff "ceremony" well enough to perform it without thinking.

SOCIAL CUSTOMS

Only those customs that are useful for playing Restoration comedy will be mentioned. Check the bibliography for works that will amplify such information.

Wine was never sipped by men, but was swallowed in a single draught. In tea scenes, the hostess will pour and either offer the guest his cup and saucer, or hand it to a servant to give to him. The cup and saucer should be handled with control and delicacy. Expressive points can be made with the cup and saucer. The timing of sipping and speaking must be absolutely precise.

Greetings between men can be made with a brief nod of the head, but they are more formal with members of the opposite sex. The gentleman bows, even to his wife, upon greeting, by stepping forward with his left foot, bending his right knee and leaning his torso forward from the hip. His lower arms should be held outward with the hands raised, palms down, and fingers bent gracefully. He may at the same time remove his hat by grasping the front brim as he steps forward and bringing it vigorously down and to his side. If he wishes to be a bit more flamboyant, he may cross his hat in several small arcs in front of him from left to right, plumes flying, before he brings it to his side. The bow may be followed by kissing the lady's hand, which must first be offered to him. He takes it gently with his fingertips, palms up and fingers bent gracefully, and gently brushes the back of her hand with his lips.

The lady's curtsey is similar to the Elizabethan curtsey. She may step forward with her left foot, then bend her knees slightly as though she were going to sit. Her torso remains erect, but she inclines her head slightly.

Her fan hand should be held away from the body, palm upward, and to the right side, while her left arm is bent at the elbow, forearm raised to the side, the palm of her hand is down, and her fingers are curved gracefully.

When the gentleman and lady depart together, he offers his arm to her by raising his elbow to the side so that his entire arm is in a horizontal position. The elbow is bent forward and the forearm offered to the lady, who extends her arm away from her body, elbow bent and forearm raised, and places her hand lightly over his wrist.

Exercises for social customs will be incorporated into the final exercises at the conclusion of this chapter.

THE "REALITY" OF RESTORATION COMEDY

A knowledge of the way of the world and of the special social code of the Restoration upper class was essential for dignified survival for each member of that class. But knowledge alone was not enough. You were a prominent candidate for ridicule if you possessed such knowledge but failed to exercise it properly, as is the case with Witwould and Petulant in *The Way of the World*. Perhaps such discrepancy is best expressed in the following discussion of Lord Foppington between Loveless and his wife Amanda, in John Van Brugh's *The Relapse* (1696):

AMANDA: Now it moves my pity more than my mirth, to see a man whom nature has made no fool be so very industrious to pass for an ass.

LOVELESS: No, there you are wrong, Amanda; you should never bestow your pity upon those who take pains for your contempt. Pity those whom nature abuses, but never those who abuse nature.

(Act II)

The meaning of "nature" in the context of Loveless's remark is an important clue for our understanding of the proper execution of the social code. Clearly one must be pitied if nature has not endowed him with a sound mind and body and the capacity to control them. It is when those endowments are misdirected that nature is abused, and its violators become "un-natural." Social deviants such as Sir Wilfull Witwould are ludicrous because of their ignorance of the social code, but our ridicule is tempered for two reasons. First, they have not had the benefit of a social education, and second, they have no pretentions to wit or social grace. More deserving of unpitying scorn are the Anthony Witwoulds, Petulants, Foppingtons, and others who *affect* wit without possessing it and who distort social propriety in their efforts to conform to it. They *affect* manners rather than *reflect* them in their efforts to prove to society that they belong in it. In this sense they are exhibitionists, constantly trying to bring attention to their "wit," their success with women, their acquisition or exaggeration of the latest fashions, and their awareness of the latest fads, such as the interspersion of French phrases (usually mispronounced) in their conversation.

Behaving "naturally" is relative because of the varied interpretations of man's nature. Since the late eighteenth century, the Western world's ideal of naturalness has been the noble savage whose natural instincts have not been repressed or violated by the tyranny of man-made rules. Today's "do your own thing" is a manifestation of this philosophy. It follows then, that for us a society such as that of the Restoration court that stressed artifice would be scorned for its "unnaturalness," just as our behavior would have been scorned by it as being "primitive," which for it represented "unnaturalness."

But there is another way of looking at criteria for naturalness. *Within* every society, affectation and pretentiousness are the critical terms applied to those who distort, exaggerate, and flaunt their social norms. True naturalness for any society really boils down to being able to assimilate one's social norms so well and so completely that its expression becomes completely unself-conscious and unlabored. It has been observed that the secret of successful verbal expression for Restoration society was a combination of true wit and its nonchalant (natural) delivery. The same principle applied to the wearing of its lavishly ornamented dress: one had to match its elegance physically, but with effortlessness (naturalness) and apparent unconcern. Finally, the same principle applied to the execution of artificial social customs whose practice was only acceptable if it appeared to be intuitive (natural) rather than learned. You are only successful with handling your fan or your snuffbox if you can convince everyone that such acts come as easily to you as breathing or any other natural function.

The modern actor is obliged to recognize these principles of naturalness if he is to perform successfully in comedies of manners of any period or place. Such comedies are intended to mirror realistically the actual or ideal external behavior of a real social group. Unfortunately, too many productions of Restoration comedy fail to make this observation because they em-

309

phasize the discrepancies between *modern* standards of normative behavior and those of the Restoration, rather than the discrepancies between the standards of the Restoration and its own deviationists.

The result is that what should be performed with the kind of naturalness demanded instead is presented as ludicrous affectation. *All* males, not just the fops, are delineated as affected and pretentious, and because they wore lace and high heels, as effeminate creatures with loose wrists, shrill voices, and mincing steps, constantly posturing and waving their silk handkerchiefs. Actresses portray the games the female characters play with heavy-handed coyness, flirtatiousness, and unceasing fan fluttering.

Because of its stress on emotional control and a protective veneer of restraint and dissimulation, the characters of Restoration comedy are too often portrayed as fashionable puppets who are never quite human. The artifice is presented without belief in a subtext in which very earnest desires and emotions exist. The contemporary actor must approach the challenge of these plays positively by accepting the characters as real people, and believing for a period of time that he must "live" with them in the reality of their life style.

EXERCISES

1. Realistically perform a simple function such as drinking a beverage, locating a book and sitting down to read, playing cards, or making a purchase.

2. Wearing a real or simulated Restoration costume, repeat your performance as naturally as possible.

3. Have someone play a musical selection from the works of Handel, Haydn, Purcell, Rameau, Lully, or any late seventeenth century composer. Repeat your selected action, allowing the rhythm and style of the music to affect you.

4. Create and prepare a pantomime for two or more characters in which you will portray a Restoration protagonist. Establish an environment such as a drawing room, dressing room, ballroom, or mall, in which some kind of social activity is taking place. It might be a dance or a gossip session during which tea is served. Create a simple given circumstance: a flirtation or intrigue, a lesson in some sort of skill. Incorporate the use of accessories and social customs. Everything must be performed with lightness, restraint, and full mastery of all social conventions. Choose a musical selection from one of the composers listed above, and time your scene precisely to it.

5. Select one of the Restoration comedy scenes listed below and do the following:

    a. Analyze the characters and their relationship.

    b. Provide an environment for the scene with appropriate furniture and properties.

    c. During rehearsals, go through the scene paraphrasing the dialogue.

    d. During rehearsals, improvise different external conditions, but play the character and the dialogue. Try playing the scene on the telephone, while eating lunch, or while playing a game (cards, checkers, darts, etc.).

    e. Work on the exact timing of your personal stage business and dialogue.

    f. Help each other to develop preciseness and clarity of speech, and ease of delivery.

    g. Get used to costumes and accessories so that their use becomes second nature.

    h. Warm up for rehearsals and performances by listening to music of the period, and, if you can receive instruction, by dancing to it.

Selected Period Scenes for the Comedy of Manners

SCENES FOR ONE MALE AND ONE FEMALE

Etherege, *The Man of Mode,* V, 1: Dorimant and Mrs. Loveit

Farquhar, *The Beaux' Stratagem,* IV, 1 and V, 2: Archer and Mrs. Sullen

Molière, *The Misanthrope,* III, 7: Alceste and Arsinoe
                IV, 3: Alceste and Célimene

Van Brugh, *The Relapse,* II, 1: Amanda and Loveless
             III, 2: Berinthia and Worthy
             III, 2: Berinthia and Loveless
             IV, 3: Berinthia and Loveless
             V, 4: Amanda and Worthy

SCENES FOR TWO FEMALES

Farquhar, *The Beaux' Stratagem,* IV, 1: Dorinda and Mrs. Sullen

Molière, *The Misanthrope,* III, 4: Arsinoe and Célimene

Van Brugh, *The Relapse,* II, 1 and IV, 2: Amanda and Berinthia

311

SCENES FOR TWO MALES

Etherege, *The Man of Mode*, I: Dorimant and Medley
Farquhar, *The Beaux' Stratagem*, I: Aimwell and Archer
Wycherley, *The Country Wife*, I: Harcourt and Horner

PART V

NOTES

1. Athena Seyler and Stephen Haggard, *The Craft of Comedy* (New York: Theatre Arts Books, 1966).
2. Phyllis Hartnell, ed., *The Oxford Companion to the Theatre* (London: Oxford University Press, 1951), p. 255. [Emphasis mine.]
3. Frederick C. Green, ed., *Comedies, Molière,* Vol. 2 (London: J. M. Dent and Sons Ltd.), p. 416.
4. Norman R. Shapiro, ed., *Four Farces by George Feydeau* (Chicago: University of Chicago Press, 1970).
5. Eric Bentley, ed., *Let's Get a Divorce and Other Plays* (New York: Hill and Wang, Inc., 1958).
6. ———, *The Modern Theatre,* Vol. 3 (New York: Doubleday & Co., Inc., 1965).
7. Mattoon M. Curtis, *The Book of Snuff and Snuff Boxes* (New York: Liveright Publishing Corp., 1935), p. 72.
8. *Ibid.,* quoted on p. 72.
9. *Ibid.,* p. 75.

SELECTED READINGS

Farce

Bentley, Eric. "The Psychology of Farce," in *Let's Get a Divorce and Other Plays.* New York: Hill and Wang, Inc., 1958.
Bergson, Henri. *Laughter.* New York: The Macmillan Co., 1913.
Dolman, John. *The Art of Acting.* New York: Harper and Bros., 1949.
Freud, Sigmund. *Wit and Its Relation to the Unconscious.* New York: Random House, 1938.
Selden, Samuel. *First Steps in Acting.* 2d ed. New York: Appleton-Century-Crofts, 1964.
Seyler, Athene, and Haggard, Stephen. *The Craft of Comedy.* New York: Theatre Arts Books, Inc., 1946.
Thompson, Alan R. *The Anatomy of Drama.* Berkeley: University of California Press, 1942.

High Comedy (Restoration)

Barton, Lucy. *Historic Costume for the Stage*. Boston: Walter H. Barker & Co., 1935.

Brockett, Oscar G. *History of the Theatre*. 2d ed. Boston: Allyn and Bacon, Inc., 1974.

Bryant, Arthur. *The England of Charles II*. London: Longmans, Green and Co., 1935.

Cunnington, C. W., and Cunnington, P. *Handbook of English Costume in the Seventeenth Century*. 2d ed. London: Faber, 1957.

Curtis, Mattoon M. *The Book of Snuff and Snuff Boxes*. New York: Liveright Publishing Corp., 1935.

Henshaw, N. S. "Graphic Sources for a Modern Approach to the Acting of Restoration Comedy," *Educational Theatre Journal,* Vol. 20: 157-170.

Holland, Norman. *The First Modern Comedies*. Cambridge, Mass.: Harvard University Press, 1959.

Longueville, Thomas. *Rochester and Other Literary Rakes of the Court of Charles II*. London: Longmans, Green & Co., 1903.

Meredith, George. *An Essay on Comedy*. New York: Charles Scribner's Sons, 1897.

Nicoll, Allardyce. *The Development of the Theatre*. New York: Harcourt, Brace & Co., n.d.

Rockwood, Jerome. *The Craftsmen of Dionysus*. Glenview, Ill.: Scott, Foresman & Co., 1966.

Seyler, Athene, and Haggard, Stephen. *The Craft of Comedy*. New York: Theatre Arts Books, Inc., 1946.

Sydney, William C. *Social Life in England*. London: Ward & Downey, 1892.

Thompson, Alan R. *The Anatomy of Drama*. Berkeley: University of California Press, 1942.

Ward, Ned. *The London Spy*. New York: H. Doran & Co., n.d.

Wilkenson, D. R. M. *The Comedy of Habit*. London: Universitaire Press, 1964.

Portraits by Sir Godfrey Knellar and Sir Peter Lely will be useful for the student of Restoration acting.

POSTSCRIPT

Completing the Complete Actor

Many aspiring actors do not realize, and many practicing actors forget, that acting is a craft. The industrial age and mass production have diminished the concept of craftsmanship as being work performed with skill and artistry. Acting, in a majority of television and film drama and stock theatres, has joined other crafts that have succumbed to assembly-line mediocrity. There is little time to study scripts, to develop rich characterizations, to rehearse enough for the creative imagination to be properly exercised, and finally to refine and perfect the results. The substitute for all this is typecasting, and the only "skill" expected from the actor is his ability to learn lines quickly, adapt to the medium, and satisfy the superficial qualities that his roles demand. Facility, not artistry, is expected, with the result that the contemporary actor strives for little else.

It is true that the craftsmanship of recent scriptwriting has created minimal challenges for the actor, but our concern is not for the actor who is content to confine his talent to such activities. That actor will be fragmented rather than complete because he denies himself the opportunity to exercise the full potentialities of his craft. To begin with, completeness can be attained only by those who seek the opportunities to perform in the type of plays and conditions that challenge both their imagination and their interpretative abilities.

If such an actor is fortunate enough to find the proper theatrical milieu, and is talented enough to be accepted into it, he must resist the temptation to rest on his laurels. Like most crafts, acting requires continued practice and thought. Because his expressive instruments are his own voice and body, he cannot afford to neglect or abuse them. Like the conscientious professional musician, he must exercise and expand the capacity and range of his instruments daily. Some of the great European repertory companies require its members, including its established stars, to attend voice and body sessions several times a week. But the really conscientious actor will not need to be forced into such activity. He wisely recognizes that his art and livelihood depend too much on the care and exercise of his voice and body, and he will see to their maintenance without external compulsion.

We have learned that fine acting requires sensitivity and imagination as well as well-developed and flexible bodies and voices. These qualities require as much continued exercise as do the body and the voice. Unless the actor is involved with a company such as the Open Theatre where the actor originates the characters he plays, he thinks of himself as being less a creator than an interpreter. But as it has been emphasized, the act of giving a character an embodiment is truly creative and requires as much awareness and sensitivity to the world as is demanded of the playwright, the painter, or the sculptor. We have seen that no one necessarily is born, or gifted, with acute perceptivity. This is a talent that is cultivated and that must be maintained and expanded if the artist is to justify the continuation of his work.

The actor, too, must never stop seeing. His observation of people, animals, and objects and his imaginative responses to them must be an habitual, never-ending process. He must make a continual practice of looking inward, and analyzing his own behavior and experience. He must continue to exploit the work of those who by their art can expand his appreciation of life, by attending museums and art galleries at least twice a year and by reading voraciously.

The actor also is involved in works of living art whose expression of ideas about the human condition must have relevance for the audience for whom it is enacted. Such ideas are not limited to one concept of human nature or human activity. We have seen, for example, that characterization is not limited to psychological behavior, but may stress man's social or political behavior. Works such as *Medea* and *Richard II* assume special values for today's audiences. The concern of the former with the human rights of women and of the latter with the misuse of power and the question of the justification of political assassination, assume special importance and focus for today's audience, and this must be realized by the actor. The actor who is out of touch with his changing world limits his personal and, consequently, his artistic, vision.

The world's changes are mirrored in its art. Our study of reality and its relation to style attempted to demonstrate the relation between notions about reality and acting conventions. Because conceptions about the nature of the world constantly are being reinforced or changed, forms of artistic expression become altered. Successful actors often do not feel the need to be curious about new developments in their craft. Why should they when they have reached a pinnacle in their chosen field? The answer is a simple one: when we lose our desire and capacity for growth we face a kind of spiritual death. This is not limited to living, but to our life's work, which like life itself, requires some sort of periodic regeneration. The artist cannot stop the normal deterioration of his body, but he can extend the scope and vitality of his vision. Actors need regularly to explore new methods to freshen and improve their work. They need constantly to experiment to find more effective ways of solving old problems, and the best ways of solving new ones.

In one sense Stanislavski's work evolved in order to find ways of dealing with the new naturalism, but it also was concerned with finding new and effective ways of consciously doing what great actors had been unconsciously doing for centuries. There are those who may feel that the devotion of so much space in this book to Greek acting style is wasteful because few actors will have the opportunity to act in Greek tragedy. These people fail to take into consideration that such efforts can only challenge and enlarge the actor's abilities and skills. One will be a better realistic actor, if this is what his future limits him to, for his experience with Greek tragedy.

The preceding reflections about the actor as craftsman emphasize the necessity of a certain self-discipline: the actor's responsibility in maintaining and perfecting his skills. There is yet another kind of self-discipline that the actor must develop before he lays claim to being a complete actor. The theatre is a collaborative art and the degree of a production's success depends upon the quality of the contributions of each of its participants. The playwright depends upon the director, designers, and actors to interpret and illuminate his manuscript. The director is responsible for a clear and *unified* interpretation of a text, but must depend upon the imagination and cooperation of the designers and the actors. The actor, unless he is performing in a one-man show, needs a director's guidance and the effective stimuli of the other actors, to whose characters his character must relate. The responsible actor will, like other responsible play participants, be a selfless artist who recognizes his dependence upon others and their dependence upon him. His work habits during rehearsals and eventually in performance require a discipline that makes successful collaboration possible.

REHEARSAL DISCIPLINE

A director is responsible for the rehearsal schedule. If he is a well-organized, efficient, and considerate person, he will present a schedule that makes the most of the actors' time, and will provide the actor with some idea of the kind of progression expected of him. This will result in the director's dependence upon the actor to make his own plan work. Clearly every minute of rehearsal time will be precious. An actor who is not punctual not only keeps everyone else waiting, but increases the amount of time needed for the play's effective progress.

All of us are familiar with the doctrine that "the show must go on," and the hyperbole that the only excuse for missing a performance is death. More actors need to be made to feel the same about rehearsals. Preparation for a performance is not unlike the construction of a building. In the latter, the roof cannot be put on without walls, and the walls cannot go up without a foundation. In the former, tempos and rhythms cannot be established until lines are learned and a pattern of movement is established. Character relationships cannot be established arbitrarily, but require a deepening day-by-day awareness of one's own character and the manner in which it must commune with and adapt to other characters. When the actor misses one day of a carefully organized rehearsal schedule, he has in effect eliminated a few "bricks," or supports, without which the finished structure will be weakened.

How easy it is to rationalize with "I'll never be missed," or "I'm ahead of the others anyway," or "I'll make it up." Such an attitude demonstrates ignorance of one's role in rehearsals, and an unfortunate self-centeredness. It suggests that the actor's presence at rehearsal is for the express purpose of developing *his* part. He does not stop to think about how his absence will affect other actors who must adapt to his presence, or the director who thinks in terms of the composition of scenes and the development of a consistent pattern of character relationships. Suppose the director wants to change the movement of a scene or develop some necessary business? During *every* rehearsal the director is attempting to determine what works and what doesn't, and how to improve each moment. He needs the presence of *all* the actors in order to make proper judgments.

A timetable for learning lines is a controversial practice. Some actors prefer to learn lines as quickly as possible so that they may be freed from the encumbrances of the script and have more time to develop character, business, and timing. Others believe that lines are better learned by the association of lines with the action developed in rehearsal. Directors have their preferences, too, and some of them employ a flexible attitude depending upon the kind of play that is in rehearsal. For example, they may believe that the fast tempo and amount of physical business in farce needs more time to develop and "set" than other genres. The actors cannot invent or respond to suggestions for struggle scenes, the comic handling of properties, and split-second reactions while holding and focussing on their scripts.

Because of the variables of line-learning, many difficult rehearsal problems arise. When an actor who believes he works best when given plenty of leeway with lines works with a director who insists upon working without scripts as soon as possible, tension results. If the director is flexible or undemanding, some actors will learn lines quickly, while others prolong their dependence on the script. The result is that the actor who knows his lines cannot progress in any scene in which character interplay is essential as long as the other actor in the scene continues to struggle with his lines.

The easiest solution to the problem is for the director to establish a reasonable period in the rehearsal schedule when scripts should be set aside. He might make some concession to those actors who have very large roles, and to those who are admittedly slower learners. It is then the actor's responsibility to comply with the director's request. In any case, it is generally true that prolonging line memorization too long will lead to disaster for everyone. No actor can be secure in performance when he is not sure of his lines, and the line-perfect actor cannot be secure in performance when he doesn't know what to expect from the others. A safe rule to follow is, at the latest, to have lines in command before the last two weeks of rehearsals begin.

The complete actor will want to create as independently as possible. Of course his imagination and inventiveness are subject to certain aspects of his relationship to the director and his fellow actors, but essentially he is expected to contribute to the development of his character and to the play as a whole. Most directors understand that this process takes time and will give the actor every opportunity to develop on his own, but such directors can only be expected to wait so long before they get nervous about the progress of the play. A frequently heard remark by actors to directors is, "Don't worry about me; I'll come through for you." Even worse is the comment, "Don't expect much in rehearsals—but I'm always great in performance!" Interestingly enough, this may prove to be true, but the results for the play itself and the other actors probably will be inadequate. Suppose you are playing Toinette in *The Would-Be Invalid*. The actor playing Argan does little but go through the motions of blocking and a few bits of stage business during rehearsals. What are you to do during performance when a character you have never seen emerges suddenly, and begins to do all sorts of funny things to you and with the furniture and props? You will probably stand by and admire his performance, which certainly is not the reason you were cast in this role in this play.

Acting is give-and-take between actors. It is the working out of a consistent interpretation by an ensemble. A performance consists of repeating the things you have developed in rehearsal, but which have been selected, heightened, and perfected with the knowledge that they are relevant and thoroughly under control. The *appearance* of spontaneity is absolutely essential, but the kind of spontaneity created by sudden inspiration during performance will usually be chaotic.

There are few things as maddening to directors and fellow actors as the actor who never remembers his blocking and stage business. Sometimes the director is responsible if he does not permit sufficient time and repetition to "set" action, or if he is ambiguous about what it is he wishes to retain. But it is often the inattentive, lazy actor who makes a shambles of rehearsals when he must be reminded over and over again of what had been developed previously. To avoid this problem, the actor should either write everything down during rehearsal, or review *in detail* what has been achieved as soon as the rehearsal is over. Too many young actors believe that the only time to think about a play is *during* rehearsal. If they are imaginative, they sometimes use this time to experiment too much. Of course the purpose of rehearsal is to experiment, but development is much faster and more rewarding if ideas and suggestions result from the actors' conscientious labors outside of rehearsal. Too much time can be wasted dealing with sudden impulses, whims, or hastily contrived irrelevancies (though these often may be useful and appropriate). The complete actor will live with his part day and night. He will work on physical and vocal details outside of rehearsal, and when not actually engaged in self-rehearsal, he will *think* about his character and the play.

There is no better feeling in the backstage life of the theatre than the experience of being part of a happy and well-integrated ensemble. Actors do not have to love one another, but they should *care* about one another. It can be stated categorically that no actor will be as good or as complete in his role as he really should be when he works with actors with whom there is only a minimum of adaptation and communion. This principle is as valid for the actors' relationship to one another as it is for their characters' relationship to one another. *Esprit de corps* happens when the performers in a company have developed respect for one another—a respect that is contingent upon several factors. All the criteria for individual responsibility itemized thus far must be included.

But there are two kinds of people who may not respect the selfless, dedicated, and truly creative actor. One is the actor who has none of these qualities; the other is the envious actor. The envious actor makes the mistake of competing rather than cooperating. He must be better than anyone else in the cast. There is nothing wrong with striving for excellence, but the justification for doing so must be based upon each actor's contribution to the ensemble and the play. When one competes, one then begins to strive for effect, and virtuosity replaces honesty. Individual performances replace a harmonious ensemble when actors act *against* rather than *with* other actors.

Working with other actors involves creating together. This can happen only when actors are willing to take the time to do so. It will happen at rehearsals when actors are listening and playing off one another, but a greater achievement is possible when they agree to work in another room when they are not required onstage, or when they make arrangments to meet outside of rehearsals in order to discuss and develop their scenes together. Farce in particular requires such extra attention to the creation of imaginative comic business and timing. Love scenes often are much more honest and inventive when the actor and actress find the time to work privately together.

Working with other actors demands patience and understanding. All actors suffer the tensions and the frustrations that occur when mistakes are made, when imaginations seem to "dry up," or when fatigue sets in. While actors have a right to expect maximum effort from one another, each must understand that his fellow actors are as human as he is. He must be patient with another's self-irritation when things are not going well, and be tolerant of certain quirks as long as they do not infringe excessively upon rehearsal progress. Temperamentalism can be annoying, but acting is a business in which the ego is sorely tried. We all want to do our best, and we do not wish to make fools of ourselves. Conscientious effort for demanding roles is emotionally draining, so that occasional depressions and flareups cannot be avoided. When actors see this happening to other actors, they must sympathize rather than complain—unless, of course, such behavior is the rule rather than the exception.

It is not usually a good idea to offer unsolicited suggestions to other actors. An actor does not appreciate too many self-appointed directors telling him what to do. On the other hand, generous praise from his fellow actors when he has achieved something really fine is one of the actor's most encouraging and uplifting rehearsal experiences. This kind of experience can only occur, of course, when the actors are *aware of* and *concerned* for one another.

Another crucial rehearsal relationship is that which exists between the actor and the director. *Everything* that has been referred to up to this point adds up to what the director should expect from the actor. Our concerns must also include, however, what the actor should expect from the director. The director's chief concern is to unify all aspects of production into a consistently interpreted performance that will possess clarity and rhythmical design. To achieve these ends, he must have control over all persons creatively connected with the production and, ideally, make the best use of their creative potentialities. The first rule that the actor must accept is that the director is the "captain of the ship." He knows, more than any other single member of the company, where it is going and the means by which he hopes to get it there. While the actor, like any member of a ship's crew, is expected to know his job and to do it well, it is the director, like the captain, who best knows the most appropriate ways in which each job must function. The actor then begins by assuming that the director has a concept about the play and is ready to guide him in accordance with it.

There are several ways in which directors communicate their ideas, and the actor must be prepared to respond to any of them. First, the director may begin rehearsals by explaining his fundamental ideas about the play's meaning, and some of the ways in which he hopes to realize them. He may comment on the play's style and genre, and explain how he already has accepted certain design concepts to express them. He may schedule conferences with each actor early in rehearsals, during which he may describe his ideas about character. In this respect, he might tell the actor everything he has thought of about the character, or he might provide a few ideas for the actor to consider. He might simply ask questions of the actor, and by Socratic means lead him or her along certain paths.

But not all directors perform their tasks in the same way. In contrast, there are directors who believe it best to say as little as possible preferring to give the actor every opportunity to discover as much for himself as he can before making any commitments. Other directors will communicate through action and fragmented commentary rather than with organized and comprehensive explanations. They may imply things in their suggestions for movement and stage business, or they may do so by means of improvisation. In such cases, the actor eventually begins to fit things together for himself and attempts to find a central core to which all the hints of the director may relate.

There are also directors who, rather than use abstractions as a kind of guideline and stimulus for the actor, will insist upon defining most of the actor's movements, gestures, facial expressions, and vocal qualities.

All of these types of directors share similar goals, but for various reasons, practice different means of achieving them. Each of them can be equally successful in terms of the final result, which is the performance. It is not the actor's prerogative to dispute the director's methods. It is his job to respond positively to them, whether he likes them or not. If he believes that he cannot tolerate the director's methods of working with actors, he had better resign rather than suffer. If he does resign, however, he might think about giving up acting altogether, for it is rare indeed for an actor to work with only his favorite directors.

A much better course is to accept the reality that not only do directors direct differently, but that actors respond better to certain kinds of direction than to others. Some actors prefer to develop as independently in a role as possible, while others want clear, definitive explanations of what is expected of them in their roles. It is possible, then, for the members of a single cast to differ widely on what kind of direction they prefer. Adaptability is probably the sanest solution to suggest. The actor should ask himself, "How can I work best with this director?" He should accept the silent challenge of the nondirective director, and believe that there is a great deal he might learn from the dictatorial one. The latter, in fact, need not exclude acting creatively. Someone may tell you exactly what you are supposed to do, but it is your job to make it spontaneous, believable, and integrated.

Directors truly are concerned with doing the best job possible, and consequently many of them will respond readily to the problems of the individual actor. If the actor wants the director to give him time to develop on his own, or if he wants immediate help, he can always approach the director and express himself. Hopefully, the director will be understanding and will either comply or explain why it is not possible for him to do so.

It has been stated that it is the actor, not the director, who is responsible for creating a character, although we have seen that some directors prefer it otherwise. There are, however, certain responses that the actor has a right to expect from his director. First, he needs to be assured whether or not he is on the right track. Is the style that he has begun to incorporate consistent with the style of the other actors and with the director's concept? Is what he is beginning to demonstrate with his character relevant to the overall conception of the play? The character's spine and his pattern of behavior must ultimately correspond to other characterizations for meaning to be expressed with unity. We have observed how, in *Miss Julie,* all the characters' patterns are related to sexual and social dominance and submission. If the actress playing Julie decides that her character is just a giddy young thing, or simply insane, Strindberg's play will lose it cohesiveness.

Second, the actor has a right to expect the director to perceive his contribution as would an audience. Are his speech and movement always clear? Is he monotonous? Has he tried to do too much, with the result that he has obscured the character and the character's intentions? Since the actor cannot "see" himself, the director should assist the actor in his selection and definition of the details of character and action.

We have spoken thus far of what might be termed the various "functional" relationships between director and actor. It is necessary to comment upon what the actor should expect in terms of a personal and emotional relationship. As with the "functional" relationship, the actor must be prepared to face varieties of personal behavior, including some that he might find offensive. Some directors are all business. They concentrate upon the play in as objective a manner as possible. They do not believe it is their job to "baby" the actor or to "charge" his emotions. There are no pep talks, only remarks as to what works and what does not work. Some directors do not feel obliged to give praise, believing that one is expected to be a whole actor and a good one, and should require no bolstering of his security.

But in this realm of directing, too, there are distinct contrasts. At the other extreme, there is the director who believes that actors need inspirational stimuli, and that personal attention and encouragement often produce better results than stage directions. And, of course, there are volatile directors whose pleadings, beratements, and tantrums often are performances in themselves.

Actors have their preferences here as well. Some want constantly to be reassured and coddled, while others are insulted by such indulgence. Some respond to the electricity of an inspirational lecture, while others are embarrassed by it. Some actors want to be told when they are doing well, while others immediately suspect a ruse when they are complimented. Once again, since actors have different expectations, no single directorial personality can hope to satisfy all of them. The result is that the actor must determine to be adaptable, and learn to cope with the natural or affected, "cool" or excitable, detached or loving director. While there are many things the actor cannot control, it is most dangerous for him to permit himself too much emotional dependence on the director. Even when he encounters a director who is willing to provide his individual needs, his work is likely to become director-centered, and all of his energies are then aimed at pleasing the director rather than pleasing himself. In rehearsal this type of actor has one eye cocked on the director, and is constantly trying to measure his reaction to what he (the actor) is doing. Such dependence can result in a loss of confidence and lead to despair when the director does not bounce with joy when each "jewel" is produced by the actor.

Hopefully, the actor will find the director rational in his response to requests for more reassurance or less patronization. Such requests, of course, should be made in private rather than in front of the ensemble.

PERFORMANCE DISCIPLINE

Many of the same rules for rehearsal discipline apply to performance. Promptness, for example, is even more crucial for performance than for rehearsals. The start of rehearsals can be delayed even though the practice is undesirable. In performance an audience expects the play to start on time, and undue delay invariably will get the play off to a poor start. Keeping an audience waiting, however, is not the only serious consequence of tardiness. Indeed, the actor may get to the theatre in time for the curtain, but may have to begin the play in a state of unreadiness. The actor has many tasks to perform before he appears onstage. He must put on his makeup, get into costume, check his properties, and be psychologically ready to walk onstage in character. All of this takes time and should not be rushed. None of these tasks are meaningless chores, but are part of the actor's transition from the real world to the world of the play. As he applies his makeup and costume, he not only becomes transformed externally, but, if he takes his time, he will feel an internal change as well.

There are stories of great actors who claim to be capable of telling jokes in the wings while waiting, then move onstage right on cue and in complete character. Actors vary in terms of their need for preparedness, but despite the claims of those who can turn their characters on and off at will, a certain amount of preparatory concentration is needed if the actor's performance is to be anything but mechanical. Some actors prefer to be alone from the time they enter the theatre until their entrance onstage, because they believe they require that time span in order to begin to think and feel as the character. Some actors like to warm up vocally and physically, and will arrive at the theatre early in order to do this. (Indeed, some directors insist on the early arrival of the entire company for warm-up exercises.) Actors can get together and run through some of their lines for pace and for sense of relationship. Preperformance improvisation is a delightful way of getting into character while inspiring fresh approaches to it.

Costumes and personal properties should be checked carefully well in advance, so that if something is missing there will be time to locate or replace it. It is not uncommon for part of a costume to disappear, or for a sword to be missing. Imagine discovering just before your entrance as Richard II that your crown is missing! Jose Ferrer tells the story of his entrance in a performance of *Cyrano de Bergerac* without his artificial nose! Adequate preparation is time-consuming, and since most of it consists of mental and emotional preparation as well as simple good sense and efficiency, the task should not be done hastily or perfunctorily.

For some actors opening night is all that matters. They are emotionally charged for it; the critics are out front, and everyone is keyed up for his first contact with an audience. The result often is a letdown in subsequent performances. Not only is the initial excitement missing, but in a long run subsequent performances become mechanical repetitions of the early ones. All the surface polish is there but the real spontaneity and involvement of the actors begins to disappear. They even begin to think about other problems while onstage, and their failure to concentrate on the play results in missed cues and dropped lines.

There are two principles that actors must observe in avoiding staleness. The first is a matter of attitude. The actor must believe that *every* audience is as important as the first, and apply the same dedication to excellence in every performance. The second is based upon a realization of the reality that despite his dedication, he can easily fall into all the snares of repetition—especially of becoming mechanical. He must find ways of sustaining interest in his role and of keeping it fresh and spontaneous. One of the methods of doing this has been described already—developing warm-up improvisations in which the character is placed into a different set of given circumstances than those in the play.

There are additional procedures that the actor can take in order to sustain his interest and enthusiasm. At some period after the play has opened, the actor should read the entire play without relating it to its present performance. It should be an objective reading. It is surprising how many new ideas and subtle new perspectives can result. The actor will undoubtedly discover that he has altered the text—not always for the better. He may find that other characters have lines relating to his character or to his responses that he had not really heard before. In performance the actor should concentrate on *really* listening and watching the other characters. He may have done this during rehearsals, but it is surprising how easy it is eventually to stop doing so. He will suddenly begin to observe new and subtle variations in other characters that may require a new kind of response.

Few of the really best actors ever believe that they could not have improved upon themselves in most of their roles. If the actor goes into performance believing that there is room for improvement, rather than believing that he has gone as far as he can go, he will constantly find dissatisfaction with certain readings, certain physicalizations, and certain reactions, and attempt to find methods of further illuminating his part. Actors should agree to additional rehearsals together during performance periods in order to solve problems that they mutually recognize, or to change action with which they have become dissatisfied. It has been repeated several times that theatrical interpretation is open to a variety of solutions. The actor who feels he is going stale might explore alternate ways of interpreting various scenes.

While changes may be helpful to the actor and actually may improve the production, they can be harmful as well. Directors who keep an eye on performances of their productions often discover the actors weakening themselves and the play with their "improvements." Sometimes actors do not realize that they are doing this. In playing comedy, for example, their timing may unconsciously change for the worse or they may push too hard for laughs. In predominantly serious plays, audiences may laugh in places where the actors had not expected such a response, with the result that the performers try to exploit this response for more laughs. Before long, the genre of the play becomes distorted—usually for the worse. It is helpful, then, for a director or stage manager to keep the actor's work in perspective.

But what about the conscious changes made by actors that have been previously advocated? Most directors will agree that such changes are often desirable for both the actor and the play, but realize that they must be kept under control. We have seen the necessity for such procedures in farce, whose action can only succeed when it is precise. The solutions are simple ones. The actor should change nothing without first discussing his new ideas with the director and the other actors. In addition, the actor should measure each new concept or inspiration by its relevance to his character and to the meaning and interpretative treatment of the play. It is, unfortunately, not uncommon for actors to "prove" their point in a dispute with a director by doing things "their (the actors') way" in performance. This sort of thing must be resolved in rehearsal, and the actor who persists in such behavior may properly be accused of lacking integrity. By such action, he is indulging his own desires at the possible expense of the play's unifying concepts. He may even make a fool of himself, which was probably the very reason that the director had previously overruled him.

All art requires its own unique disciplines. Theatrical art is no exception, and it demands more, perhaps, than most other arts, because of its collaborative, interdependent nature. An awareness and conscientious application of such discipline is one of the integral and necessary components that comprise the complete actor.

Index